Be Strong and Show Yourself a Man

By

Mark Adcock

Be Strong and Show Yourself a Man

Copyright 2012 by Mark Adcock

TABLE OF CONTENTS

Introduction

Let me begin by thanking you for taking the time to listen to my humble opinions regarding biblical manhood. I am in no way to be considered an expert. There are certainly men out there, like John Piper and Wayne Grudem, who have written extensively on the topic of biblical manhood, offering deep views founded in scholarship. Because of the academic flavor of those writings, I fear that few men in the church today are willing to do the hard work to unpack the treasures found in their writings. Instead, we often migrate to the writings that are available in layman's terms. Yet many of those writings, in my opinion, are founded upon either an inadequate or incomplete foundation. To put it simply, they are founded more upon the psychology of our day than upon the foundation of God's Word. I do not claim to have a deep understanding, but I do believe that God has placed within my heart and mind some thoughts on this subject that are needed in today's church. I pray that as you read and study this work, you will find your biblical calling to be a strong and courageous man who is willing to sacrifice yourself for the glory of your God and the good of those you love.

The early chapters of this book are designed to force you to ask the hard questions about your faith. Are you really saved? What does it mean to be "born again?" Are you building upon a solid foundation or are you falling to the schemes of the evil one and building upon sand? These early chapters are not meant to give you a "paint-by-number" approach to becoming a REAL Man of God. They are intentionally designed to get to the heart of who you are and why you do the things you do. Much of the contemporary writings are behavioral. But we should take seriously what Jesus said in Luke 6:45, "...out of the abundance of the heart his mouth speaks." Identity in Christ leads to Godly behavior. My intent is not to give you a list of things to do to appear to be a Godly man. Rather, I want you to become a man who has a heart for God and therefore displays His character.

Once we get beyond the foundational issues, we will turn our attention towards how a man can impact the people around him for God's glory and for their good. I believe a Godly man makes a profound difference in those he comes into contact with because he is God's instrument to deliver His love to the world. In this section I will rely upon the work of many. I am especially grateful for the work of two men whose contemporary writings have helped me develop a deeper understanding of my own calling. Voddie Baucham's work Family Driven Faith, which presents a man's responsibilities in the context of his family, challenges a man to be a prophet, priest, provider and protector in the home. I love his categories and find them to be challenging and yet extremely practical. Stu Weber has similar work that can be found in his book, Four Pillars of a Man's Heart. Webber defines these four pillars as being a king, warrior, mentor and friend. The latter half of this book will look at how Scripture calls each of us to rise up and to become leaders in our marriage, home, church, community and in the world.

I have attempted to structure the book by addressing concentric circles. When you throw a stone into a still pond of water, you begin to see ripples that affect the whole pond. If there is no point of impact, then there is no effect. The impact that begins to affect our world is that experience of being radically changed by a personal relationship with Jesus Christ. When we come to have a vibrant relationship with Christ, then "Living Water" begins to rush into the lives of those around us...first to our wives and then to our children. As the ripples reach farther and farther out into the world, we see our communities affected and eventually, the world is touched and changed.

Jesus spoke of concentric circles just before he ascended to heaven.

"...you will receive power when the Holy Spirit has come upon you, and you will be my witnesses in Jerusalem and Judea and Samaria, and to the end of the earth." (Acts 1:8)

In that statement, Jesus was speaking geographically. The disciples who heard his comments were in the area of Jerusalem. Beyond the outskirts of Jerusalem was Judea and beyond that Samaria and then still further off was the world unknown. The story of Acts was the fulfillment of Jesus' calling to go and witness to the wonders of Christ in the immediate area surrounding Jerusalem. But when Stephen was stoned to death in Acts 7, the disciples began to scatter into the surrounding lands of Judea, Samaria and even beyond. As they went, they witnessed to the glory of God.

I believe that when Jesus Christ becomes Lord of your life, the grace of God flows in concentric circles. First, your wife is affected by Living Water, and soon after your children are blessed. That flow of grace and mercy continue to create positive change in your workplace, your church, the community you live and eventually the Great Commission is a reality as we preach, teach and bring hope to the world.

I also want to reveal up front that I have a personal belief that we are experiencing a crisis in the world today and that crisis has even reached the church. It is a crisis in the area of leadership. We see it in every area of society. A presidential race is taking place as I write this. A major theme is that of leadership. I have recently read from history books that tell the stories of World War II. A significant piece to achieving victory was that of strong leadership. Where are the leaders of our day? This book is a shot over the bow of masculinity. Are you are REAL Man? Are you leading those who God has placed under your care?

When it comes to the sports fields of America, we see people rise up and make a bold investment of time, energy and commitment. But in the home we are severely lacking. What if we were as passionate about winning for the Lord as we are winning on the fields of challenge.

Vince Lombardi was perhaps the greatest football coach to ever live. But he had a bigger perspective than just the game. Look at what he had to say regarding leadership:

"Leaders are made, they are not born. They are made by hard effort, which is the price which all of us must pay to achieve any goal that is worthwhile."

"It is essential to understand that battles are primarily won in the hearts of men. Men respond to leadership in a most remarkable way and once you have won his heart, he will follow you anywhere."

"Leadership is based on a spiritual quality --- the power to inspire, the power to inspire others to follow."

"Having the capacity to lead is not enough. The leader must be willing to use it."

"Leadership rests not only upon ability, not only upon capacity – having the capacity to lead is not enough. The leader must be willing to use it. His leadership is then based on truth and character. There must be truth in the purpose and will power in the character." (cite: http://www.vincelombardi.com/quotes.html)

My friend, there is a crisis looming in America. It is a crisis in leadership. It is also a crisis in manhood. We need men who are strong and courageous. We need men who are willing to dig deep and build strong character that leads to strong families. When King David was on his death bed he made a profound statement to his son, Solomon. That statement is the title of this book... Be Strong and Show Yourself a Man. May God give us the strength to walk in all His ways, the courage to stand against the raging tide of culture; the clarity to understand the difference between right and wrong, the conviction to walk in righteousness even when its hard, the compassion to love when it is easier to hate, and the passion to do it all for the glory of the Lord. 1st Kings 2:1-4

Be Strong and Show Yourself a Man

Chapter 1– What Does It Mean to Be a REAL Man?

"I'm a man!" my brother exclaimed. "I'm a REAL Man." The comment was not exactly what my mother expected to hear when she picked my younger brother up from his intermediate school in the quaint little town of Lake Jackson, Texas. At first it seemed like a bit of fantasy, but as my brother began to reveal the details of his day, it became apparent quickly that what had taken place that day over my brother's lunch hour was not so innocent. A couple of the older boys from the school had cornered my brother and told him that in order to show himself to be a man, he had to do exactly what they demanded. Now, I know that there is something in the chest of every boy that wants to prove himself to be a man, and my brother, Sam, was no different. I am sure if I had been cornered, I would have done the same thing he did. I would have tried to man up and show courage, bravery and toughness. But do those qualities make a boy a man? And just what does it mean to be a REAL Man?

That day, the two boys told my brother that in order to be a real man, he had to allow them to, bit-by-bit, peel every layer of skin off the back of his hand. And he had to suffer this without a single tear or complaint. Showing toughness and determination, Sam passed the test. For an hour or so the two boys peeled the skin off the back of his hand until it looked like a raw piece of steak. Blood oozed from his raw hand, but he never shed a tear or offered a complaint. Why? Because he wanted to show himself to be a REAL Man.

Today in America, we are dealing with a crisis. "Where did all the REAL men go?" It seems to me that our young men are struggling to grow up. Extended adolescence for many is lasting into their early thirties. Boys are not marrying or getting jobs like they used to do. In fact, in his book entitled <u>Family Driven Faith</u>, Voddie Baucham shares some statistics showing that the number of males between the ages of 22 and 34 who still live at home with their parents, have no job, and play six hours of video games per day on average, has increased by 100% in the last decade. (Cite: <u>Family Driven Faith</u>. Page).

Notes and Quotes:
In the Introduction,
there was mention of
Acts 1:8. In the space
provided, what
relationship in your
life is represented by
Jerusalem?
Spouse - Family
Judea?
Church family
Samaria?
Workplace
The ends of the earth?
Citizens of U.S.

But this problem is not only found in young males, it is rearing its head among all ages. We have lost sight of what it means to lead our families. We are rapidly approaching the time when 50% of the children of America will go to bed at night without a father in the home. And the breakdown of the family structure is leading to a moral decay that is crippling our nation. I am not saying that males are the only ones responsible for the place we find ourselves, for I believe that all of us, male and female alike, have fallen prey to Satan's schemes that have led to this crisis. We must reverse course if we are going to bring hope back into our children's lives. It is time for every Christian man to drive a stake in the ground and say, "Not on my watch. Not in my family!" It is time for the men of America to take a stand and be counted. And the place I propose you start is in your family and in that church. If Christian men do not stand up and lead the way, it will not happen.

My brother, Sam, soon learned that being tough did not make him a man. There is more to a man than being brute tough. Being a man is about character. Being a man is about honoring God no matter what the cost or how it feels; it's about sacrifice of self, loyalty, and living out the two greatest commandments: Love the Lord your God with all your heart, with all your mind and with all your strength, and love your neighbor as yourself. This is a book designed to call you to become a REAL man. May God bless you as you strive to "Be Strong and Show Yourself a Man!"

Age Does Not Make You a Man

The year was 2007 and the Oklahoma State Cowboys had just beaten Texas Tech in a wild football game. But when Oklahoma State Coach Mike Gundy entered his press conference, he did so with an ax to grind. His focus was not on the big win. Rather he was there to do battle with a young female reporter by the name of Jenni Carlson of the Oklahoman newspaper. Earlier that week, Carlson had written what Gundy believed to be an inappropriate article regarding one of the quarterbacks on his team. She had attacked his character, even though all he was guilty of, according to Gundy, was playing poorly in a football game. As Gundy ranted and railed, he became more and more agitated, heaping insult upon insult on the young reporter. Finally, the now infamous words came spewing out of his mouth. "Come after me," he said. "I'm a man! I'm forty."

When the three minute and twenty second tantrum was over it went viral. In fact, some have recently joked that Youtube.com should name a wing of their office building after Gundy because his outburst paved the way for their site and future. The reactions to his antics were mixed. Some in the media agreed and applauded as he stormed out of the press room. Others spoke about the need and right of the media to be able to write about such things as this quarterback's poor play. Some fans thought it was high time that a coach would take up for his players in this way. Even the quarterback in question, Bobby Reid, had mixed reactions to Gundy's tirade and believes that Gundy's remarks actually damaged him and his future career. Regardless of who is right and who might be wrong in their accounts of this now infamous chapter of American sports folklore, this moment lives on as one of the wildest tirades in American history.

Was Coach Gundy right? I'm not talking about his coming to the defense of his player. Nor am I talking about whether or not it is appropriate for the media to take shots at a young athlete's character when they fail on the field. I am asking this question with regards to what it means to truly be a man. Does age make one a man? Just because you might have turned forty years old does not make you a man. The fact is, being forty does not make you an adult male. I propose to you that being a man has nothing to do with age.

> I remind you that there is a crisis looming in America. It is more lethal than cancer and more devastating than any tsunami. It is the loss of manhood in America.

So just what does it mean to be a man? If we could only come to grips with that question and see a new generation of young boys rise up and show themselves to be men. Again, I remind you that there is a crisis looming in America. It is more lethal than cancer and more devastating than any tsunami. It is the loss of manhood in America. I am not naïve enough to think that this book will single-handedly change the course of history. If only it were that easy. This is simply my humble attempt to drive a stake in the ground and take a stand. It is a stand for God, faith and family. It is built upon the foundation of God's design and upon the timeless truths found in His Word. My friends, it is not too late. We can change the future. Our children don't have to grow up fatherless. God's way is better than our way. The call today is for us to be strong and courageous; it is to swim upstream against the

Notes and Quotes:

1 Timothy 4:12

In the space provided, make a list of things you believe to be vital in a REAL Man's life:

Faith
Temperment
Hope
Purity
Strength of Character

Notes and Quotes:

culture; it is to deny ourselves and begin to carry the cross. So rise up and show yourself a man!

Chapter 2– The Call to Be a REAL Man

"1 When David's time to die drew near, he commanded Solomon his son, saying, 2 "I am about to go the way of all the earth. Be strong, and show yourself a man, 3 and keep the charge of the LORD your God, walking in his ways and keeping his statutes, his commandments, his rules, and his testimonies, as it is written in the Law of Moses, that you may prosper in all that you do and wherever you turn..." 1 Kings 2:1-3 English Standard Version.

Just what does it mean to "show yourself a man?" That question is one that I have asked a thousand times in the last few years. As a man who is beginning the third trimester of life, I think it is time for me to figure out this thing called manhood so that I might leave a legacy of faith to those who God has placed in my life. The first trimester of life is largely a time of preparation. The second trimester is the battle to establish life- to raise a family and to create a place in this world. The final trimester of life should be the period in which we establish our legacy- how we will be remembered. I have reached that place in life and ask myself often, "What impact will I leave on my family?"

I don't want this question to be a selfish one. I do not want to be remembered in such a way as to "toot my own horn." Rather, I want to honor God with the way I live my life. I want to point all those who I come in contact with towards Him and show them the godly way to live. I want to be an example. I want to do that for my wife and my children and especially for my grandchildren. This is my time to impact their world for the sake of Christ! I pray that you will begin to see this as your time to shape your family as well.

Oh how I wish I had learned these things earlier in my life. It certainly would have made life easier for one family for sure. I have to tell you that many of the lessons of this book are founded upon things learned in the midst of the battles of my life. Sometimes they were battles between God and I, and sometimes they were battles that took place between my wife and I. Almost always they were battles that were a result of my selfishness and worldliness. But I thank God that in time He has matured me. He has done what He promised in His Word- He has lifted me up. I can tell you that the words of Peter are true when he writes:

"6 Humble yourselves, therefore, under the mighty hand of God so that at the proper time he may exalt you, 7 casting all your anxieties on him, because he cares for you. 8 Be sober-

Notes and Quotes:

minded; be watchful. Your adversary the devil prowls around like a roaring lion, seeking someone to devour. 9 Resist him, firm in your faith, knowing that the same kinds of suffering are being experienced by your brotherhood throughout the world. 10And after you have suffered a little while, the God of all grace, who has called you to his eternal glory in Christ, will himself restore, confirm, strengthen, and establish you. 11 To him be the dominion forever and ever. Amen." ~1 Peter 5:6-11.

I am so grateful for God's timing and the blessings that have come after years of failure and perseverance. Please don't read this to mean that I have arrived. I am not yet close to the place I long to be, but I thank God that He has begun a good work in me and will be faithful to complete it (Philippians 1:6).

I share the last paragraph because I want you to know that it is not too late for God to bring change to your heart and life. Start where you are right now. Invite God to do His work in you and begin a journey that will bless your heart and the lives of those you call family. But most of all, it will bless God, for the journey you are about to embark upon is an act of worship unto Him.

I agree with Stu Weber who said, "Sometimes a man comes to his senses a little (or a lot) later in life. Sometimes by the time he finally picks up the crown, his little kingdom is in disarray. Some of the ways of his family are set – and they may not be healthy. He'd love to go back and undo some of the things that he's done, and do some of the things he left undone...but none of us have that opportunity. Nevertheless, at whatever point we wake up to our responsibilities... God calls us to take a stand and, in His strength, to point the way." (Footnote: Four Pillars of a Man's Heart by Stu Weber. Multnomah Press, 1997. Page 111.)

My personal journey into Biblical Manhood seemed to begin just a few years ago. But in the past year I have learned that it actually began long ago. Perhaps it began when my parents started praying for me as a small boy, that I might grow to be a Godly man. Certainly it grew as my wife asked God to help me begin to stand tall and lead our home. One thing that I know contributed to my journey into manhood was the prayer of an elderly woman who asked God to make me a man who was strong in the Lord. Her name was Annie Fox. In January of 2011 Annie went to be with the Lord at the age of 93. She had asked many years earlier if I would be willing to preach her funeral. I was humbled at her request and agreed. Now that day had come. Ann was a dear woman who I had met in the mid 90's. She was the first senior adult member of the church plant that I pastored. Immediately we connected and I knew from the very first day forward that she was a woman of prayer. Upon learning of Ann's death, I went to the home of her daughter and son-in-law and gathered information about their desires for her funeral. Years ago I learned to ask to borrow the Bible of the person whose funeral you are preaching. If they were a faithful follower, there would be evidence in those pages to help preach their own funeral message. And in Ann's Bible the pages were filled with all kinds of notes and highlights.

The page that grabbed my attention most was the one that held the passage from 1 Kings 2. *"Be strong, and show yourself a man..."* That verse was highlighted and a line was drawn from it to the margin. In rather feeble looking handwriting she had penciled my name and the date of 6/20/99. This revelation hit me like a two-by-four between the eyes. This woman had prayed these verses over me some twelve years before. And the beneficiary of that prayer was me. God honored that prayer in His time by lighting a fire within my heart to become that man...a man strong in the Lord who would one day show himself to be godly and mature in faith, a man who would learn to walk in His ways. Now, my prayer is that God will finish His good work and help me to finish strong for His glory and for the benefit of those who I love.

As an act of thanksgiving for Annie's prayer so long ago, I have begun to pray that prayer on behalf of the young men of my life...for my son and son-in-law and the young men who I have been privileged to counsel and to pastor. And while it is done in a general way, I have prayed for you, the man who would one day read this book. My prayer is the same prayer that Ann prayed for me. Lord, may the men who read this book become strong in faith and show themselves to be godly men who will follow hard after You with a thirst for Your righteousness. I pray this prayer because I know firsthand what it did in my life and I believe God has led you to this book so that you might be challenged to rise up and become that man of faith.

As I write this book I have a two-fold objective. First, to educate the men who read it to purse biblical manhood in a way that will bless God, their wives, children and grandchildren. And secondly, to inspire men to rise up and become all that God created them to be for His glory and for the blessing of future generations.

This year I have been blessed with becoming a grandfather. What a privilege. I am blessed with opportunity. But what will I make of that

Notes and Quotes:

opportunity? I was reading recently and came across the testimony of a young man whose father contracted cancer just before this son went off to college. The cancer spread rapidly and soon the father lay on his deathbed. In their final conversation the son asked the father, "What do you want me to do with my life?" Listen to the way the young man described his dying father's answer:

"You told me to please God and I would please you.

You told me to love my younger sister and brother, to hug them and tell them they were special.

You told me God was good and I could trust him.

You told me to study the book of Romans hard because that's where you found your peace and that's where I would find mine.

You told me it is better to give than to receive, far better, and to learn this and live by it.

You told me I had given you deep joy as a father just by being your son.

You told me I was a man of God and had your deepest blessing, and that we had the same heart for Jesus.

You told me that true obedience is learned through suffering.

You told me to remember heaven.

You told me you were going home to meet Jesus.

It's been seven years since we had that conversation and I remember everything you said. God has been so gracious, and I'm trying my best to love and follow him like you did. Sometimes I worry about whether I'll ever be as good a Christian, husband, and dad like you were, but then I am able to rest in peace because you taught me that the Father loves and accepts us regardless of whether we succeed or fail.

> **The future generations of your family may well rest on the choices you make today.**

Thank you for making Jesus and the gospel so easy for me to love and trust, and for building a godly legacy. I love you, I miss you, and I will see you again in heaven." (Footnote: Dad, Thank You For Building a Godly Legacy, by Steve Sakanashi. Found at http://blog.marshill.com/2011/06/19/dad-thank-you-for-building-a-gospel-legacy).

Men, we can do it! We can rise up, be strong and show ourselves men who shape the lives of those entrusted to our leadership. The question is not can you, but rather, will you? The future generations of your family may well rest on the choices you make today. Your faithfulness to God is important if you are to develop a credible testimony before your wife, children and grandchildren. Never forget that what you do matters! But what matters most is not what you do, but who you are. We will unpack this more as we move forward.

Let the journey begin!

A Portrait of a Real Man...David
A Man Defined by His Heart...An Imaginative Look at a Tender Moment

The final hours of his life had finally come. Like many families, the people gathered and waited to hear the last words of this man revered by many. He had accomplished so much in his life; in fact, he was legendary. Everyone had heard the stories of how, as a teenage boy, he had taken on the giant Philistine and won. If that had been the only victory in his life, it would have been enough to grant him a place in history. But there was so much more to remember.

Gathered around his bedside were many who loved him. From sons to servants, they all loved him. His breathing was becoming more and more labored. Just as the people thought he would draw his final breath, he called out for his son, Solomon. In an impassioned plea, he gave one final appeal to the young man who would now reign as king...

"I am about to go the way of all the earth. Be strong, and show yourself a man, and keep the charge of the LORD your God, walking in his ways and keeping his statutes, his commandments, his rules, and his testimonies, as it is written in the Law of Moses, that you may prosper in all that you do and wherever you turn, that the LORD may establish his word that he spoke concerning me, saying, 'If your sons pay close attention to their way, to walk before me in faithfulness with all their heart and with all their soul, you shall not lack a man on the throne of Israel.' "(1 Kings 2:2-4 ESV)

After David had delivered these final words, he closed his eyes and died. The people who had gathered mourned and remembered. David had sat on the throne of Israel for forty years. He had not been perfect, but he had been noble even when he had failed; for he had come back to God with a humble heart. Truly, he had been a man "after God's own heart."

As the people sat and processed their loss, they began to talk about the things that had made David great. Some said it was his victories on the battlefield that would define his legacy. Others ventured to speak of the way he treated the people of his kingdom. But Solomon, who had received the impassioned plea to rise up and be a strong man, knew what the key thing was that had made his father great...it was his heart. Not only was David a "man after God's own

Notes and Quotes:

heart," but he was also a man who had a heart for God. Being a REAL Man requires that a man look deep into his heart and deal with his character and identity.

From the very moment that David splashed onto the scene of history in 1 Samuel 16, it was his heart that defined him.

One by one Jesse's sons
Stood before the prophet
Their father knew a king
Would soon be found
And each one passed
Except the last
No one thought to call him
Surely he would never
Wear a crown

But when others see a shepherd boy
God may see a king
Even though your life seems filled
With ordinary things
In just a moment He can touch you
And everything will change
When others see a shepherd boy
God may see a king

(From: http://www.elyrics.net/read/r/ray-boltz-lyrics/shepherd-boy-lyrics.html)

Samuel was a prophet who was told by God to go to Bethlehem and seek out a man named Jesse. While there, Samuel was to secretly anoint a new king for Israel. When he arrived there, he found a whole household of potential candidates, for Jesse had seven sons. The first brought to Samuel was the oldest; his name was Eliab and he was a man of great physique. He was incredibly handsome. Samuel was impressed. His immediate thought was that this man would make a great king for Israel. But God interrupted Samuel's thinking and spoke these words to him, *"Do not look on his appearance or on the height of his stature, because I have rejected him. For the Lord sees not as man sees: man looks on the outward appearance, but the Lord looks on the heart." (1 Samuel 16:7).*

When finally the last son of Jesse was presented, David, who was said to be small in stature, was the one God had chosen to be the king. Why? Not because of his appearance, but because of his heart.

Throughout all the days that David reigned, he was concerned about his heart. As he wrote you see his passion regarding the heart.

> *Create in me a clean heart, O God,*
>
> > *and renew a right spirit within me.*

(Psalm 51:10 ESV)

> *Who shall ascend the hill of the LORD?*
>
> > *And who shall stand in his holy place?*
>
> *He who has clean hands and a pure heart,*
>
> > *who does not lift up his soul to what is false*
>
> > *and does not swear deceitfully.*
>
> *He will receive blessing from the LORD*
>
> > *and righteousness from the God of his salvation.*
>
> *Such is the generation of those who seek him,*
>
> > *who seek the face of the God of Jacob. Selah*

(Psalm 24:3-6 ESV)

> *Search me, O God, and know my heart!*
>
> > *Try me and know my thoughts!*
>
> *And see if there be any grievous way in me,*
>
> > *and lead me in the way everlasting!*

(Psalm 139:23-24 ESV)

As we begin this quest to become REAL Men of God, we must do so by engaging our hearts. David was considered a great leader because he did many great things for the people of Israel. But when God looked at David, he did not see his accomplishments, rather he saw his heart. It was that way from the very beginning. And when the Apostle Paul wrote that David was "a man after God's own heart," he understood that it was not David's behavior that defined him in God's eyes. No, it is not the external that matters most to God but the internal. It is not the behavior that matters most but the character. Being a REAL Man is about the state of your heart!

Chapter 3- Out of the Overflow of the Heart

"For no good tree bears bad fruit, nor again does a bad tree bear good fruit, for each tree is known by its own fruit. For figs are not gathered from thornbushes, nor are grapes picked from a bramble bush. The good person out of the good treasure of his heart produces good, and the evil person out of his evil treasure produces evil, for out of the abundance of the heart his mouth speaks."

(Luke 6:43-45 ESV)

It is important for us to realize as we begin this journey to become REAL Men, that Christ-like behavior is not founded upon the actions of our lives, but rather it is founded upon our identity in Christ. Being a Christian man is not so much about acting a certain way that appears Christian, rather it is about BEING a Christian man. And out of our being we do what honors God.

For those of us who desire to rise up and be REAL Men after God's own heart, we quickly come to a problematic place. Because of Adam and Eve's failure in the Garden of Eden, our hearts are tainted even from the point of our conception. David wrote in Psalm 51:5 , *"Behold, I was brought forth in iniquity, and in sin did my mother conceive me."*

An investigation of our hearts before the sanctifying work of God reveals great concern. Just look at what Scripture teaches us about our hearts prior to God's transforming work.

> *The heart is deceitful above all things,*
>
> > *and desperately sick;*
>
> > *who can understand it?*

(Jeremiah 17:9 ESV)

> *We have all become like one who is unclean,*
>
> > *and all our righteous deeds are like a polluted garment.*

Notes and Quotes:
Prior to God's work on a
man's heart, what does
Scripture teach about the
natural state of the heart?
Have you fallen for Satan's
scheme to try to convince
you that you have no
hope because sin is too
powerful for you to
overcome?

We all fade like a leaf,

and our iniquities, like the wind, take us away.

(Isaiah 64:6 ESV)

The LORD saw that the wickedness of man was great in the earth, and that every intention of the thoughts of his heart was only evil continually.

(Genesis 6:5 ESV)

Now before you get too depressed at the terrible condition of your heart, remember that we are not defined by the psychology of man, because that requires us to deal only with the natural man and there is no acknowledgement of God's work in our lives. We are not forever trapped as the Genesis 3 man who is defined by sin and a corrupt heart. No, we are defined by the theology of man; that we were made in the image of God and because of Christ we can experience redemption. We have the capacity to take on the communicable attributes of God and live differently. We cannot change our own hearts for we are powerless apart from God's gracious act of transformation. But we thank God that He planned all along to send Christ to redeem us and give us hope. The good news is that God is our heart surgeon who takes away our wicked, hard heart and replaces it with a new heart.

Note: Many men, even Christian men who attend church regularly, see themselves powerless against the sinful nature that seems to have its way in their lives. Many have come to the wrongful understanding that they are stuck with no hope of a future because they are unable to overcome this depraved nature that has corrupted them. It is like they have recorded their life on an old cassette deck. The tape that records their life has become mangled to the point that every time they want to rewind their life and have a "do over," the tape gets stuck at the Fall of Genesis 3 and never can find its way back to the point of Genesis 1 where man was made in the image and likeness of God. The truth is that we cannot in our own power find our way back to that place of new beginnings. We do not have enough money or character to pull that off. But resetting your life is within the power of God. The reset button is called redemption. And because of the cross of Jesus Christ, we can start fresh and new. Keep reading and find out more about how God wants to grant you a fresh new start.

How does He accomplish this amazing and gracious feat? By doing some radical surgery on your heart!

I will sprinkle clean water on you, and you shall be clean from all your uncleannesses, and from all your idols I will cleanse you. And I will give you a new heart, and a new spirit I will put within you. And I will remove the heart of stone from your flesh and give you a heart of flesh. And I will put my Spirit within you, and cause you to walk in my statutes and be careful to obey my rules.

(Ezekiel 36:25-27 ESV)

Thanks be to God that we who have been born again have been given a heart transplant. We are blessed beyond measure. Our lives have a hopeful foundation because of Christ. Listen to what Jesus said when the disciples asked why he spoke in parables.

"This is why I speak to them in parables, because seeing they do not see, and hearing they do not hear, nor do they understand. Indeed, in their case the prophecy of Isaiah is fulfilled that says:

"You will indeed hear but never understand,

and you will indeed see but never perceive.

For this people's heart has grown dull,

and with their ears they can barely hear,

and their eyes they have closed,

lest they should see with their eyes

and hear with their ears

and understand with their heart

and turn, and I would heal them.

But blessed are your eyes, for they see, and your ears, for they hear. For truly, I say to you, many prophets and righteous people longed to see what you see, and did not see it, and to hear what you hear, and did not hear it."

(Matthew 13:13-17 ESV)

Jesus said that the people who have not had this heart transplant are unable to see with their eyes the glory of God. Nor are they able to hear from the Lord. Their hearts are unaware. But for those of us who have experienced regeneration, we have been given a gift. We now can see the difference between darkness and light. We are now able to distinguish the voice of God. We are now set free to love with a love that is selfless. We are no longer trapped by Genesis 3 and the Fall of Man, but we have been given redemption and can now be defined as God intended, by the image of God that He placed within us.

Notes and Quotes:

According to Ezekiel 36, who is it that provides the power for change?

Have you had a heart transplant?

Notes and Quotes:

Capacity does not equal

change. How have you

made your heart available

to God to do His work?

The sinful nature is still a part of our flesh. But because Jesus died on the cross, our sins were buried with him and we have been given a spirit that has ushered us into a new life.

I want you to know that if you know Christ, if you have been born again, if you have been redeemed by the blood of Christ, then you have been given a new heart and have the capacity to develop within your heart, the character of God. But unfortunately many of us have never filled the spiritual warehouse of our hearts with the things that grow us to be more and more like Christ. Instead, we often consume the things of this world and as a result, find that our Christianity is diluted by a heart that is in disorder and convoluted. Sections of our hearts are devoted to God, while other sections of our hearts are devoted to self. And the overflow of our hearts is conflicted because we have not keep our hearts pure.

Years ago I sat at the hospital while a man from my congregation went through a difficult open heart surgery. Several bypasses were done to give him the opportunity to continue to live. Thankfully, the surgery was successful. When the doctor came out to speak to the family about how the operation had gone, I was invited to go along. The surgeon came in and offered the minimal report. Surgery had gone well. He had been able to accomplish what he had gone in to do and the patient would be able to enjoy life much more once he had recovered from the trauma of the surgery. Just about the time the surgeon appeared to be turning to leave, a friend of the family asked the doctor, "Well is he going to be okay? Will this be something that will reoccur?" The doctor, who did not specialize in bedside manner, gruffly stated, "I am just a plumber. I went in and changed all the pipes. His heart now has the capacity to function properly and give him a long life. But if he continues to put all that garbage back into his body, he will find himself back here sooner than later."

The doctor was right. Just because we have been given the capacity does not mean that we will use it in a way that will lead to lasting change. We must begin the process of filling the spiritual warehouse of the heart with the things that show devotion to the Almighty. We must invite God to change us so that we look more and more like Him. So as we launch into this adventure, let us set our minds upon the goodness of our God who says:

I will give them a heart to know that I am the LORD, and they shall be my people and I will be their God, for they shall return to me with their whole heart.

(Jeremiah 24:7 ESV)

> *Blessed are the pure in heart, for they shall see God.*

(Matthew 5:8 ESV)

Years ago I was blessed to be able to sit under great teachers who helped me to learn how to use God's Word to help others to become more like Christ. As a result of these teachers' investments in me and my ministry, I now spend much of my time doing biblical counseling and personal discipleship. In my counseling, I have found that men usually fall into one of three categories.

Man is good and can accomplish all that needs to be accomplished alone.

This understanding is founded upon Humanism. There is no acknowledgement of God in any way. Man is reliant completely upon self. This is called practical atheism. (Atheism is, in a broad sense, the rejection of belief in the existence of deities. In a narrower sense, atheism is specifically the position that there are no deities. A practical atheist [my term] is a person who may say they believe in God, but live as if He does not exist.)

Example: Stan (not his real name) came to my office and asked if I would help through a problem that he was having. He prefaced his confession with this statement. "I don't want you to think badly of me because I am a really good man." He went on to say that his mother had taught him well the things of God. But he, in spite of this amazing goodness, had made a number of mistakes that were haunting him. As his story unfolded he told of three failed marriages. And now, he was in intimate relationships with multiple women, none of which knew about the other women in his life. And he was so busy trying to manage all the lies that he was miserable. Yet, he continued to come back to his goodness over and over again.

His arrogance was astounding. He rationalized and trivialized. In the end he said, "I just can't bear to hurt any of them." What he really meant was, "I am so good and wonderful that these women need and deserve a man like me in their lives. I can't help it if I am so wonderful that every woman needs me. They would be lost without me!" This man said with his mouth that he believed in God and was saved. But he was living as a practical atheist. With no respect for God at all; seeing no need for God in his life.

Notes and Quotes:

Have you ever felt that because of your sinful nature, you were stuck with no hope of pleasing God?

Notes and Quotes:
Have you ever felt that
because of your sinful
nature, you were stuck
with no hope of pleasing
God?

Man is depraved and in need of a Savior.

This understanding teaches that man cannot accomplish anything of lasting value apart from God. It is founded upon the psychology of man. It is also founded upon a partial, incomplete theology of man. But without a deeper, more complete understanding of theology, psychology leads to a futile place that says, "I am stuck here. Because of sin I will never experience what my life ought to be." Man is reliant upon Jesus as Savior. This is called salvation.

Example: Let's call him Ed. Ed sits across the table from me at lunch. I have asked for the meeting because I want to do some pastoral care. I care about Ed. And over the past few years I have had the opportunity to counsel Ed regarding what he says is a "raging addiction to pornography." Ed knows that he is a sinner. He understands that his looking upon a woman with lust is sinful. But he has fallen for Satan's lie that he just can't help it. He has a sinful nature and is just stuck here. He proclaims his salvation with great vigor. But his philosophy is that he is really good at sinning and God is really good at forgiving, so they have the perfect relationship. He just keeps on sinning and he believes God understands and will respond with mercy and grace.

Or let's consider Brian's story. Brian is a man who struggles to understand grace. He is constantly overwhelmed by his sinfulness. His heart is contrite. But he has bought Satan's scheme that he will never experience anything beyond the massive guilt that he carries. The way he carries himself seems to constantly proclaim his guilt-ridden life. He says that he knows that Christ died for him, and without a Savior, he would be lost forever. But he has no victory. He is stuck with a sinful nature that offers him no hope.

Much of the literature in the church today is written around this philosophy.

Man is made in the image of God and has the capacity to experience godly change.

This is founded upon a deep understanding of theology. Because of Christ, we can experience redemption...we can be bought back and transported to the place of new beginnings. We can experience new life and with God's help cultivate a new heart. Man is reliant of the Lordship of Christ. This is called sanctification.

Example: David is a young man who came to see me to talk about his battle with sin. He grew up in a Christian home and learned early in life about the things of God. But as soon as he became a teenager, he ran down the road called Prodigalism. He said, "I honestly just spit in the face of God." That road led him to a life of radical sin which led to brokenness. He had a child out of wedlock and eventually married the baby's mother. Together they wallowed in sin until one day, God broke his heart.

David sat across from my desk having recently come home to God. He was humble and ready to grow. He said to me, "I know God has forgiven me, but now my question is how can I become the man of God that I believe He wants me to be? I have so many scars and I see myself as ugly in the presence of a beautiful God. Help me to change!"

As we move forward, I will attempt to present evidence that in order for man to understand himself, he must first understand God. Therefore, a good theology of God gives birth to a theology of man and offers a platform which can lead to one's growth and maturity.

Notes and Quotes:

The 'Y' Diagram...Out of the Overflow of the Heart

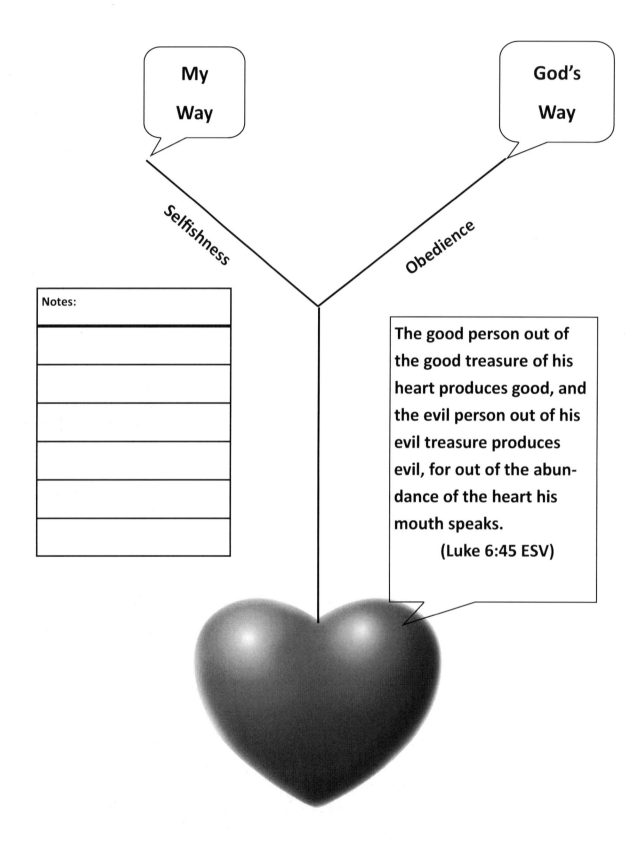

Chapter 4- A REAL Man Understands Himself in Relationship to God

27 So God created man in his own image, in the image of God he created him...~Genesis 1:27.

Many in the church have written on the subject of what it means to be a man. And I am sure that these men have great intentions. But I am concerned that too often their starting point regarding man is founded upon a psychology of man rather than upon a theology of man. Allow me a moment to explain.

When a man bases his understanding of himself upon psychology rather than theology, he sees himself from a worldview rather than a God view. The important question to ask here is not "What do I think about myself as a man and how am I to approach living this life?" Rather the real question should be "What does God think about my life as a man and how I should approach life?" If we begin with psychology we will find that our starting point is Genesis chapter 3 where Adam and Eve sinned and the fractured world that resulted from the fall. When we begin with this logic, we quickly must address the many wounds of this world. Many writers speak of wounds inflicted by parents who were not godly and the brokenness of this harsh world. The problem is that if we begin with man and his view from a broken place, we will spend our time trying to fix the problems of life rather than embrace God's sovereign plan for our lives.

 If we look through the eyes of psychology we will look to cope rather than to live victoriously in Christ. We will also explain away our shortcomings as a result of all the ways we have been hurt and affected by the sins of others. We will come to say that "We just can't help it." Stu Weber says, "We've got all the psychology in the world and little of biblical reality." (Footnote: Four Pillars of a Man's Heart. Multnomah Press, 1997. Page 107.).

There is a movement within the church to define man according to his innate, primal urges. This is more Freudian than biblical. If we listen to this perspective we get the picture that man is some chest-bumpin', butt-scratchin', scrappy, burly, manly man who is all about adventure; he is boisterous, arrogant, and proud of it! This view also says that unless man pursues living in this primal way, he will never be happy. He is wired this way. I will propose in the pages that

Notes and Quotes:

In what ways do the roots

of psychology become of

concern for the Christian?

follow that God is none of these things. He is holy, faithful, consistent, and gracious and that because we have been made in His image we should be about developing these qualities and in doing so we will find joy and happiness.

The problem with basing our approach to manhood upon psychology is that the roots of psychology are foreign to the gospel of Jesus Christ. Here is what psychology has taught us:

"Jean-Jacques Rousseau, (one of the founders of psychological thinking) says, 'You are an individual with a mind, but you don't really need God and his grace to help you. You don't need to look outward to God. You need to look inward to self. You're not really a sinner. You're basically a good person. What you need to do is not seek God's love, but love yourself. You need not seek God's acceptance through Jesus. You need to learn to accept yourself as you are.' Give yourself a big hug, as it were. That's Rousseau. And so we don't need God. We need to love ourselves and accept ourselves – not think so negative, that we're sinners, and not have that kind of condemning sort of self-assessment.

Well, this continues forward to a man named William James, one of the dominant psychologists in the history of America. And he said, 'Not only are you a pretty good person, and not only are the answers in you instead of in God, you don't really need God at all. What you need is a highly-trained specialized psychiatrist. You need a therapist. You need a psychologist.' Of course a therapist would come up with that idea. 'You don't need God, you need me.' And, 'You don't need God to walk with you, you need me to walk with you.' And, 'You don't need God to speak to you, you need me to speak to you.' And, 'You don't need God to assess you, you need me to assess you.'

And the assumption was that we're really, in many ways, a machine – that the human body is a machine and that, through clinical psychology and therapy, you can fix people by reordering their understanding and their component parts psychologically... it (psychology) omitted God, who is the great counselor. The Bible calls Jesus, in fact, Wonderful Counselor. We're not opposed to Wonderful Counselor Jesus and counselors who counsel with, for, like, through, to Jesus, but this is counseling without Jesus, without God, without an acknowledgement of human sin. And this is having someone else, other than Jesus, be your functional savior. You don't go to Jesus to get your life together, you go to a professional. And the goal of the professional is not to help you get to know Jesus at all.

Well, this leads as well to a man named Abraham Maslow. He comes up with something you may have heard called the hierarchy of needs, and your greatest need is not to glorify God, but to glorify self. Self-actualization – you want to achieve your full potential, you want to make all the money you can make, you want to be as healthy as you could be, you want to be as successful, as powerful, as influential, as affluent as you could possibly be. You want to be all you can be." (Footnote: http://marshill.com/media/doctrine/image-god-loves)

We must begin with a good theology rather than psychology. We must realize that God is the architect and Creator. A look at the theology of man does not begin with Genesis 3 but rather with Genesis 1 when God makes man in His image. What an amazing thing to think about. We were made with some resemblance to God. We are to be image bearers of the Most High God. It is impossible to understand man unless first you study the One who made man. When we look into the face and majesty of God, we not only begin to see Him as He is, but we begin to see ourselves as we are.

We will not find the essence of man by looking inward. We must look upward if we are to find our meaning and purpose.

In Isaiah 6 the prophet has an encounter with the Almighty that first enlightens the prophet to who God is but then leads him to an accurate understanding of himself.

Isaiah's Vision of the Lord

1 In the year that King Uzziah died I saw the Lord sitting upon a throne, high and lifted up; and the train of his robe filled the temple. 2 Above him stood the seraphim. Each had six wings: with two he covered his face, and with two he covered his feet, and with two he flew. 3 And one called to another and said:

"Holy, holy, holy is the LORD of hosts; the whole earth is full of his glory!"

4And the foundations of the thresholds shook at the voice of him who called, and the house was filled with smoke. 5And I said: "Woe is me! For I am lost; for I am a man of unclean lips, and I dwell in the midst

Notes and Quotes:

of a people of unclean lips; for my eyes have seen the King, the LORD of hosts!"

6Then one of the seraphim flew to me, having in his hand a burning coal that he had taken with tongs from the altar. 7And he touched my mouth and said: "Behold, this has touched your lips; your guilt is taken away, and your sin atoned for."

Isaiah's Commission from the LORD

8And I heard the voice of the Lord saying, "Whom shall I send, and who will go for us?" Then I said, "Here am I! Send me."

Notice that the first thing that happens when Isaiah stands in the presence of God is that he is captured by the greatness and majesty of the Almighty One. He notices how incredible God is in intimate detail. He speaks about His throne and robe and angels. It was quite an experience. It was an experience that Isaiah had on many different levels. He saw with his eyes and heard with his ears. He even felt the earth quiver and smelled the smoke of His majestic presence. The only sense not engaged in verses 1-4 was taste. But then in verse 7 the angel is dispatched to take a coal from the altar and place it upon his lips. God is a God who is to be experienced. And when we experience Him, something else happens. Not only do we begin to understand Him as He is, but we also begin to understand ourselves and who we are. Notice that standing in the presence of God, Isaiah suddenly sees his sinfulness and need for Him. "Woe is me! For I am lost..." Our understanding of our manhood is not found in psychology but in our study of Him who created us. C.S. Lewis said, "The real test of being in the presence of God is that you either forget about yourself altogether or see yourself as a small, dirty object." When we see and understand God, we will find our understanding of self. Let us begin by acknowledging that...

"8For my thoughts are not your thoughts,

neither are your ways my ways, declares the LORD.

9 For as the heavens are higher than the earth,

so are my ways higher than your ways

and my thoughts than your thoughts."

~Isaiah 55:8-9

Finally, from the encounter that Isaiah has in the throne room we see that once Isaiah sees and comes to understand God and who He is, and himself in light of the Holy One, then he begins to understand the call of God upon his life. If we are going to come to understand how we are to live as godly men in a broken world, we must first study God deeply and pursue Him with all our heart, mind and strength. Then we will begin to see ourselves and our calling in the light of His purpose for our lives. Nothing short of this understanding of manhood will sustain us through the trials of this life. Without this sound theology of what it means to be a man, we will fail to rise up and be men of God.

Created in the Image of God

Just what does it mean that you were created in the image of God?

We have the capacity to develop some of the same attributes that God displays

If we are created in the image of God then we have the capacity to look like Him in character. While not all of the attributes of God are communicable attributes, there are some attributes of God that can be experienced and seen in the lives of every person. These communicable attributes include:

God has given us a spirit- God Himself is spirit. He has no physical features. When He chose to come to earth in the form of a man, he put on flesh so that we might understand Him and His love for us. But He is spiritual. And because we are made in His image, He gave us a spirit as well. When this physical life draws to its final conclusion, all that remains is the spirit. It is the spirit of man that will experience eternity.

The moral attributes of God- Many of the attributes of God that we have opportunity to display in our lives fall under the category of the moral attributes of God. By definition moral means pertaining to, or concerned with the principles or rules of right conduct or the distinction between right and wrong. (Footnote: http://dictionary.reference.com/browse/moral). Because God is truth and is not capable of any wrong, He is moral in all His ways and in all His character. While our nature is not capable of perfection this side of heaven, we do have the ability to make moral decisions that reflect the image of God. Here is a list of some of the moral attributes of God that we can cultivate in our lives:

Goodness- God is the final standard of good. He is incapable of anything other than good. We are certainly capable of walking outside of the goodness God desires. But the fact that we have been given the capacity to choose goodness shows that we are born in the image of God.

Love- God eternally gives of himself to others. We can imitate this communicable attribute of God by loving Him back and by loving others

Notes and Quotes:

What is the difference between communicable attributes and non-communicable attributes?

"Love is willing self-sacrifice for the good of another that doesn't demand reciprocation, or that the person being loved is deserving." ~Paul David Tripp

Notes and Quotes:
Make a list of Godly
attributes that you would
like to see cultivated in
your heart:

with a love that comes from God as well. In 1 John 4:11 we are taught that because God has shown His love for us and because we are the beneficiaries of that love, we ought to love others. Paul David Tripp offers this definition of love: "Love is willing self-sacrifice for the good of another that doesn't demand reciprocation, or that the person being loved is deserving." (Quote from Paul David Tripp found in <u>What Did You Expect?</u>)

Mercy, Grace and Patience- According to Wayne Grudem, these three attributes of God may well be explained as three specific works of the attribute of goodness mentioned above. I agree with his assessment but also find it helpful to break them out separately so that we can study them in a more in-depth fashion. However, this study is not about an exhaustive look at the attributes of God. Rather it is simply to show how we have been given the capacity to resemble God by displaying certain attributes that are a part of His nature. For those who have a regenerate heart, certainly mercy, grace and patience are attributes that we are called to cultivate in our lives.

Holiness- Most who read this will know that God is holy. This means that He is perfect in all His ways. Many have fallen for Satan's scheme believing that they cannot experience this attribute in their lives. But this is certainly one of the communicable attributes of God. We can choose to not sin. Therefore, we can choose to be holy. In Leviticus 19:2 God told Moses to gather the people and to tell them, "You shall be holy; for I the Lord your God am holy." Wayne Grudem writes, "God's holiness provides the pattern for his people to imitate." (<u>Systematic Theology</u>, page 202). Because we have been made in His image, we have the capacity to choose to be holy. In our humanity, we fail, but God has given us the ability and opportunity to live above sin. This is important as we study the difference between the psychology of man and the theology of man. As I mentioned earlier, if you base your understanding of man on psychology, you will make Genesis 3, the fall of man, your foundation. But a theology of man goes back to Genesis 1 and the fact that God has made man in His image with the capacity to choose something other than his sinful, selfish nature. It is refreshing to realize that we have been made in His likeness with the capacity to pursue holiness. This is a critical piece in building a foundation for biblical manhood.

Righteousness- This term is both moral and ethical. God always acts in accordance with what is right and is incapable of anything less than righteousness. He is the standard bearer and creator of the high calling of righteousness. Because we have been created in His image, we too can choose to walk in this way. And in so doing, we reflect His character.

Much more is available for study regarding the attributes of God. Two sources that I would recommend are the two volume set by A.W. Tozer entitled <u>The Attributes of God</u>, and Wayne Grudem's rather exhaustive book entitled <u>Systematic Theology</u>. You will be blessed to study this deeply. But for the purpose of this book and study we must move on. Before I do, however, let me restate my point one last time. If we base our view and understanding of what it means to be a man upon psychology, then we will make the fall of man in Genesis 3 the foundation of our belief and understanding. And if we base our view of man on Genesis 3, we will see ourselves to be victims of this sin cursed world who are unable to do anything else except pursue our own selfishness. God's word tells us that we are made in the image of God. Therefore, we have the capacity to reflect Him in the ways we approach life. If we unpack 1 Kings 2:1-3 we will see that the way a godly man shows himself to be a man is by "walking in his ways and keeping his statutes, his commandments, his rules, and his testimonies..." Men, it is time for us to rise up and show ourselves to be men who bear the image of our Creator!

Because we are created in the image of God we can exercise dominion

26 Then God said, "Let us make man in our image, after our likeness. And let them have dominion over the fish of the sea and over the birds of the heavens and over the livestock and over all the earth and over every creeping thing that creeps on the earth."

27 So God created man in his own image, in the image of God he created him; male and female he created them.

28 And God blessed them. And God said to them, "Be fruitful and multiply and fill the earth and subdue it, and have dominion over the fish of the sea and over the birds of the heavens and over every living thing that moves on the earth."

(Genesis 1:26-28)

Because God has made man in His image and because of the way that He ordered creation, we have been charged with the responsibility to "take dominion" over certain aspects of creation. To take dominion means that we are to exercise authority and be responsible for certain things which God has entrusted to us. The study of this God-given au-

Notes and Quotes:

Notes and Quotes:

Is man more than just an

animal? Why?

thority and responsibility is important to our becoming godly men and will be unpacked in a future chapter. But for now, we must recognize that God made man to exercise authority and to be responsible within the framework of His designed sovereign will. Much of the latter part of our study will focus on how to "take dominion" of the things God has placed in your care.

Dominion must be exercised. There is no way to passively "take dominion." It requires action. Passive dominion is nothing more than a title. Many men today are falling short of God's call upon their lives because they are not actively living out this call. We must come to understand what it means to exercise dominion over the things that God has placed under our care in this world. Much of the remainder of this book will address how we fulfill our God-given calling to exercise this authority and take responsibility for the people who have been placed in our care, our wives and children. We must actively pursue this calling and attack the passive nature that pervades our culture and renders male responsibility impotent and unnecessary.

Psalm 8 is a wonderful commentary on what our role is when it comes to taking dominion. Take a moment and reflect on these words of Scripture.

"1 O LORD, our Lord, how majestic is your name in all the earth! You have set your glory above the heavens. 2 Out of the mouth of babies and infants, you have established strength because of your foes, to still the enemy and the avenger.

3 When I look at your heavens, the work of your fingers, the moon and the stars, which you have set in place, 4 what is man that you are mindful of him, and the son of man that you care for him?

5 Yet you have made him a little lower than the heavenly beings and crowned him with glory and honor. 6 You have given him dominion over the works of your hands; you have put all things under his feet, 7 all sheep and oxen, and also the beasts of the field, 8 the birds of the heavens, and the fish of the sea, whatever passes along the paths of the seas.

9 O LORD, our Lord, how majestic is your name in all the earth!"

Notice that Psalm 8 helps us as men to find our place in God's order of creation. Verses 5-8 tell us that we have been made below the place of the Creator, and above all the things of this earth. And we have been given responsibility over the things of this earth.

"What is our place? Well, it is under God and above the rest of creation. Every flaw anthropologically speaking either presses us up too far, to where we're God, we're divine, there's a spark of the divine within us, we're not sinners, we're basically good, that we are like God or we're our own little God, or it pushes us too far down where we are just basically animals. Okay? Heard one quote this last week in the paper, and that was from a religious leader – very well known – said, "There is goodness and the divine within each of us." That's too high. I was listening to talk radio on that same day and there was a guy who called in, said, "I keep cheating on my wife, committing adultery. She found out. She's really angry. What do you think about that?" And the radio show host said, "Well, just tell her you're an animal. You know, you're just a highly evolved animal with a job and that's the way we are as man." I said, "No, we're not animals." We're human beings crowned with – I love the language here – glory and honor. You can't say, "I'm just a highly evolved animal with a driver's license." No, you're an image-bearer of God with moral accountability, responsibility." (Footnote: Quote from Mark Driscoll found at http://marshill.com/media/doctrine/image-god-loves).

Does Genesis 3 change who I am as a man?

Certainly when sin entered into the world everything changed. Life is harder. The curse has affected all of us and every aspect of life on this earth. But does it change who I am called to be as a man? Does the image and likeness of God persist in men and women after sin and the fall and the curse? The answer is yes. Genesis 5, Genesis 9, and James 3 all continue to say that though sinful, we are still God's image-bearers.

In Genesis 9 we read of God's covenant with Noah after the flood has destroyed the earth. The reading of this chapter shows many similarities to the original creation story. Even though sin has entered into the world and God has shown his judgment, He continues to call Noah to the very things he called Adam to in Genesis 1. *"1 And God blessed Noah and his sons and said to them, "Be fruitful and multiply and fill the earth..."*

Scripture teaches that we are to tame our tongues and not allow them to curse others, for they have been made in the image of God. We must deal with the curse of sin. James writes: *"9 With it (the tongue) we bless our Lord and Father, and with it we curse people who are made in the likeness of God. 10 From the same mouth come blessing and cursing. My brothers, these things ought not to be so. 11 Does a spring pour forth from the same opening both fresh and salt water? 12 Can a*

Notes and Quotes:

Notes and Quotes:

fig tree, my brothers, bear olives, or a grapevine produce figs? Neither can a salt pond yield fresh water."

(James 3:9-12)

From these passages we can see that the fact that man is an image-bearer of God is still relevant even after sin enters the picture in Genesis 3. And James calls us to be accountable and to be an image-bearer of God even in this sin cursed world. Let us never allow our sinful nature to become a license to wallow in sin. Rather let us keep our eyes upon the call of God to bear the image of Him who created us. Let us rise up and pursue holiness and show those who we love and who we are called to lead the majesty and glory of God. It is our highest calling- to become like Him. It is our spiritual act of worship.

Chapter 5- A REAL Man is Twice-Born

As you begin this quest to be a real man, realize that the point of embarkation is the place where you become "born again." Without being born again, you will never become a real man. Because being a REAL Man revolves around character, and character is taking on the likeness of God. Without a personal relationship with God through Jesus Christ, no one ever excels in the area of character development. Apart from God, you will forever be trapped in a Genesis 3 fallen world. But with a legitimate experience of new birth, you begin to see the old man pass away and the new man begin to grow and develop in the image of God.

In John 3, a man who seems to have it all together comes to Jesus under the cloak of darkness to find answers to his haunting questions about life. While he is very religious, he knows that there is something lacking. Having heard that Jesus is a great teacher, the man comes in search of answers.

Here is how it is recorded by the Apostle John:

>Now there was a man of the Pharisees named Nicodemus, a ruler of the Jews. This man came to Jesus by night and said to him, "Rabbi, we know that you are a teacher come from God, for no one can do these signs that you do unless God is with him." Jesus answered him, "Truly, truly, I say to you, unless one is born again he cannot see the kingdom of God." Nicodemus said to him, "How can a man be born when he is old? Can he enter a second time into his mother's womb and be born?" Jesus answered, "Truly, truly, I say to you, unless one is born of water and the Spirit, he cannot enter the kingdom of God. That which is born of the flesh is flesh, and that which is born of the Spirit is spirit. Do not marvel that I said to you, 'You must be born again.' The wind blows where it wishes, and you hear its sound, but you do not know where it comes from or where it goes. So it is with everyone who is born of the Spirit."

>Nicodemus said to him, "How can these things be?" Jesus answered him, "Are you the teacher of Israel and yet you do not understand these things? Truly, truly, I say to you, we

Notes and Quotes:

Have you been born again

again? Describe what

happened to you? Was

there an obvious change?

Is there a difference

between knowing Jesus

as your Savior and know-

ing Him as your Lord?

speak of what we know, and bear witness to what we have seen, but you do not receive our testimony. If I have told you earthly things and you do not believe, how can you believe if I tell you heavenly things? No one has ascended into heaven except he who descended from heaven, the Son of Man. And as Moses lifted up the serpent in the wilderness, so must the Son of Man be lifted up, that whoever believes in him may have eternal life. (John 3:1-15 ESV)

Friends, I must stop at this point and ask you to examine your heart. Are you stuck in religion without any evidence of the kingdom in your life? Many have fallen prey to the lie that going to church and trying to live a good life is all that is required. But the truth of the matter is that without an experience of new birth, you will never be an authentic, real man. Everything short of new birth rings hollow when the storms of life begin to rage.

Last Easter Sunday, an elder in my church, Rick McFarland, shared his testimony about his experience of being born again. He spoke about his intellectual understanding of Christianity prior to coming to new birth. He had grown up in the church and learned all the stories of faith. As a young boy he had prayed a prayer and asked God for forgiveness. And in that moment, he sought Christ to be his Savior. But the knowledge of God had done little to change his life. Rick had failed to invite Christ to be his Lord. He chased after the things that people in the world chase after. But when he got to the end of each pursuit, everything led to emptiness. Then a crisis overwhelmed him. He and his wife had a son born premature. For days they waited and watched to see if the baby boy would survive. During that waiting, the man realized that while he knew a lot about God, he had no personal relationship with Him. So in the moment of crisis, Rick cried out to God and was born again. Life has never been the same since. Some who read this will come to realize that while they know a lot about God, they have no experience of second birth. Realize that what happened to Rick can happen to you as well. God can and will use the circumstances of your life to draw you to Himself and give you the amazing gift of new life. And new life always begins with new birth.

A.W. Tozer calls the man who has been born again twice-born. He writes, "there is yet one distinction which we dare make, which indeed we must make if we are to think the thoughts of God after Him and bring our beliefs into harmony with the Holy Scriptures. That distinction is the one which exists between two classes of human beings, the once-born and the twice-born...Those who are twice-born crystallize around the Person of Christ and cluster together in companies, while the once-born are held together only by ties of nature, aided by the ties of race or by common political and social interests…What we need to restore power to the Christian testimony is not soft talk about brotherhood but an honest recognition that two human races occupy the earth simultaneously: a fallen race that sprang from the loins of Adam and a regenerate race that is born of the Spirit through the redemption which is in Christ Jesus. To accept this truth requires a tough-mindedness and a spiritual maturity that modern Christians simply do not possess. To face up to it hardly contributes to that "peace of mind" after which our religious weaklings bleat so plaintively. For myself, I long ago decided that I would rather know the truth than be happy in ignorance. If I cannot have both truth and happiness, give me truth. We'll have a long time to be happy in heaven." (Tozer in Man: <u>The Dwelling Place of God).</u>

What Tozer is teaching us is that there should be an obvious difference between the way a born again man lives his life and the man who does not have a spirit that has been regenerated by new birth. Many of the men I counsel know about God but have no assurance of salvation. Recently I sat with an intelligent young man who was struggling with his faith. He had grown up in the church and knew the teachings well. However, he had no assurance of salvation. When I posed the question, "Have you been born again?" his response startled me. He said, "You tell me. Roll the dice." As you read this book, I ask that you would respond to the same question I asked him. I ask it not to produce guilt or frustration but to help you to determine if you have taken the first steps of becoming a real man. Have you been born again?

Examine yourselves, to see whether you are in the faith. Test yourselves. Or do you not realize this about yourselves, that Jesus Christ is in you?—unless indeed you fail to meet the test! (2 Corinthians 13:5 ESV)

The premise of this book is that a REAL Man knows God intimately. He has a relationship that goes beyond that of acquaintance. A REAL Man is born again and is therefore a child of the living God. He has a new identity. And out of that new identity, he acts differently; he walks differently and talks differently. Some who read this will understand what I am talking about because they have experienced this new birth and life is so much different than what it used to be. But some who read this will sit at this point wondering if they have experienced new birth. They will be like the young man who said, "You tell me. That's the million dollar question. Roll the dice." If you are that man, I want to take you back to the story of Nicodemus in John 3. What was it that Nicodemus did

Notes and Quotes:

A REAL Man is twice-born.

What does this phrase

mean to you?

Can a man have assurance

of salvation?

Are you saved?

Notes and Quotes:

when he realized that he didn't have an authentic experience of faith? He sought out Jesus in his quest for a new beginning. God has designed the emptiness that haunts us prior to new birth to lead us on a journey for new life. The promise of God found in Jeremiah 29:13 is this:

You will seek me and find me, when you seek me with all your heart. (Jeremiah 29:13 ESV)

The Greek word to seek is Zeteo. It is a wonderful word that calls us to salvation. If our heart has been quickened by the Holy Spirit then we will enter into a quest to find Him. And nothing will fill our emptiness until we are born again. Don't stop until you know for sure that you are twice-born. You will never be satisfied until you have confidence that you are a new creation.

"Ask, and it will be given to you; seek, and you will find; knock, and it will be opened to you. (Matthew 7:7 ESV)

Some will say that not all will be saved. That is a true statement founded in reality. But it is not because God does not want all to know Him. In fact Peter writes, *"The Lord is not slow to fulfill his promise as some count slowness, but is patient toward you, not wishing that any should perish, but that all should reach repentance."(2 Peter 3:9).* My friend, if you question whether or not you are born again, don't sit idle and just wait. Set out on the adventure of a lifetime and search for Jesus with all your heart. When you seek him with all of your heart, Jeremiah says that you will find him. Don't settle to just know about him. Seek and you will find. This is the beginning point of every REAL Man. If you are reading this and have not yet given your heart to Christ, turn to Appendix One and look at a step-by-step plan for becoming a Christian. Then, after you have this foundational relationship with God established, return to the next chapter and begin to allow God to make you a REAL Man.

Group Discussion Questions for Chapters 1-5:

1. What do you think about the author's explanation of the difference regarding the theology of man vs. the psychology of man?

2. How does redemption bring us back to the "Imago Dei?"

3. Do you feel stuck because of your sinful nature?

4. What is the difference between salvation and sanctification?

5. John 15 is the story about the vine and the branches. If we abide in him, Jesus says, we will bear much fruit. Where is the fruit in your life?

Notes and Quotes:

6. Can a man know for sure that he is saved?

7. Why do you think that the author begins with a call to be right with God and growing in faith in a study on Biblical Manhood?

8. Capacity does not equal change. If God has given you a new heart, what have you done to show yourself a man?

Chapter 6–So You Just Had a Heart Transplant

What if you were just regaining consciousness after receiving a new heart? How would you act? How would you feel? I am sure those first few moments of new life would be intense. It would almost be like starting over completely. At first you would be careful when you moved, perhaps even afraid to do so, fearing that you might somehow damage the work that had been done inside. A new Christian, just born again, is like that in many ways. I remember the night that I received Christ. I was only ten years old and yet when I arrived home that evening and went to my room to go to bed, I had this feeling unlike any I had ever felt before. I realize now that the feeling I had was brought on by the realization that I had a new heart, and the questions began to flood my mind as I tried to get to sleep. What do I do now? I really didn't know, and the pastor who prayed with me gave me no instruction regarding what to do with this new life. There were anxious thoughts too. Anxiety by definition is fear of the unknown. What would this decision to live for Christ mean for my future? Would I enjoy it? That probably wasn't an appropriate question because it was founded upon my selfish nature. But I asked it nonetheless.

Bob Aronson will never forget the day that the phone rang and the person on the other end said, "Mr. Aronson, we have you a new heart." For twelve years Bob had ridden a downward spiral. He first noticed the symptoms of his heart condition in 1995. After testing it was determined that he had a condition called Cardiomyopathy. As every day passed, Bob got weaker and weaker. By 2006 he was spent. Bob describes it this way: "I was horribly discouraged with my debilitation. I had to stop and rest even during a brief walk from the family room to the bathroom in our home." But on August 21st of 2007, the phone rang, and his life would never be the same again.

Before I continue on with this writing, let me stop and ask an important question. Have you received a new heart? Have you been given new life? We ended the last chapter asking that question, and before we go forward, I want to again remind you that without a new heart, you will surely die. In his testimony about his journey to receive a new heart, Bob tells that one of the most surreal moments was when he arrived at the Mayo Clinic and went to the admissions desk and said, "I am here for a heart transplant." If you have not bowed your heart to the Lord

Almighty and told Him you have come for a new heart, do it now. Again, if you have questions about how to become a Christian, you can read Appendix One for instructions as to how to proceed.

For the new believer, coming to faith in Jesus Christ should be life changing. Scripture teaches that the old is passed away and all things become new. In an instant, one is transported from darkness to light. But learning to walk in that light is a process. There are many emotions that are associated with a radical change such as this. One of those emotions is thanksgiving.

Just imagine how Bob felt waking up in that recovery room knowing that he had received the gift of a new heart and new life. Here is what he had to say about the responsibility he feels to make the most of the gift he has been given.

"I can hear it, I can feel it, and I can feel its effects — but this heart doesn't belong to me," says Aronson. "Just saying that is important because it reminds me that I must take very good care of it. With this gift comes great responsibility and I enthusiastically accept it. I owe my life to my donor and his family. I live because of their compassion and I pray that they know that their loved one lives within me and I will take extra special care of this precious gift."

"Christian spirituality is a spirituality of grace in which an awakened heart responds to God's mercy by giving all." (Cite: Quote by Gary Thomas in Thirsting For God. Page 59).

What Bob came to understand in those precious days after his heart transplant was that in order for him to live, someone else had to die. A loved one had to make a difficult and noble decision - to give life to someone else meant certain death for the one they loved.

When you came to Christ, God Almighty knew that your new life would require the painful death to His very own son. That thought alone should flavor the rest of your days. Jesus died so that we might have life. That sacrifice has been made. Now the real question is this: what will you do with the gift? How will you live with this new heart? You have some important choices to make. (Cite: Bob's story can be found at http://www.mayoclinic.org/patientstories/story-402.html)

Surrendering Your Old Heart is Required

In order for Bob to receive a new heart, he had to part with his old, worn-out heart. He could not live with both. It is important for us to realize that walking in new life means totally surrendering the old life.

Therefore, if anyone is in Christ, he is a new creation. The old has passed away; behold, the new has come. (2 Corinthians 5:17 ESV)

For many, we do not understand this concept of addition by subtraction. Some just want to keep their old worn-out depraved heart and add a new heart. This will never work. Had they placed a new heart into Bob's body and somehow tied it to the old one, the old one would have quickly destroyed the new one. Often we are cautioned in Scripture to be single-minded as we walk in faith. For the double-minded man is "unstable in all his ways." (James 1:8).

For a man to walk into the future with a new heart, he must put the past behind him. This means that he must have sincerely confessed his sin. But most importantly, he must walk in the forgiveness God has granted him. Man of God, you must not allow the failures of your past to stagnate or ruin your future. Learn to walk in forgiveness. Surrender that old life completely and enjoy a new beginning.

"We want to baptize our old nature rather than trade it in. We're not told to wash the old nature, however, but to kill it. True Christianity includes an utter, absolute, and complete surrender to God." (Cite: Quote by Gary Thomas in Thirsting for God. Page 99).

While we are on this subject, it is also important to note that surrender is not only putting your past behind you, but it is an everyday exercise of the Christian. We are also called to surrender our everyday to the Lord. Perhaps the place this is most important is when it comes to dealing with our will.

And he said to all, "If anyone would come after me, let him deny himself and take up his cross daily and follow me." (Luke 9:23 ESV).

Henry Drummond wrote, "The end of life is to do God's will...that is the object of your life and mine—to do God's will. It is not to be happy or be successful, or famous, or to do the best we can...it is something far higher than this—to do God's will." (Cite: Quote from Henry Drummond in The Greatest Thing in the World. Page 125).

"I am slowly learning that the real test of true faith is not how successful I am, but how surrendered I am. In the Christian faith, we are called to die daily (see for example, Luke 9:23). A Christian with his or her own agenda is like a horse with a head on both ends. This person will always be in a 'push me-pull you' struggle with God." (Cite: Quote by Gary Thomas in Thirsting For God. Page 97).

Notes and Quotes:
Do you find that walking in
forgiveness is easy or
difficult?
What would full surrender
look like in your life?

A Portrait of a REAL Man...Eric Liddell, the Flying Scotsman

A Man Surrendered

The year was 1924 and Eric Liddell was considered to be the favorite to win the gold medal in the 100 meter dash at the Olympic Games in Paris, France. Most people had already conceded the title of fastest man in the world to him even before the race was run. But something outside of Eric's control stole that title from him before he was even able to compete. That something was his deep love for the Lord.

When the schedule for the Olympics was made public in the weeks that led up to the games, Liddell noticed that the preliminary races for the 100 meter were on Sunday. Without even a second thought, he withdrew from the competition. Why? Because Eric believed that in order to honor God in all his ways, he must live a life of "complete surrender." He could not and would not compete on the "Lord's Day."

When news reached the people of Scotland, they were completely perplexed and amazed at the lack of respect that Liddell displayed for his country. His popularity quickly eroded and his character came under attack by many of the politicians of his country. When the Prince of Wales tried to pressure Eric to compromise his beliefs, Eric responded by saying, "God made countries, God makes kings, and the rules by which they govern. And those rules say that the Sabbath is His. And I, for one, intend to keep it that way."

As the games drew nearer and nearer, the people of Scotland could not believe that Liddell loved God so much that he would give up the amazing benefits that would come by winning a gold medal. His faithfulness, in their opinion, had cost him his chance at fame and fortune.

Sunday passed and the lane where Liddell was to race remained empty. In the minds of most people, Eric had blown his chance. The 100 meter race was his only shot at gold. But God had different plans for Liddell. Eric was also entered in the 400 meter race and it was not held on Sunday. Liddell was not competitive at this distance. But when that race was run, God opened the floodgates and Liddell blew away his competition and won going away.

Eric's unwillingness to compromise his faith was a demonstration of his philosophy of life—a phrase that he would later use during his work on the mission field in China—"Complete Surrender." Eric believed that there was no goal higher than serving God; there was no political or national allegiance that was greater than his allegiance to the Kingdom of God.

Perhaps you know about Eric Liddell from the movie about him, Chariots of Fire. If you've seen the movie, you know that Eric ran "for the glory of God," and that when he won, he won "for the glory of God." Perhaps you remember this quote from the movie, in which Eric says, "I believe God made me for a purpose, but he also made me fast. And when I run I feel His pleasure." (Cite: http://www.sermoncentral.com/sermons/complete-surrender-to-christ-the-king-jonathan-twitchell-sermon-on-lordship-of-christ-99251.asp).

Do you not know that in a race all the runners run, but only one receives the prize? So run that you may obtain it. Every athlete exercises self-control in all things. They do it to receive a perishable wreath, but we an imperishable. So I do not run aimlessly; I do not box as one beating the air. But I discipline my body and keep it under control, lest after preaching to others I myself should be disqualified. (1 Corinthians 9:24-27 ESV)

Chapter 7- Strengthening Your Heart

For anyone who has had radical heart surgery, cardiac rehab is a requirement to bring strength to the muscle of the heart. In the case of a heart transplant, the process of strengthening the new heart within the body is of great importance.

Let me remind you that the heart is like a spiritual warehouse that houses your spiritual identity in Christ; it is your spiritual DNA. Now that you have a new heart, with the capacity to warehouse the character of God, it is important what you allow to be placed in the empty warehouse.

My first job was that of a warehouseman for a commercial sub-contractor in Baton Rouge, LA. I started at the bottom sweeping floors and cleaning toilets. But over time I was given more and more responsibility. The warehouse was old and packed with all sorts of leftovers from jobs that had been finished long before. My job was to try to keep the inventory orderly so that products could be easily found and distributed to jobs. But over the years, the warehouse became so cluttered that the task to keep it orderly and functional was all but impossible. Not only did we have a mountain of "leftovers" to deal with, but the warehouse had become a catchall for many of the employee's recreational pursuits. There were farm implements, deer stands and duck blinds, four wheelers and the like. Before too long, that warehouse was so packed and cluttered that nothing could be found. You could hardly walk.

One day the owner of the company, realizing that space had become an issue had to make a decision. Either we were going to have to do away with much of the clutter or we were going to have to build a new warehouse. He chose the latter.

When the new space was finished, the bosses became very intentional in the decisions of what would be allowed into the new warehouse and what would be banned. For months that new warehouse was filled and the inventory grew. I, along with the other warehousemen, took pride in keeping that new space orderly and useful. But over the years we all became compla-

Notes and Quotes:
What traits do you see in
your heart today?
What needs to be
removed?
What needs to be added?

cent. I am sure you can guess what happened. Eventually the new warehouse was just as cluttered and unusable as the first warehouse.

Guarding Your Heart

Just like the new warehouse I mentioned above, your new heart will eventually become cluttered with the things of this world unless you work diligently to protect it. We in America have become so consumed with distraction that this will be difficult for most to apply. Most of us have become convinced that multi-tasking is a good thing. So we are constantly juggling all kinds of things as we do life. Our relationship with the Lord should not be just another ball that we throw into a juggling act, or an attempt to keep all the plates of our lives spinning without them crashing to the ground. No, we must turn off the TV and cell phone and carve out quiet times with the Lord in order to experience intimate relationship with Him. In future chapters, we will look at how we also need to develop uncluttered time in order to develop intimacy with our wives and children.

As we journey to become REAL Men, we must develop a focus. One of the many problems that we have in the world today is that we are easily distracted. Let's take a moment and look at the lie that multi-tasking is a good thing. New research is proving that multi-tasking is actually making us less effective and efficient, and even worse, it is attacking intimacy and the ability to have deep personal relationships. The technology age has made it all but impossible to focus on one important task unless one has trained himself to be "single-minded."

"Multi-tasking, for most Americans, has become a way of life. Doing many things at once is the way we manage demands bearing down on us at warp speed, tame a plague of helpful technological devices and play enough roles — parent, coach, social secretary, executive — to stage a Broadway show. But researchers peering into the brains of those engaged in several tasks at once are concluding what some overworked Americans had begun to suspect: that multi-tasking, which many have embraced as the key to success, is instead a formula for shoddy work, mismanaged time, rote solutions, stress and forgetfulness. Not to mention car crashes, kitchen fires, forgotten children, near misses in the skies and other dangers of inattention." (sited from We're All Multi-tasking, But What's the Cost? Found at http://www.umich.edu/~bcalab/articles/LATimesMultitasking2004.pdf)

The truth of the matter is that Satan is using our infatuation with doing more in less time to distract our gaze away from the things that matter most. And for a REAL Man, our gaze must become fixed on God. As I mentioned early on in this book, I am taken with Isaiah's experience in Isaiah chapter 6 as he is transported in a vision to the Throne Room of God. And there his gaze becomes fixed on the majesty and glory of the Almighty. When he begins to see God clearly, he begins to understand himself as well. If we are to become REAL Men, we must turn our gaze back to God. We must become single-minded and not double-minded!

Nancy Missler writes, "a person is single-minded when he continually chooses to relinquish himself (all his thoughts, emotions and desires that are contrary to God's) so that God's Life from his heart can come forth. In other words, only one life is being lived, Christ's." (cited from Single-mindedness vs. Double-mindedness Part 2 found at http://www.khouse.org/articles/2003/484/).

"Double-mindedness, obviously, is the enemy's game plan. He knows that double-mindedness will: keep us unstable in all our ways (James 1:8); quench the light of the knowledge of Jesus in our lives (Luke 11:34c); and finally, 3) cause us to fall (Luke 11:17)...Every kingdom divided against itself is brought to desolation; and a house divided against a house falleth." (Luke 11:17) (cited from ibid)

Let's take a moment and analyze our schedules and the schedules of our families. How busy is too busy? It seems that every season of life is busier than the last. I know of families who are so torn apart by schedules and activities that they have lost their ability to relate to each other. The people who are to be most important in their lives are but strangers sleeping in the same house. And I know firsthand what it is like to have a schedule so busy that I do not take the time to sit in the Presence of God and experience renewal and growth. Satan is using business to divide and conquer.

It isn't that we plan to allow our gaze to wander away from God and onto the things of the world. It simply happens if we are not intentional about setting our gaze. It seems that distractions are more prevalent today than in past generations. Families are seldom connected to one another or to God. We seem to never experience the wonder of walking with Christ. If only we could find the time to worship together and experience God pouring out amazing blessing. When we do find mo-

Notes and Quotes:

Consider your schedule and your family's... Are you too busy for God?

Notes and Quotes:
Are you consumed with
WANDER or WONDER?

ments of blessed connection with the Lord, or a season of revival, before we know what happened we are running off to the next athletic season for Junior, or we throw ourselves into that play that our daughter always longed to be able to be a part of. We think, "Oh, it will just be a few weeks." But excellence on the playing field leads to more opportunity. Junior is invited to play on a traveling team that is gone weekend after weekend. The sport is not evil, but Satan uses it to turn our focus away from that which is most important, and we soon find ourselves having moved from the WONDER of God to place of WANDER. My friend, if you are going to show yourself to be a man, you will have to take back your schedule and refocus your gaze. And that will also require you to exercise leadership within your family to bring your wife and children to a place of understanding that God must be first in your life and home.

In the Old Testament, there is a book called Judges. For a period of some 350 years, the Israelite people found themselves in a ruthless cycle. It began with God's amazing blessing which brought them to a very peaceful place in life. But in this place of peace and blessing, the people allowed their gaze to stray away from the One true God to the false gods of the culture around them. Once their focus left the Almighty, their hearts were easy to stray away as well. And having lost their focus, the people found themselves in the place of struggle. Over and over the pattern was lived out, and the people, in their place of trouble, finally recognized their desperate need for God and cried out to Him. Then God would send a Judge to lead them back into a vibrant relationship with Himself.

The REAL Man of God is one who will be used by God to lead his family back into a vibrant relationship with the Almighty. We must return from the places of distraction and put our eyes on Him once more. When Jesus ascended, he sent the Holy Spirit who is available to help us break the cycle of the Judges and to develop a single-minded focus on the God of our salvation. A REAL Man understands God and is focused on Him at all times, even in the midst of a busy season, he intentionally carves out moments of worship for himself and for his family.

"Living a busy life is like running a marathon—we tax our ability to care, our ability to focus, our strength to manage disappointment, our sense of peace and rest. Consequently, we live on the edge of exhaustion, irritation and anger." (Cite: Gary Thomas in <u>Thirsting for God</u>. Page 127).

Oh, man of God, you must "Turn your eyes upon Jesus, Look full in

Notes and Quotes:

His wonderful face, And the things of earth will grow strangely dim, In the light of His glory and grace." (Helen H. Lemmel, 1922. Public Domain). **Developing a Quiet Heart**

I have recently studied four ways to develop a quiet heart that is available to God for intimate relationship. They are: 1) The disciplines of a captivated heart; 2) A bridled tongue; 3) A limited curiosity; and 4) A slow reentry into daily life after a time of prayer. (Cite: Gary Thomas in Thirsting for God. Pages 123-130).

How does a man take captive his own heart for God's glory? You must begin by limiting some things so that you have the energy to concentrate on the important things. On the athletic fields of life, we are diligent about the time of preparation. If you were going to play an important basketball game tomorrow night for a championship, you would not stay up all night tonight or expend all your energy running a marathon. Why? Because you would want to be at your best when you stepped onto the court tomorrow. The discipline of developing a captivated heart is similar to this. We regulate our lives in such a way that we have more energy and focus when we come into the presence of God so that our times with Him are more productive and blessed.

"The more people rejoice over something outside of God, the less intense will be their joy in God; and the more their hope goes out towards something else, the less there is for God." (Cite: Quote by John of the Cross in The Ascent of Mount Carmel, in Thirsting for God, page 123).

What does it mean to have a bridled tongue? One way to keep your heart focused on that which is important is to be "slow to speak and quick to listen." According to the writer of Proverbs, the mark of a spiritual man is a listening heart, not a lecturing tongue.

When words are many, transgression is not lacking,

but whoever restrains his lips is prudent.

(Proverbs 10:19 ESV)

"Oddly, those who talk the most often pray the least, frequently giving the excuse that they simply have no time." (Cite: Gary Thomas in Thirsting for God. Page 125).

Notes and Quotes:

Why should we limit our curiosity? Because when we become involved in all the things of the world that we have no business involving ourselves in, our minds and hearts quickly become distracted, cluttered and divided. It is good counsel to concentrate on the things that are important to you. Some of us are too involved in opinionizing about everything under that sun and yet do not have enough time to focus on what is truly important.

Climacus said, "Stay away from what does not concern you, for curiosity can defile stillness as nothing else can." (Cite: Climacus in The Ladder of Divine Ascent. Page 273.

And why should we tarry after times of prayer? Because the afterglow of prayer brings serenity, clarity and wisdom. Often we do not invest in quiet moments with God like we ought to. I want you to hear me... REAL Men pray. And it is more than a sentence or two as you race at breakneck speed to get to your next adventure in life. No, I am talking about a lingering time in the presence of God. Many will say, "I just don't have time for that." Be honest—we all have the same amount of time every day. It is not a matter of time but rather a matter of commitment.

"After prayer, be careful not to agitate your heart, lest you spill the precious balm you have received. My meaning is, that you must, for some time, if possible, remain in silence, and gently remove your heart from prayer to your other employments; retaining, as long as you can, a feeling of the affections which you have conceived." (Cite: Francis de Sales in Introduction to the Devout Life. Page 75).

How do you get something into your heart?

Diet Matters to a New Heart

As you begin to fill your new heart with the things of God, you must be intentional. It is not enough to just guard your heart from outside intruders who want to fill it with their own toys, you must also begin to fill your heart with the things of God. One of the awesome things about having a new heart is that we can choose what we put into that spiritual warehouse. In a human body that has received a new heart, diet is of the utmost importance. In your spiritual warehouse, what you consume matters.

In my example of the warehouse, my boss began by asking himself, "If I could only house one product in my new warehouse, what product would I choose?" He chose a directional fissured ceiling tile that was our most popular product, Armstrong 755B. If you could only have one quality or characteristic in your heart, what would you choose? I suggest you start by praying for God to fill your heart with that in abundance.

As I have pondered that question, I originally thought that I would choose love. After all, love is a powerful thing. It melts hearts and brings hope to hopelessness. I certainly want love to be available in ample amounts in my new heart. But love did not win my heart as the most important virtue I could pursue. Instead, I choose truth. Why? Because the Truth will set you free.

Consider a few things that make truth essential as you pursue a new life.

> *Behold, you delight in truth in the inward being,*
>
> > *and you teach me wisdom in the secret heart.*

(Psalm 51:6 ESV)

This Psalm teaches us that God takes delight when we cultivate truth in our hearts. If we truly want to bring delight to our Heaven Father, then we will pursue truth.

> *The sum of your word is truth,*
>
> > *and every one of your righteous rules endures forever.*

(Psalm 119:160 ESV)

If we have the truth in us, then we have the fullness of God's Word in our hearts. God's Word is true. And if we had to sum the entirety of His Word up, we could package it in one word...truth. We also learn here that truth is eternal...it "endures forever."

> *So Jesus said to the Jews who had believed him, "If you abide in my word, you are truly my disciples, and you will know the truth, and the truth will set you free."*

(John 8:31-32 ESV)

> *Jesus said to him, "I am the way, and the truth, and the life. No one comes to the Father except through me.*

(John 14:6 ESV)

Certainly we want Jesus in our hearts. And since he is THE Truth, what better characteristic to begin filling our hearts with.

Next, make a short list of essential things that you want to be displayed

Notes and Quotes:

Notes and Quotes:
Which of Blackaby's
characteristics would you
most like to cultivate?

in your heart and ultimately in your life. I have become more and more attracted to humility as I have developed this book.

Gary Thomas says that "Humility and honesty are essential ingredients of an authentic and mature Christian life." (Cite: <u>Thirsting for God</u>. Page 132).

Christian classics throughout the years have lifted up humility as one of chief virtues that is necessary in order to build a holy life. Perhaps Fenelon said it best.

"All the saints are convinced that sincere humility is the foundation of all virtues. This is because humility is the daughter of pure charity, and humility is nothing else but truth. There are only two truths in the world, that God is all and creature is nothing." (Cite: <u>Christian Perfection</u>. Page 205).

Why is humility so important? Consider one last quote on this subject.

"Here is what makes humility the most powerful of virtues: True, God-breathed humility makes sin impossible. If I am humble, I can't sin sexually against another person, because of the thought of abusing someone for my own pleasure would be abhorrent. I couldn't steal from them, because I would rather be wronged or even go hungry than to take what rightfully belongs to someone else. I couldn't use gossip as a way to be accepted in the crowd, because I would be more concerned about someone else's reputation than my own. I couldn't be materialistic, because I would be moved by compassion for others more than I would by my own perceived wants and needs. Humility undercuts virtually every temptation. To grow in humility is to pull up sin by its roots." (Cite: Gary Thomas in <u>Thirsting for God</u>. Pages 133-134).

There are two lists of virtues that I would suggest you consider before we leave this portion of our study. The first list comes from Galatians 5:22-23 which we have come to know as the "Fruits of the Spirit." Surely you will find a number of characteristics here to place in your spiritual warehouse.

But the fruit of the Spirit is love, joy, peace, patience, kindness, goodness, faithfulness, gentleness, self-control; against such things there is no law.

(Galatians 5:22-23 ESV)

The second list comes from Henry Blackaby in his book entitled <u>The</u>

Notes and Quotes:

<u>Man God Uses</u>. Blackaby says that the man God uses has eight specific characteristics in his heart and life. They are: Holiness, A Pure Heart, A Contrite Heart, the Fear of God, Faithfulness, Obedience, a man who Seeks and Loves God, and finally a man who is a Servant of the Lord.

As you can see, the possibilities are endless. Your heart should become a blending of Godly characteristics that melded together form your personality and character; to put it simply, the new you. Remember, you are a "new creation." The old has passed away and all things have become new.

So, how do you get these things into your heart? It was easy to fill that new warehouse years ago. I just drove a forklift over to a semi-load of product and hoisted it up and carried it in. The spiritual forklift that is needed to accomplish this work is called prayer. Begin to ask daily, in very specific ways, for God to cultivate these things in you. And then wait patiently for Him to accomplish his good work. But realize that this endeavor requires a partnership between you and God. You cannot afford to be lazy! Men, we are often passive when it comes to spiritual formation. We just sit back and say, "God, if you want to accomplish this in me, then you are going to have to do it in spite of me." This is sin. We must be active in the process of becoming.

Teresa of Avila said, "If you do not strive for the virtues and practice them, you will always be small in the faith." (Cite: <u>The Interior Castle</u>. Paulist Press. 1979. VII:4:9).

"Cultivating virtues is a necessary part of the Christian life. 'That's just the way I am' is a confession of sloth, not humility. It's admitting that we are too spiritually lazy to change, too selfishly indifferent to the way our weaknesses and lack of virtue hurt people. Whether we have a bad temper or an overly indulgent lifestyle, we injure others, weaken our witness, and grieve our Lord." (Cite: Gary Thomas in <u>Thirsting for God</u>. Page 50).

So get off the couch and get busy! Stop with all the excuses. God is able and will accomplish it if you will invite Him into your heart to do His good work.

Now to him who is able to do far more abundantly than all that we ask or think, according to the power at work within us, to him be glory in the church and in Christ Jesus throughout all generations, forever and ever. Amen.

(Ephesians 3:20-21 ESV)

Chapter 8- Faith Without Works is Dead...Time to Go to Work

Therefore, my beloved, as you have always obeyed, so now, not only as in my presence but much more in my absence, work out your own salvation with fear and trembling, for it is God who works in you, both to will and to work for his good pleasure.

(Philippians 2:12-13 ESV)

Once your new heart has been filled with the virtues of God, you must exercise it to grow and mature in your faith. Think of this like an athlete who is training for a major competition. Scripture is full of illustrative examples suggesting that we should pursue spiritual training in much the same way an athlete trains.

I have fought the good fight, I have finished the race, I have kept the faith. Henceforth there is laid up for me the crown of righteousness, which the Lord, the righteous judge, will award to me on that Day, and not only to me but also to all who have loved his appearing.

(2 Timothy 4:7-8 ESV)

Therefore, since we are surrounded by so great a cloud of witnesses, let us also lay aside every weight, and sin which clings so closely, and let us run with endurance the race that is set before us, looking to Jesus, the founder and perfecter of our faith, who for the joy that was set before him endured the cross, despising the shame, and is seated at the right hand of the throne of God.

(Hebrews 12:1-2 ESV)

This new heart must be exercised and trained in much the same way that one trains for competition on the court or field. It amazes me how men will go to great extremes to become profi-

What kind of spiritual

exercise program are you

on?

cient in their recreational endeavors, but when it comes to being proficient in their spiritual endeavors, they shirk their responsibility and wimp out in fear. Call a man a wimp on the football field and he will fight you to the end. Call him a wimp in his spiritual life or family life and he will often put his tail between his legs and limp away whining as he retreats. We must prepare to fight the good fight of faith with the same tenacity that we would use if we were going to war or battling for a Super Bowl.

Both of my children played sports in high school. I was amazed at the discipline they developed and displayed as they prepared over time to do their very best. My son Morgan played football. I often wondered if the tremendous sacrifice he made to develop his skill on the football field was worth it. That is until one night. It was the first game of his senior year. For three years he had stood on the sidelines with his helmet strapped on ready to play, only to never have his number called. As a parent, I felt for him. All the work he put in seemed for naught. The hours in the weight room, the family vacations missed because he was working to be ready; all of it seemed but a waste. But finally after three years of preparation and hard work, he became a starter. That night as they announced the starting lineup my wife and I stood so proud as we heard his name spoken over the loud speaker. Our team played against Manuel High School, and Morgan played great. I will never forget that night as he arrived home after the game. He was exhausted but so invigorated. He sat on the couch, and we discussed in detail every play. And then he said, "If all I ever got to experience in my football life was this one night, all the hard work would still be worth it."

My daughter, Amye, was a distance runner. Thinking back I wish I had kept track of how many miles she ran over her career in cross country and track. Some weeks, her training required at least sixty miles of running. Often her legs ached and she battled shin splints and stress fractures. During her senior year in high school she faced the hardest part of her career. Her iron levels dropped to the place that she could not even run a mile. We had to radically address her diet and make sure she was getting enough rest. For several months we poured all the nutrients we could into her body. Finally after several months of uncertainty and struggle, her body began to respond to the nutrients we were inputting. The result was that she recovered just in time to qualify for the state finals in the mile. The race took place on the Indiana University track. Thousands of fans filled the stands and cheered. The gun sounded and Amye ran an awesome race, finishing 14th in the state. For us, the joy we felt was magnified by the adversity she had overcome. She had fought the good fight and she had finished the race. But most importantly, she had kept the faith! Training is required if we are to accomplish all that God placed us on this earth to accomplish.

I want you to know that becoming a Strong Man of God will not be easy. It will cost you much. Someone has said that salvation is free but maturity comes with a price. I agree wholeheartedly. I am not calling you to an easy road. This journey will not be over in a week or even a year. It will take the rest of your life. But in the end, when you hear those precious words, "Well done thou good and faithful servant," you will realize that all the effort was worth it. If you rise to this challenge, you will miss some of the things this world has to offer. But you will gain far more than you sacrifice; you will gain eternity.

"The focus on our ultimate salvation rather than persistent growth has been a convenient but spiritually depleting lapse. Growth is painful. It is most frequently the result of enduring difficulty and pain. Unless we are strongly motivated to grow, the effort required will be too great, and we will excuse ourselves from the obligation by saying, 'Jesus already did it for me.' In such a context, this is not a statement of faith; it is a statement of slothfulness. Scripture is bursting with references urging us to grow." (Cite: Gary Thomas in Thirsting for God. Page 20).

Develop a Training Program

The obvious- Prayer, Bible Study, Worship

For most, we have an understanding that the basics of prayer, Bible study and worship are essential to our becoming the men that God calls us to be. I call these three areas, the "Just Do It!" pieces to our training program.

These three areas are like the staples that form the base of every good recipe. It would be hard to bake a great desert without eggs and sugar. These three, prayer, Bible study and worship, can also be seen as the foundation upon which a Christian life is erected. Without a good foundation, the house will not stand. The Rock, of course, is Christ himself. But prayer, Bible study and worship are the anchor bolts that keep one connected to the source of life and strength. Let's take a moment and look a little deeper at each of these disciplines.

Prayer- Years ago I attempted to define prayer in my own words. Here is the definition I came up with then. Prayer is the kindling God uses to

Notes and Quotes:

What other things might be included in the obvious section?

Notes and Quotes:

set ablaze your heart for Him; it is the first movement of a sacred dance from mourning to joy; it is the doorway to communion and it is the highway to purity. Prayer is the chisel of change; it offers vision when darkness consumes and patience when confusion confounds. While Scripture is the road map to life everlasting, prayer is the vehicle we use to travel the pathway that leads to perfect peace. Pray, O child of God, pray without ceasing and travel the journey hand in hand with the author of your destiny. "For I know the plans I have for you," declares the Lord, "plans not to harm you but to prosper you; to give you hope and a future." (Jeremiah 29:11). Pray until you find your way Home! And when you arrive at such a blessed place, you will dance with the One who brought you there, Christ himself.

Prayer is, simply put, communication with God. You will never become the man of God that you were made to be apart from prayer. In the definition above, it says that prayer is the chisel of change. I believe that is accurate. Without prayer we become static in our journey. Some people have a false impression of prayer. They think that prayer is all about changing God's mind with regards to what they want and desire. But how can an unchangeable God, who is the same yesterday, today and forever, change His mind about anything? Prayer is not so much about changing God as it is changing us. When we pray, God hears our prayer and answers every time. Sometimes he says yes, sometimes he says no and sometimes he says wait. When he says no or wait as we ask over and over again for what we desire, then God uses our prayer to launch us on a journey to find God's will and way. Why am I not getting what I pray for? That question leads to a crisis of belief and that becomes the curriculum of change in our lives.

Realize that as a staple, prayer is a non-negotiable. You cannot live as a Christian man and never pray to a Holy God. Take a moment and study these passages about prayer and see if you do not arrive at the place of saying prayer is truly essential for every Christian.

And we urge you, brothers, admonish the idle, encourage the fainthearted, help the weak, be patient with them all. See that no one repays anyone evil for evil, but always seek to do good to one another and to everyone. Rejoice always, pray without ceasing, give thanks in all circumstances; for this is the will of God in Christ Jesus for you. Do not quench the Spirit. Do not despise prophecies, but test everything; hold fast what is good. Abstain from every form of evil.

(1 Thessalonians 5:14-22 ESV)

Watch and pray that you may not enter into temptation. The spirit indeed is willing, but the flesh is weak."

(Matthew 26:41 ESV)

> *Rejoice in hope, be patient in tribulation, be constant in prayer.*

(Romans 12:12 ESV)

> *Is anyone among you suffering? Let him pray. Is anyone cheerful? Let him sing praise.*

(James 5:13 ESV)

Bible Study- When it comes to the staple ingredients of a Godly life, the study of God's word is often one of the weak links in the lives of many men. In my experience as a pastor, Biblical illiteracy appears to be running rampant in our homes and in our churches. If we are going to become REAL Men of God, we must come to a deep understanding of God's Word.

Several years ago I had a life-changing experience as I was sitting in a classroom studying about how to become a Biblical counselor. The session that evening was about God's Word. I had been to Bible college and to seminary, so I thought that this class would be just a review for me. I had studied God's Word through much of my adult life and had read the Bible through from start to finish on several occasions. But on this night, I saw God's Word through new eyes. The instructor that evening walked a group of about 25 men and women through approximately 20 passages that simply spoke about God's Word. Most of those passages are printed below. Before you read them now, stop and pray that God would allow you to see them with new eyes and a new heart. And then allow the Word of God to bathe your soul. Enjoy!

> *Your word is a lamp to my feet*
>> *and a light to my path.*

(Psalm 119:105 ESV)

> *The sum of your word is truth,*
>> *and every one of your righteous rules endures forever.*

(Psalm 119:160 ESV)

> *All Scripture is breathed out by God and profitable for teaching, for reproof, for correction, and for training in righteousness, that the man of God may be complete, equipped for every good work.*

(2 Timothy 3:16-17 ESV)

Notes and Quotes:

> Is not my word like fire, declares the LORD, and like a hammer that breaks the rock in pieces?

(Jeremiah 23:29 ESV)

> Do not add to his words,
>
> > lest he rebuke you and you be found a liar.

(Proverbs 30:6 ESV)

> For the word of God is living and active, sharper than any two-edged sword, piercing to the division of soul and of spirit, of joints and of marrow, and discerning the thoughts and intentions of the heart.

(Hebrews 4:12 ESV)

> But be doers of the word, and not hearers only, deceiving yourselves.

(James 1:22 ESV)

> The law of the LORD is perfect,
>
> > reviving the soul;
>
> the testimony of the LORD is sure,
>
> > making wise the simple;
>
> the precepts of the LORD are right,
>
> > rejoicing the heart;
>
> the commandment of the LORD is pure,
>
> > enlightening the eyes;
>
> the fear of the LORD is clean,
>
> > enduring forever;
>
> the rules of the LORD are true,
>
> > and righteous altogether.
>
> More to be desired are they than gold,
>
> > even much fine gold;
>
> sweeter also than honey
>
> > and drippings of the honeycomb.

(Psalm 19:7-10 ESV)

> Your words were found, and I ate them,

and your words became to me a joy

and the delight of my heart,

for I am called by your name,

O LORD, God of hosts.

(Jeremiah 15:16 ESV)

That night as these passages were read, something profound happened to me. I fell in love with God's Word. It wasn't that I had never cared for His Word before then. But things were different following that evening. I no longer saw the Bible as just words on a page. No, these were God's WORDS, spoken to me. It became personal that night. I pray that as you begin to train yourself to be a workman who can "rightly divide the Word of Truth," that you too will fall in love with the Word of the Lord.

Worship- Some will look at my inclusion of worship as a staple ingredient in Godly training and say, "How can this be true? Isn't worship about giving God glory and not about what we receive?" I agree completely that worship is not so much about us as it is about God and giving Him glory, honor and praise. But remember the story that I shared from Isaiah 6. Isaiah comes into the Throne room of God and in an amazing encounter with God, he suddenly finds a new understanding of self. When we come before God and worship Him, not only is He glorified, but we are changed.

Another aspect of worship that lends itself to our growth and maturity is when we listen to the preaching of God's Word in the context of corporate worship. Martin Luther said, "The greatest act of worship is the preaching of the Word." We must remember that God's Word never returns unto Him void. It is powerful, and therefore, worship is a vital part of God's designed plan to change us into the likeness of His Son.

And let us consider how to stir up one another to love and good works, not neglecting to meet together, as is the habit of some, but encouraging one another, and all the more as you see the Day drawing near.

(Hebrews 10:24-25 ESV)

We should understand that we do not mature in faith in a vacuum apart from other people. No, we need each other. So the writer of Hebrews calls us to spur one another on to acts of good works and to not forsake the gathering of the church. Why? Because we are to help one another to become Godly.

Notes and Quotes:

Do you agree that worship is necessary for growth?

Notes and Quotes:
What other, not so
obvious ways can you
think of to train yourself?

The not-so-obvious:

Rising early, Journaling, Meditating on the Word, Partnering, Personal Trainer

Rising Early- I have to admit that as I write this training method, I am not incredibly excited about this discipline. I love to sleep in late. But the more that I study this method of spiritual discipline and put it into practice in my life, the more convinced I am that there is great wisdom in rising early and seeking God to start your day.

A while back I preached a sermon about developing a spiritual quiet time to devote your full attention to God. I included in that challenge a statement that said, "God is not so interested in what time of the day you choose to honor Him with your time as he is interested in you spending time with Him every day." After that service, a wonderful lady gently approached me and challenged me to think about that statement. She said she believed that she could build a Biblical case that God wanted our time and attention first thing in the morning based on the story of the manna that God provided the Israelites; perhaps even before the sun would break the horizon.

> *My heart is steadfast, O God,*
>
> > *my heart is steadfast!*
>
> *I will sing and make melody!*
>
> > *Awake, my glory!*
>
> *Awake, O harp and lyre!*
>
> > *I will awake the dawn!*

(Psalm 57:7-8 ESV)

"...how odious we must appear in the sight of Heaven if we are in bed shut up in sleep and darkness, when we should be praising God, and are such slaves to drowsiness as to neglect our devotions for it." (Cite: William Law from <u>Serious Call</u>. Page 189.

Can we be honest, men? Our culture is falling more and more into laziness. The Biblical term for this is slothfulness.

> *Slothfulness casts into a deep sleep,*
>
> > *and an idle person will suffer hunger.*

(Proverbs 19:15 ESV)

A note from the ESV Study Bible regarding this verse says, "The lazy person is always too tired to work. Then his laziness becomes more and more severe until he is in dire poverty." It would be easy for us to place this simply into a physical context, but what if we apply it spiritually. If we become spiritually lazy then that laziness will multiply itself until we reach the place of spiritual poverty.

Do not be slothful in zeal, be fervent in spirit, serve the Lord. Rejoice in hope, be patient in tribulation, be constant in prayer.

(Romans 12:11-12 ESV)

A byproduct of rising early and spending time with God is that it puts us on a schedule that places us at a place of weariness during a time period when Satan seems to do his best work late in the evening when we are perhaps more vulnerable to sin. A young man made a bold statement to a friend following his release from the county jail. He said, "I can tell you one thing, I am never going out after 1 AM again." When the friend inquired why not, the young man said, "Because that's when all the trouble starts! Everyone in that jail got in trouble after midnight!" Perhaps your being up or out late will not bring added temptation to your life, but for some there is probably some truth in this.

"As a sin-laden man living in a sinful world, I've found I'm much more vulnerable to particular types of sin after nine at night than I am when I arise at five in the morning, except perhaps for such attitudinal sins as the slavish pursuit of money or selfish ambition." (Cite: Gary Thomas in Thirsting for God. Page 52).

I am not saying that in order for you to be strong and show yourself a man that you have to rise early. But for some, this is a wonderful discipline that leads them into Godliness.

One final thought regarding this before I move on. Rise early and spend an hour in study and prayer before the sun comes up. Then stop and allow your eyes to feast on the glory of God's creation just as the sun breaks the horizon. Do it and just see if your heart does not burst with worship! Mine did.

Fasting- There was a day when fasting would have fallen under the obvious category. But in this day and age, fasting has become all but obsolete in the church. In fact, in his book Celebration of Discipline, Richard Foster says that he could not find even a single book that was written on the subject of fasting between 1861 and 1954. And certainly in today's church, fasting has fallen by the wayside.

Notes and Quotes:

Notes and Quotes:

John Wesley said, "Some have exalted religious fasting beyond all Scripture and reason; and others have utterly disregarded it." (Cite: Celebration of Discipline. Page 47).

Fasting is referred to throughout Scripture as the abstaining from eating food for a spiritual purpose. Probably the most remembered fast was when Jesus fasted for forty days in the wilderness and was tempted by Satan in Luke 4. If you take a few moments and study, you will find many passages in Scripture that speak of this discipline.

The practical application of this discipline is that one would refrain from eating for the purpose of pursuing God on a deeper level. When I fast, I do so to focus my prayer life. Every time I feel those pains of hunger, I allow the Lord to use those pains to drive me deeper into prayer. So I find that I do pray more often and with more intensity.

The question most have when we speak about it is, "Should I fast?"

"And when you fast, do not look gloomy like the hypocrites, for they disfigure their faces that their fasting may be seen by others. Truly, I say to you, they have received their reward. But when you fast, anoint your head and wash your face, that your fasting may not be seen by others but by your Father who is in secret. And your Father who sees in secret will reward you.

(Matthew 6:16-18 ESV)

Notice both verse s 16 and 17 begin with the words "...when you fast." Certainly as Jesus taught in the Sermon on the Mount, he assumed that fasting would continue as the church moved forward. It was not a question of if we would fast or not, but rather when we would fast. It is also important to realize that fasting is not to be placed on public display; it is not to be bragged about or made the focus of our righteousness. Rather, we should fast in secret so that we receive no glory.

To answer that question mentioned above, Should I fast? I suggest you pray about it and explore what God wants you to do with regards to this discipline. And then do whatever He lays on your heart.

"Fasting must forever center on God. It must God-initiated and God-ordained." (Cite: Ibid. Page 54).

Perhaps as a part of your new spiritual training program, you will feel led to include fasting in your disciplined approach. For further study of this discipline I suggest you read Richard Foster's Celebration of Discipline. Perhaps as a part of this study, you may simply want to fast for a meal and see what God will teach you. Or perhaps you will want to fast

Notes and Quotes:

for a day or even a day each week. My purpose in bringing this to you is that you might have another opportunity to grow in faith.

Journaling- For some people, journaling becomes a great tool for growth in their walk of faith. I try to always keep a notebook close by to record important thoughts, quotes and passages that come to me as I study. Some people see this to be something similar to a spiritual diary to record each day's thoughts and experiences. I have participated in this type of journaling at different points in my Christian walk, but do not do it on a daily basis. I occasionally will go back and read what I wrote weeks or months or even years ago. What I see is that I am prone to write when I am overwhelmed with God's blessing and when I walk through trials. In these postings of my thoughts and feelings there are lots of written prayers. I find that writing my prayers in times of distress helps me greatly to focus and ask God for specific things rather than general things. But while I do not journal in this way every day, I do use a journal simply to record important findings in my study almost daily.

"There are many ways to communicate and spend time with the Lord. One of the most effective and useful tools you can use to draw closer to God is Christian journaling. Every Christian should read and pray every day. It is a wonderful way to grow spiritually. However, through journaling, a Christian can grow even more because it takes more thought and motivation. Christian journaling combines prayer, scripture reading, and deeper analysis of God's teachings all into one. It is an excellent way to spend time with God and truly draw closer to him." (Cite: http://www.squidoo.com/christianjournaling101).

For step-by-step instructions on journaling I suggest you read Journaling as a Spiritual Practice: Encountering God through Attentive Writing, (InterVarsity Press, 2008).

Meditate on God's Word- Now friends, I want to be very careful with this discipline. This is not some eastern mysticism that is prevalent in the world today. Rather this is simply the art of stopping and lighting upon a particular piece of God's Word and hovering there for a period while asking God to deepen our understanding and experience.

This Book of the Law shall not depart from your mouth, but you shall meditate on it day and night, so that you may be careful to

Notes and Quotes:

do according to all that is written in it. For then you will make your way prosperous, and then you will have good success.

(Joshua 1:8 ESV)

> *Blessed is the man*
>
> > *who walks not in the counsel of the wicked,*
>
> *nor stands in the way of sinners,*
>
> > *nor sits in the seat of scoffers;*
>
> *but his delight is in the law of the LORD,*
>
> > *and on his law he meditates day and night.*

(Psalm 1:1-2 ESV)

As you meditate on God's Word, you will be blessed. Too often we read the Bible as if it were some novel that we are striving to finish. But that approach to God's Word usually leaves us empty. I want to encourage you to find those wonderful jewels of wisdom in the Scriptures and then think deeply about them. One author says we are to "muse" about the richness of God's Word.

"To muse means to "ponder, consider, and study closely." This is the aspect of meditation that most people are aware of: taking hold of a promise or a truth and going over it again and again; not going over it in order to memorize it, but squeezing out all the richness; thinking on it and allowing it to wash through your inner man." (Cite: http://hopefaithprayer.com/scriptures/three-ways-to-meditate-gods-word-dennis-burke/).

"Bible reading is like the potatoes in your spiritual diet. You must have meat in your diet to remain healthy. The meat comes as you chew on a promise. Let it circulate through you. Squeeze the life of God from it.

This will bring the greatest discovery of revelation knowledge you have ever known. As you meditate, you will receive fresh revelation for yourself. There is no substitute for knowing you have heard from the Holy Spirit. There is no replacement for time spent in meditation and fellowship with God.

He will become intimate with you. This is the desire of God: to have an intimate relationship with His children. The Apostle James said, "Draw nigh to God, and he will draw nigh to you" (James 4:8)." (Ibid).

Partnering- If we are honest, it is often difficult for us to train alone. When my daughter, Amye, was at the top of her athletic career, she was often given a personalized training program to complete on her own. These became the hardest days. Why? Because she wanted and needed her teammates in order to do the things that were necessary to become strong and to excel. Without a partner, she seldom pushed herself to greater heights. But with a partner who encouraged her, she flourished and the routine became a relational opportunity to not only do the hard work, but it was her avenue to grow in relationship as well. In fact, the girls she ran cross country with still hold a special place in her heart.

Partners are not mentors but rather peers who are at a similar place in their journey of faith. Sometimes we find great strength in working together to accomplish goals.

My friend, Randy Kimberly, found himself at a difficult spot in life. He was significantly overweight and knew that without some discipline in his life, the extra weight would probably shorten his life and certainly limit his mobility and opportunity to enjoy life. Randy would tell you that he is not a very disciplined man.

One day Randy and his wife Debbie decided to partner together in order to try to lose some weight. The plan would primarily be to insert daily exercise into his life. An amazing thing happened. Together they were able to do what Randy could never do alone. The pounds began to drop off. And the byproduct of the partnership was that Randy and his wife had special times to talk and connect. After a year or so Randy came to me at the door of the church and said, "I have lost 98 pounds... be praying God will help me get to 100 this week." The next week he broke the century mark. How did he do that? How did he lose more than 100 pounds without surgery? He did it one day at a time with the help of a friend.

Perhaps you struggle to stay on task when it comes to spiritual training. Partner up with someone who will encourage you as you encourage them. The results will amaze you. And you will also experience the precious byproduct of a deeper relationship!

Spiritual Director- While the partner mentioned above is a friend or peer in your journey of faith, the Spiritual Director is a mentor. This should be a man who is more mature than you are who can speak into your life with Biblical truth. He should be credible in his witness of

Notes and Quotes:

Notes and Quotes:

Christ. However, you must realize that this man, while more mature than yourself, is on his own journey towards holiness and has not yet arrived. You can ill afford to take your eyes off of Christ and place them upon any man. A Spiritual Director can and will fail at times and you should expect there to be times when his human nature will show forth, even as he strives to honor Christ and walk in such a way that he can say to you, *"Follow me as I follow Christ." (1 Corinthians 11:1)*.

Recently I preached a sermon on David's fall as he committed both adultery and murder. Thankfully for David, there was a man in his life who was Godly enough to confront him with his sin, even though that confrontation could have ended in his death. The mentor was a man named Nathan. And his confrontation with David gave the King opportunity to confess and repent. Everyone needs a Nathan in their life; someone who will bring the Truth even when it is not popular to hear.

Many have heard the name Augustine. He was a man who lived in the 300s. He is noted as an early father of Christian theology and left a work that is often quoted thousands of years after his death. The work was called his Confessions. Early in his life, Augustine saw no need for God and was by his own definition a true scoundrel. But eventually God broke his heart and he came to faith. Listen to what he says led to spiritual growth and maturity in his life.

"To Milan I came, to Ambrose the Bishop...To him was I unknowingly led by Thee, that by him I might knowingly be led to Thee. That man of God received me as a father...I hung on his words attentively." (Cite: Confessions. V:23).

Milan was the place Augustine came and Ambrose was the person that spoke Truth into his life. I again say every man needs a mentor... a Nathan or an Ambrose.

We live in the day of personal trainers. The gym craze has taken over in a massive way. People boast of their attempt and desire to get in shape physically. But often they say, "The spirit is willing but the flesh is weak." Therefore they seek out a gym that will offer them personalized instruction and training. The church should be about this type of personalized training in a spiritual sense. Who has God placed in your pathway to help you grow and become all that God desires you to be?

"Even the most mature Christian, according to John Climacus, hasn't outgrown the need for the input of others. Any one of us could be led astray. 'A man, no matter how prudent, may easily go astray on a road if he has no guide.'" (Cite: Climacus quoted in Thomas' Thirsting for God. Pages 254-255).

Francis de Sales said, "Wouldst thou walk in earnest towards devotion, seek a good man, who may guide and conduct thee; this is the best advice I can give thee." (Cite: Ibid. Page 254)

Now you may be asking at this point, "Do I have to have a spiritual director in order to grow in faith?" The answer to that question is no. There is no Biblical mandate that such a mentor is required. This is simply a suggestion born out of practical experience through the ages. However, due to the passive nature of man, especially when it comes to spiritual and relational things, having such a man in your life can be a huge catalyst for growth. Consider this by taking it to the Lord and asking for wisdom and direction on this matter.

My final word here is to realize that this is for more than just bringing to light sin in your life. It is also to bring a healthy dose of encouragement to inspire you to soar above the worldly philosophies so that you might bring honor and glory to your Heavenly Father and experience His abundant blessing!

Discussion Questions on Chapters 6-8:

1. If you had just received a heart transplant, how concerned would you be about making sure you were diligent in caring for your new heart?

2. What have you done to maintain a healthy heart spiritually?

3. What do you need to do in order to keep your new heart strong and healthy so that you might honor God in all that you do and bring grace to the ones you love?

4. Part of this lesson was on developing a spiritual diet. What are the things that you believe you need to do to input Godly character into your life?

5. What is God's role in what goes into your heart? What is your role?

6. We covered some obvious disciplines that train us and bring strength of character to our lives. Which of these three, prayer, Bible Study, or worship, is easiest for you to invest in and which is the most difficult for you? Why?

7. Of the not so obvious methods that were mentioned, what are you

Notes and Quotes:

Notes and Quotes:

most likely to incorporate into your future walk of faith? Why?

8. What other things come to your mind that are Godly disciplines that help a person grow in faith?

Concentric Circle #2- Our Judea... Impacting the People Closest to You for God's Glory

From the very beginning, God has laid on my heart that this book was to be about a man's impact on the world around him. In order to understand that calling to impact the world for Christ, it was important to begin with a good understanding of God. Now that we have established that foundation, let's launch into the heart of the issues involved. How does a man impact his wife and children with the gospel? Should he be single, divorced or widowed, then what is his obligation to the furtherance of the kingdom? What will your legacy be? These questions and more will be addressed as we move forward.

Remember the ripples of water that flow out from the impact point where the stone broke the surface of the water? We have studied the stone which represents God in our lives. The deeper our understanding of him, the larger the impact He has on our lives and the bigger the waves that result. If we have a puny understanding of God, then we will have a puny impact on others. But if we have an accurate understanding of the majesty and glory of God, the waves will have tremendous impact on those who are close to us.

This section deals with the people who are closest to you. For most who read this, it will be their wives and children. For some, it will be their mothers, fathers, sisters and brothers. And for others it will be their peers: the people they room with, work with or do life with. In every man's life, there are people who stand in those most cherished spots. If you are not married, then apply these principles to your closest relationships and allow God's living water to flow out to those you love most.

The first four areas that we will look at as a man impacts the lives of his loved ones will be a man's call to be a protector, a provider, a prophet/mentor and a priest. These roles are significant and provide a context for you to become a minister to those you love. Every man is called to be a shepherd, to care for the people who are entrusted to his care by the Almighty. We must prepare ourselves to be used by God for His glory and to deliver His blessing to those we love. This is your Judea, the next place you must concentrate. Take the gospel of hope to those who are most precious to you and deliver God's love with both passion and compassion.

Chapter 9- Protector, Defender, Soldier, Warrior

4 Love is patient, love is kind. It does not envy, it does not boast, it is not proud. 5 It is not rude, it is not self-seeking, it is not easily angered, it keeps no record of wrongs. 6 Love does not delight in evil but rejoices with the truth. 7 It always protects, always trusts, always hopes, always perseveres.

8 Love never fails. (1 Corinthians 13:4-8 NIV).

If you are a REAL Man who has a vibrant, growing relationship with Jesus Christ, then you have been called to protect and to defend. To put it simply, as the Apostle Paul did, love always protects! When things in life get really hard you must adopt a military attitude that is often talked about in Scripture as the attitude of a soldier or warrior.

The structures of our lives are under attack, but some men seem to not even notice. They are so busy chasing after careers or hobbies that they do not realize that Satan is waging an all-out assault on the family, on marriage, and on the church. Sound the alarm!!! Danger is lurking just outside your door. REAL Men of God realize that they have a God-given duty to protect.

Let's begin by asking what or who we are to protect. Well, the obvious place to begin would be with our families - our wives and children. And that certainly will require a significant amount of our energy and attention, but before we get to the home, let's consider a couple other things that must be protected in order for our focus on our home to be effective.

We Protect and Defend the Reputation of God

When you became a Christian and received that new heart, you enlisted in the army of the Lord. When someone enlists in the army of the United States of America, they take an oath to support and defend the country. It goes something like this: "I, [name], do solemnly swear (or affirm) that I will support and defend the Constitution of the United States against all ene-

Notes and Quotes:

mies, foreign and domestic; that I will bear true faith and allegiance to the same; that I take this obligation freely, without any mental reservation or purpose of evasion; and that I will well and faithfully discharge the duties of the office on which I am about to enter. So help me God." (Cite: http://en.wikipedia.org/wiki/ United_States_Uniformed_Services_Oath_of_Office).

You are probably wondering where I am going with this thinking. I believe that as a Christian man, I bear the responsibility to protect and defend the honor and reputation of my God. I realize that God can more than take care of Himself. But I believe I bear a responsibility to protect and defend the Name of the Lord. I am so tired of men claiming to be in Christ, and yet by the way they live their lives, they drag Him through the mud and filth with very little awareness that they are harming his reputation in the world. The credibility of their testimony and of the church is weakened, if not destroyed, by the lack of reverence and respect that is shown as they chase after earthly, fleshly things that in no way bring honor and glory to the one they "call" Lord. I wonder, "If there was a Christian uniform that proclaimed boldly that we were soldiers of the Most High, would we act in disgraceful ways, publicly humiliating the One we have pledged to serve?" This last question has drawn my attention over and over for one reason. How ironic that He gives grace even when we offer disgrace. That's amazing to me. My friend, if you are a Christian, you carry the name of the Lord on your person. It is like a uniform that announces to the world, "I am a Christian."

We often talk about testimonies in the church. A testimony is simply a person's own story of how he/she came to Christ and what God has done in and for him/her. What if the last month of your life was your written testimony? Would it be an honorable discourse about the Lord?

Warning: Did you know that other people, Christians and non-Christians can see your Facebook posts? Because of social media, our lives are perhaps more transparent to the world than they have ever been. Now, I am not saying that we as Christians can't use this avenue for God's glory. But it is alarming to me when I see a man or woman profess Christ on one day and then lift up Satan on the next. Some will say, "Well I didn't lift up Satan, that was just some innocent fun." Or they may say, "I still have to battle that sinful nature, and I am not perfect and never will be!" But my friends, that is just the problem. We see ourselves powerless against sin. When Jesus died on the cross, not only was the penalty of sin broken, but the power of sin as well. Christian man, you do not HAVE to sin. We have a choice. Will we ever conquer this struggle this side of heaven? No, but we must fight! So many men are passive when it comes to going to war with evil. We must not walk in "cheap grace" with no intention to honor God. We must fight the good fight of faith and defend the character and majesty of our God. We must protect and defend our God.

We Protect and Defend the Gospel

Never in the history of the world has the gospel message come under such attack. That is my own personal opinion, but here is why I believe this statement to be true. In past decades and centuries, the existence of evil has been just as active as it is today. But one thing has changed significantly. In the past, when evil reared its head and tried to deceive and destroy, the majority had some relationship and understanding of Truth. The Bible is a book of absolute Truth. And in the past there was some national submission to it as an anchor to bring us to an understanding of right and wrong. But today all the "isms" have infiltrated the thinking of both Americans and the world. No longer do people revere God's Word and allow it authority. Humanism, atheism, relativism, me-ism, and scores of other "isms" have all found their way to the table of modern day thinking. We have thought ourselves into a dilemma. We have thought ourselves to the place of proclaiming ourselves and our minds to be god. As a result, we have lost faith. *"Now faith is the substance of things hoped for, the evidence of things unseen." (Hebrews 11:1).* That is right, faith is believing in what you cannot see. And this is where our problem was born. Our culture tells us that if you can't wrap your mind around something and understand it in an exhaustive way then it is unbelievable. But God is indescribable and incomprehensible. A.W. Tozer said that if you ever reach the point that you think you understand God, then you don't; because God is way beyond our ability to understand. Scripture would agree.

> *For my thoughts are not your thoughts,*
>
> > *neither are your ways my ways, declares the LORD.*
>
> *For as the heavens are higher than the earth,*
>
> > *so are my ways higher than your ways*
>
> > *and my thoughts than your thoughts.*

(Isaiah 55:8-9 ESV)

We have a responsibility as men of God, to step up and battle for the

Notes and Quotes:

gospel message, to fight for Truth.

See to it that no one takes you captive by philosophy and empty deceit, according to human tradition, according to the elemental spirits of the world, and not according to Christ.

(Colossians 2:8 ESV)

For though we walk in the flesh, we are not waging war according to the flesh. For the weapons of our warfare are not of the flesh but have divine power to destroy strongholds. We destroy arguments and every lofty opinion raised against the knowledge of God, and take every thought captive to obey Christ, being ready to punish every disobedience, when your obedience is complete.

(2 Corinthians 10:3-6 ESV)

As you read these verses, you cannot help but see the warrior mentality called forth by the Apostle Paul. Our weapons are not of this world. But we are called to go to war against philosophies that stand against the knowledge of God. We must, according to Stu Weber, run to the places where evil attacks and wage war.

REAL Men step up to fight evil on a daily basis. It is not enough to just try and avoid it or coexist with evil. We must face it down and fight to eliminate it wherever we find it in our culture.

A British politician, Edmund Burke said, "All that it necessary for the triumph of evil is that good men do nothing." (Cite: Stepping Up: A Call to Courageous Manhood).

Do not be overcome by evil, but overcome evil with good.

(Romans 12:21 ESV)

In his book entitled Spirit Warriors, Webber says that one of the problems that we have fallen into, perhaps as a result of our politically correct culture, is that we simply try to contain evil rather than destroy it. He uses the tragedy at Columbine High School in Littleton, CO to make his point. When the shooting began, officers arrived fairly quickly. They could still hear the guns blazing inside. But instead of running to the guns and facing the evil and destroying it, they simply tried to contain it. They set up a perimeter and waited for backup. All the while, the massacre inside continued on until the two gunmen took their own lives. Still for hours, the wounded lay on floors bleeding to death. What if the first officers on the scene had run into battle to eliminate the evil that threatened the innocent? Perhaps some who died might well have lived.

Men, we must do better. We cannot allow evil to exist in our backyards and not expect it to wander over and take a shot at our son or daughter playing unaware. We must not become idle or lazy in our battle against the evil one. The cost of our passivity will be tremendous.

We Must Protect and Defend Our Hearts and Minds

You will notice that in Colossians 2:8 Paul tells us to see to it that no one takes you captive. Earlier in this study we talked about the need to guard our hearts. This is simply a reminder that we are all susceptible to the schemes of the devil. Guard your heart and mind so that you do not fall to sin.

Keep your heart with all vigilance, for from it flow the springs of life. (Proverbs 4:23 ESV)

Do not be anxious about anything, but in everything by prayer and supplication with thanksgiving let your requests be made known to God. And the peace of God, which surpasses all understanding, will guard your hearts and your minds in Christ Jesus. (Philippians 4:6-7 ESV).

Do not be conformed to this world, but be transformed by the renewal of your mind, that by testing you may discern what is the will of God, what is good and acceptable and perfect. (Romans 12:2 ESV).

My flesh and my heart may fail, but God is the strength of my heart and my portion forever. (Psalm 73:26 ESV).

Men, this is about spiritual warfare. And I want you to know that God has not left us defenseless. We have been more than provided for. When you study Ephesians 6:10-20, you will see that two of the pieces of the armor of the Lord are specifically designed to protect your mind and your heart, the breastplate of righteousness and the helmet of salvation. If you give yourself to pursuing righteousness, your heart will be protected. And dwelling on what Christ has done for you by dying on the cross to offer you the free gift of salvation will act as a protection for your mind. We must be prepared when Satan comes calling or we will surely die.

Notes and Quotes:

Chapter 10- The Basic Principles of Marriage

Before I attempt to discuss being a protector of your wife, I want to take a few pages and speak about God's intentions for marriage. This is not a book on marriage. However, a man cannot discuss becoming a REAL Man of God without looking at one of the foundational callings of a man, that of loving and leading his wife. So let's ask ourselves, "What is God's plan for marriage?"

There are at least four reasons that God designed marriage.

1) It is not good for man to be alone. (Genesis 2:18). When God created the heavens and the earth and then covered the earth with all the beautiful plants and creatures, He completed his work with this statement: "And God saw everything that he had made, and behold, it was very good." (Genesis 1:31 ESV). When God then made Adam, He said, "It is not good for man to be alone." We cannot infer from this that God made a mistake and created Adam less than perfect. God could have made Adam complete, not lacking anything. Instead, God chose to make Adam incomplete and then created him a wife to complete him. In Genesis 2:24 we learn that the man and woman together become one. This is God's design. We must recognize that God's intention is that a man would marry a woman and that together they would do life. Some will say that it is not God's intention for every man to marry, and I would agree with this statement. But celibacy and singleness is a gift that some (few) are given for the purpose of honoring God in a special way. But for most, God's design is that we will marry a woman and our marriage would be a significant piece of our testimony.

2) God made marriage for procreation. It has always been God's design for families to continue from generation to generation. The way that God continues mankind is through the union of a man and a woman.

3) God made marriage as an instrument of sanctification.

4) God made marriage as an illustration.

Notes and Quotes:

God Intends for Marriage to Last a Lifetime

And Pharisees came up to him and tested him by asking, "Is it lawful to divorce one's wife for any cause?" He answered, "Have you not read that he who created them from the beginning made them male and female, and said, 'Therefore a man shall leave his father and his mother and hold fast to his wife, and the two shall become one flesh'? So they are no longer two but one flesh. What therefore God has joined together, let not man separate."

(Matthew 19:3-6 ESV)

Divorce in America has led to a crisis in the home that is tearing away the stability of our culture and nation. Fatherless homes are becoming more and more the norm rather than the exception. Children who grow up without a father in the home are more vulnerable than ever.

Most of you have heard that the divorce rate in America is about 50%. This figure has been widely spoken about in churches concerned about the state of marriage today, and rightly so. That statistic is often disputed by sociologists and psychologists. But every finding that I have come across in my research shows that marriage is in trouble in America. According to the Forrest Institute that did a recent study on the divorce rate, the number of first marriages that end in divorce is 50%. But usually when a person gets divorced they look to remarry. That is when the numbers begin to soar and spiral out of control. The divorce rate of second marriages is 67%. And third marriages end in divorce 74% of the time. (Cite Jennifer Baker of the Forrest Institute. See http://www.divorcerate.org/).

I recently heard a new term that seems to describe today's cultural view of marriage: disposable marriage. Even in the church we have fallen prey to a shallow view of an institution created and ordained by God to be the most sacred of human relationships. We have cheapened it and trivialized it. Here are just a few ways that we have come to make marriage disposable.

We have walked away from God's standard to abstain from sex before marriage and to stay sexually pure until we marry. Premarital sex has become the norm in our society and even in the church we have adopted a "don't ask, don't tell" approach. Not long ago I had a couple come to me for premarital counseling, and they offered me the fact that they were sexually active and felt no guilt or shame. Then they said they had made a very intentional decision after studying God's Word and finding nowhere in the Bible that indicated that sex before marriage was a sin. Unfortunately, recent Bible translations have left out a word that would have perhaps helped them understand God's call to purity - fornication. Most translations have generalized a number of sexual sins into a broad category called "sexual immorality." Fornication by definition is "voluntary sexual intercourse between two unmarried persons or two persons not married to each other." (Cite: www.dictionary.com). As a culture we have turned our backs on a call to remain sexually pure until marriage. We have labeled this call and commandment to be "old fashioned" and cheapened marriage in the process.

We have adopted a "divorce for any reason mentality." In Scripture there are only two reasons why a Christian should ever divorce their spouse; 1) Marital unfaithfulness (see Matthew 19) and 2) Abandonment (see 1 Corinthians 7). But culture has led us down the path to a place where people, even in the church, divorce for reasons that are far from the Biblical standard. "I just don't want to be married anymore," a lady said to me recently. "We just fell out of love," another will say. Disposable marriage is a result of a casual view of sin and a rampant attack of Satan against God's institution of marriage. We have walked away from the integrity that was and is, and always will be, God's intended purpose for marriage. The vow has been desecrated and the integrity of a people has fallen to the place of crucifying the standard of God in order to get what we want. God has forever called us to crucify the selfish, sinful desire so that God's standard might shine forth as Truth. This is the way to Godliness. We must restore the standard. It begins with each Christian man first living to God's standard of "until death do us part," and then teaching that standard to our children.

We have made marriage disposable by teaching that it is only about one's happiness. As I mentioned above, one of the four reasons God designed marriage was for the purpose of our sanctification. Marriage is the most intimate of human relationships. Your wife will come to see you at your best, but she will also come to see you at your worst. God intends for the marriage relationship to act like sandpaper to round off all the rough edges of your character so that you might, more and more, come to look like Jesus Christ. I agree with Gary Thomas in his book Sacred Marriage when he says that he believes that marriage is more about making us holy than making us happy. In this egocentric culture we have lost our concern to bring God pleasure and have replaced it with seeking our own.

I must acknowledge that we do not live in a perfect world. Divorce

Notes and Quotes:

happens, and often it happens when one partner in a marriage does not want it to happen. We must not condemn those who have experienced the pain of divorce as a result of having been sinned against by a spouse unwilling to honor God. We must also offer forgiveness to every person who will come confessing their failure and desire to pursue God's way into the future. We must offer mercy to those who do not even recognize their sinfulness which has led to brokenness. But we must call the men of the church to be strong and courageous and live to the call of Scripture to honor their vows and walk in righteousness in spite of what the world declares. Again I say, we must drive a stake in the ground and kick Satan out of our homes and out of our marriage beds. When we fail, we must confess and then walk in repentance for the glory of God and for the benefit and blessing of those we love. We can do better. We must do better. Let's take back marriage and give our kids a chance at faith and victory!

God Intends for the Husband to Lead His Wife as Christ Leads His Church

For the husband is the head of the wife even as Christ is the head of the church, his body, and is himself its Savior. Now as the church submits to Christ, so also wives should submit in everything to their husbands.

(Ephesians 5:23-24 ESV)

Men, we need to rise up and show the world what God's love looks like by loving our wives with a love that goes beyond understanding. It must be a sacrificial love that does not demand reciprocation and it must be lavishly offered even when our wives do not deserve it. God's love is unconditional and available even when we do not reciprocate. And certainly God's love is always present even though we in no way deserve it. For more on this definition of love, see Paul David Tripp's book entitled <u>What Did You Expect?</u>

Chapter 11- Being Your Wife's Protector

Husbands, love your wives, as Christ loved the church and gave himself up for her...

(Ephesians 5:25 ESV)

I must begin this chapter with an emphatic statement: There is no human relationship on earth more important than the marriage relationship! Why? Because the marriage relationship is to be a picture to the world of Christ's love for us.

There is great concern in the world today that men not be put in a position to dominate a woman. And I believe that because many men have abused their role, we have adopted a philosophy that stereotypes men to be abusive, controlling and overbearing. The cultural picture is that if a man leads then he is stifling his wife and using her as a doormat to get what he wants.

I want to say straight up that a man who abuses his wife is sinning against her and against God and must be held accountable for his sin. God's intent is that a husband would lead his wife in the same kind of loving way that Christ leads his church. How did Jesus show love for the church? He died for her. In the same way, men, we must lead with a sacrificial love that is always founded upon loving God with all our hearts and placing others, especially our wives and children, ahead of ourselves.

Jesus bore the descriptive title of "Good Shepherd." As you read throughout Scripture about a shepherd's concern for his sheep, we begin to get a beautiful picture of a protector. When the sheep find themselves in harm's way, the shepherd risks everything to bring security and safety. Men, we are to be shepherds and not ranchers. We are not to drive our wives and children in the direction we want them to go, even if that direction is good and right. Rather, we are to lead them there. How? By creating a deep and trusting relationship that is founded upon a lavish love. This type of love can only be found in God...for God is love.

Our culture has gotten it wrong!!! It is not ungodly for a man to lead his wife. It is Biblical. But the world has adopted a philosophy that has been lifted up against "the knowledge of God."

Notes and Quotes:

Corinthians 10:4-5). And we must boldly proclaim Truth to a world lost and broken.

There was a day when unions in this country were needed and effective in providing protection for workers who were being abused by employers who saw their employees as tickets to more prosperity. In their greed, employers often forced their workers to endure horrific conditions that were destructive. Those unions did an admirable service to society. But over time, those unions overstepped and became almost abusive towards the employers, and the stalemate that has been created in society has bred conflict and even violence.

In the same way, feminism in its early days seemed to have a good and Godly agenda; to seek a place of equality for women who were experiencing less than God intended for them to experience. And to a degree, this brought issues to the table that were healthy to uncover so that women would not be hurt or abused. But the feminist movement has gone too far to the place where their agenda is not equality but to bring conflict and even violence into the marriage relationship.

Listen to the feminist agenda today as you read the following quotes:

"Under patriarchy, no woman is safe to live her life, or to love or to mother children. Under patriarchy, every woman is a victim, past, present, and future. Under patriarchy, every woman's daughter is a victim, past, present, and future. Under patriarchy, every woman's son is her potential betrayer and also the inevitable rapist or exploiter of another woman." (Cite: Andrea Dworkin in <u>Our Blood: Prophecies and Discourses on Sexual Politics</u>. Page 20).

Another writer goes on to say that virtually all heterosexual sex is rape. (Cite: Robin Morgan in <u>Theory and Practice: Pornography and Rape</u>.

Again I say, we as a culture have gotten it WRONG! God called men to lead. There are Godly ways to do so, and there are sinful ways to do so. We must learn to lead with love. But we have cowered in cultural fear for too long. We must take back marriage and show the world how to live it out so that God receives glory and both men and women find the special, blessed, God-created space upon which they are to stand, live and grow. This is a battle we must fight. And more than simply fight the battle, we must win so that our sons and daughters have hope for a Godly future.

So how do you protect your wife?

Protect the Institution of Marriage- Do not allow culture to paint a dismal view of something God created and intends for good. Ask for spiritual vision so that you might see clearly. We must be able to see the broken philosophies of this world and bring the Truth of God's Word to shed light reality. God wants to give us spiritual vision so that me might bring blessing into our wive's lives.

Stand Between Your Wife and Evil- In a physical sense, this seems like a no-brainer. If you went to the door and there were men standing there with masks and guns who asked if your wife was home, you would quickly understand that your wife's life was in danger. A Godly man would fight all the way to the finish, if necessary, out of love for his wife. He would protect her at all cost.

Not long ago I was given the blessed opportunity to officiate at the wedding of my daughter, Amye, to a great young man, Mike. One of the greatest joys of that celebration, as her father and as her pastor, was to write the vows that Mike would agree to if he was going to marry my daughter. As I sat and prayed and then began to pen the words that I believed Mike needed to vow in order to have my daughter's hand in marriage, one phrase came back to me over and over again. At first I thought it was too radical to include. It was too countercultural. But in the end, the Holy Spirit won out and I placed that phrase in Mike's vows to be promised on their wedding day. I knew all along that Mike had to embrace it and then repeat it. The phrase was this: "...and if necessary, I will die for you." Mike, being a man in pursuit of God, gladly spoke those words. But I realize that just speaking them is not enough. In the case of hardship and adversity, should the circumstance ever degenerate to the place where he might stand between my daughter and evil, will he live them out then? I believe he will. Because I believe my daughter chose well, a REAL Man of God.

But what about spiritually? Do you know and understand when evil comes to destroy her walk of faith? Be aggressive when your wife comes into contact with evil and fight for her. This is war! When Satan comes calling, do not allow your wife to be easy prey. Remember, our weapons are not of this world. In your role as husband exercise the following three things daily:

Prayer- Men, we must lift our wives to the Most Holy and ask for His protection. This is not a prayer that is only sounded in the midst of need. It is a daily, continual appeal for God to be active and attentive to the needs of our wives. When Paul tells us to put on the full armor of

Notes and Quotes:

Notes and Quotes:

God, he concludes by calling us to pray at all times about all things. (Ephesians 6:18). Some have said that prayer is our primary weapon in spiritual warfare. I agree! Pray for your wife at all times, and when evil comes, become even more focused in your prayers for your wife.

Presence- Men, when your wife is struggling with an attack from the evil one, you must sacrifice lesser things to be present for her during the most intense time of the battle. I recently had a man call me and ask if he could bring his wife in for a time of spiritual counseling, prayer and encouragement. He went on to say that she was struggling greatly due to the pain of multiple losses. To make this call was an incredible Godly act. But what he did next was even more amazing. When I asked about scheduling the appointment, he said that he would rearrange his life and schedule to come with her to simply be by her side as she faced the terrible sorrow and pain. That, my friend, is presence. And that man did exactly what he said. He cancelled his plans at work and came week after week to simply sit by her side as she battled confusion, disillusionment and loss. Your prayers are vital, but so is your presence.

Perspective- When your wife is facing spiritual warfare, it is important that you keep a sense of Godly perspective. To her, everything may appear hopeless. Your job is to encourage, not with idle or empty words, but with God's Word. You are to "wash her with the water of the Word." (see Ephesians 5:25-27). Seek out Biblical hope in the Scriptures and don't buy in to the thought that she is stuck here for the rest of her days. God says that in Christ, we are "more than conquerors. "We can do" all things through Christ who gives us strength." "All things do work together for good for those who love the Lord and are called according to His purpose." (see Romans 8). When she finds herself in the depths of despair without any hope, you must keep your focus on Christ and the hope found in him. Remember those old movies where a scuba diver is trapped far beneath the surface because something happens to the oxygen supply. They appear doomed. But suddenly someone notices their struggle and zooms in and shares their tank of air and slowly, without panic, they rise out of the depths to see a new day dawn. Men, that is your role and calling in your ministry to your wife. The tank of oxygen you offer her is your constant focus on Jesus Christ. Remember he is the author and protector of your faith and the faith of your wife. Do not fall into panic! Trust God, and offer His perspective.

In the movie <u>Fireproof</u>, there is a scene where the husband must fight

Notes and Quotes:

to keep his wife. An outside party is trying to woo her away from him and into a relationship that is obviously contrary to the ways of the Lord. In this particular scene, the man goes to the office of the intruder and boldly states that this intruder must leave her alone. It could not have been a comfortable position for that husband or for the one he confronted, but what he did was Godly. He stepped between his wife and evil and fought for God's glory and her good.

When You Protect Yourself from Lust, You Protect Your Wife from Heartache

Men, if you are honest, you will agree that sexual lust runs rampant in our society. Not only is it ever present, but it is flaunted and even celebrated. When you protect yourself from the advances of sexual lust, you give your wife a wonderful gift and protect her from terrible pain and heartache. We must pray every day with the Psalmist:

> *Create in me a clean heart, O God,*
>
> *and renew a right spirit within me.*

(Psalm 51:10 ESV)

King David wrote this psalm in the aftermath of his sin with Bathsheba. David was a "man after God's own heart," yet he experienced a season in his life when he stopped guarding his heart and gave in to the lusts of his flesh. The results were devastating. To cover up his sin, he had Uriah killed. His children were thrown into a tailspin that led to all kinds of evil including rape, incest and murder. After confession, David came to realize the importance of having a pure heart. We don't have to experience such tragic failure to see our need for a pure heart. Seek after it by asking God to grant you victory over the flesh.

The following are a few things a man can do to protect his heart:

Practice radical amputation- When you recognize that certain things lead you into temptation, cut them off quickly. DO NOT FLIRT WITH EVIL! Do not think, "I can handle this in moderation." Cut it off. Jesus said, "If your eye causes you to sin, gouge it out." Ouch! "If your hand causes you to sin, cut it off." In this day of rampant sexual promiscuity, it is vital that we build systems that will protect us so that we keep the evil far from our hearts. I suggest that every man have a filter on their computer to lock out pornography. But now, this means you must also take control of the content that comes into your life by way of smart phones. The evil one is crafty and will do everything possible to place those images before you. If not on your computer, TV, or phone,

Notes and Quotes:

then in real life. One man who was battling lust said, "I can't even go to a ballgame on a summer day because women dress themselves in ways that lead my mind to the place of sin." Men, if it causes you to sin, cut it off! This will not only protect your heart but it will also show honor to your wife.

"But among you there must not be even a hint of sexual immorality, or of any kind of impurity, or of greed, because these are improper for God's holy people." (Ephesians 5:3 NIV).

Become transparent with your wife and with a mentor- After God fashioned Eve as a helper and completer for Adam, he placed them in the Garden of Eden and blessed them with a wonderful, open marriage. In fact, Genesis 2:25 says that both the man and the woman were naked and yet they felt no shame. That is a beautiful picture of intimacy. It is also the picture we should lift up as a standard for marriage. Just one chapter later though, Adam and Eve sinned in the Garden and their very first reaction to sin was to take leaves and cover themselves. Sin leads to cover up. It has been that way ever since Genesis 3. You can avoid much pain and heartache and protect your wife by living your life as an open book. Secrecy is the environment in which sin flourishes. Men, we need to walk in the light. Often I have the privilege of helping a couple overcome infidelity and save their marriage. One step in that journey is to bring light to the darkness. You cannot live in darkness and expect to achieve victory. Men if you want to bring blessing into the life of your wife, you need to walk with her transparent and vulnerable. This is the only environment where trust is grown. Do not allow for a system in your home where she has to ask you where you are at, what you are watching and who you are seeing, for this leads to fear, anxiety and insecurity. Give her a gift. Allow access to your cell phone, your email, your Facebook account. Let nothing in the darkness for Satan to use to entice or deceive you. Also, as we talked about earlier in this book, cultivate a relationship with a spiritual director or mentor who you will be honest with. There is strength in numbers. Make sure you are a part of a church family where the men are binding together to learn and to lead. This too is vital. "God intend for us to fight sin as an army, not a soldier." (Cite: Gary Thomas in Thirsting for God. Page 91).

Live out repentance- Unfortunately, we in the church often major on confession and minor on repentance. Let us learn to walk in repentance so that we experience the sanctifying acts of the Holy Spirit and the miracle of a changed life. All too often, men only deal with the act of confession. We know that God's Word says that He is faithful and just to forgive us and to cleanse us from unrighteousness. (see 1 John 1:9). Therefore, we use confession as a spiritual bar of soap to clean us up after a daily walk or wallow in the mud. Men, to protect your heart, you must learn to walk in repentance. Repentance is to turn and walk in a new direction; it is to experience a Godly change of heart, character and behavior. We must repent, so that times of refreshing may come into our lives and into the lives of our wives. (see Acts 3:19).

Protect Her Reputation- Now this next statement is not going to come as a big shock to you. You are not married, nor will you ever be married, to a perfect person. Your wife is a sinner just like you are. If you are blessed like I am, she is a sinner who has been redeemed by the blood of Christ, and is in the process of being changed day-by-day and year-by-year into the likeness of Christ. But I can guarantee one thing, she will sin against you. How you respond to her sinning against you is important. A Godly man protects the reputation of his wife and gives her a place of love to stand even in the midst of her failure. Don't throw your wife under the bus! Your job is to lead her into righteousness, not paint her with the broad brush of condemnation. Like you, your wife is a person in progress of being changed. You can either help her to become more like Christ or you can make her process of becoming like Christ hard to accomplish. It is not your job to punish. It is your job to lovingly rebuke in a Biblical way when she falls short of God's standard. But we as husbands need to protect our wives from public humiliation that is founded upon our own quest for superiority and victory.

When your wife fails, and she will, don't publicly call attention to it but rather gently and lovingly address it in private for her benefit and not to put her in her place. Biblical exhortation is a Godly thing when handled appropriately. You protect your wife when you care enough to confront her sin. She, like you, will have some blind spots in this journey, and you are called to help her see clearly by bringing light to the darkness. But your motive must be pure. You must do it not to get the upper hand but because you have concern for her and her eternity. Your Godly reproof is a protection for her. And as you do it in private with a lavish love, you protect her reputation and her witness.

Chapter 12- Protecting Your Children

It was the spring of this past year. I was in my office doing what I often do, listening to the story of the brokenness of a person who God loves as much as He loves me. But this day was different than most in that the person sitting across from my desk was a fourteen year old little girl. Now, I know that she probably did not see herself as a little girl. And I know that in the world today, our children grow up much faster than we would ever want or could ever imagine. But in my mind, fourteen is a child who should still be living under her father's umbrella of love and protection. She was not an adult in any way.

That afternoon, tears welled up in her eyes as she spoke of her dilemma. She was pregnant and did not know what to do. I knew the facts before she ever arrived to meet with me. But as she teared up, and I could see her heart and her pain, my blood pressure began to rise and I found myself angry.

The reason that I was angry was because this child was not protected. She needed protection, and not in the form of a spermicide or condom, rather she needed a father who was living out his calling to be the protector of one of the most precious, entrusted things in his life.

Now, I must say that she and the boy who she had premarital sex with were both responsible for their actions. But I had to ask myself, where was her father on the day she conceived? Was he working late? Did he know where she was and who she was with? What kind of father had he been to this point in her life? Had he shown her Godly affection as she grew to be a young woman, or had he felt uncomfortable and awkward? Had he and his wife told her what to expect as she began to have interest in boys? Had they taught her to remain pure for that was God's design and intent? On the day that she conceived, that little girl needed a protector in so many different ways. What if he had been there for her and stopped the act of disobedience? Perhaps this man had just been so busy trying to provide for his family that he didn't think he had the time to be his little girl's protector. Maybe he had delegated this daughter's protection to his wife and she was not available on the afternoon in question. Or maybe he simply was not pre-

Notes and Quotes:

pared or equipped for such a responsibility. Whatever the case, his little girl needed her father's protection, and in a moment of great need, he was not there.

Just so you know, a sovereign God made something beautiful out of this situation, and a dear family received a child they desperately wanted and could not conceive. But the consequences will walk forward in the lives of all who participated.

Fathers, the moment you are entrusted with raising a child, you are called by God to be his/her protector. You must take this calling seriously and stand in the gap, or the results can be devastating to your child and to your family.

When we look back at the Hebrew culture, a baby girl was given a special place in her father's heart and home. She was a delicate treasure. When Scripture speaks in Genesis 2:24 of a man's responsibility to leave his father and mother and cleave to his wife, the intent of that verse in the Hebrew tradition was not that the woman would leave. At least not until her husband had prepared a life for her, and then he would come to receive his bride. The wedding ceremony would symbolically include the passing of this precious daughter from the umbrella of her father's love and protection to the umbrella of her husband's love and protection. And it would happen in an instant. Before the "I do," she was under her father's love and protection. And after the "I do," she stood with her husband under his love and protection. In that moment, a new family is born. We still see this carried out in the traditional wedding services of our day when the pastor says, "Who gives this woman to be married today?" The father's reply in this day is normally, "Her mother and I." But Biblically it should have been her father's place to be the third "I do."

Some of you may be asking, "but what about the father of the baby conceived? Didn't his father have some responsibility to protect him as well?" Absolutely he did. But the young man that fathered this child came from a fatherless home. He had no role models to show him what it meant to be a REAL Man. Men, I want you to see fatherhood as not only a responsibility but also as an amazing privilege.

So, what should we as men protect our children from?

Children Need to Be Protected from the Outside World

Someone once said, "Keep out of your child's life anything that will keep Christ out of his heart." That is good counsel. In order to accomplish this, you must become a good disciplinarian of your children.

Be Strong and Show Yourself a Man

Notes and Quotes:

While children hate to be disciplined, it leads to a blessed place called righteousness. Scripture teaches us that no one likes or enjoys discipline, but the results of discipline are wonderful in our lives.

For the moment all discipline seems painful rather than pleasant, but later it yields the peaceful fruit of righteousness to those who have been trained by it.

(Hebrews 12:11 ESV)

Men, realize that when a child is loved enough that he/she is disciplined, he/she begins to flourish and walk in the security of knowing that someone is watching out for him/her; therefore, he/she does not need to fear.

When my son, Morgan, was two years old, we moved into a small farm house on a very busy country road just outside of Anderson, IN. Upon moving in, I made a quick assessment of the dangers that lurked in that house for my son. My investigation revealed two areas that could prove to be dangerous for him. The first was that the highway we lived on had a speed limit of 50 miles an hour. And people seldom seemed to keep that law. They soared by at an alarming rate of speed unaware that my little boy might be playing nearby. The second thing that I found was that the steps to the basement were very steep and a two year old could quickly lose his/her balance and topple down injuring him or herself.

To try to protect my son I did two things. I went to the local hardware store and purchased a can of spray paint and a new lock. When I arrived home, I took my two year old son out to about 15 feet from the road and painted a bright red line across the driveway. Then I told Morgan, "This line is here to protect you from wandering into the street and getting hit by a car. Never cross this line. If you do cross this line, you will be in trouble, and Daddy will spank you." It was a good plan; it showed him his limits. And at two years old he could not really understand the devastation of wandering into the street and being hit by a car. He could, however, understand what a spanking was, and he wanted no part of that discipline. After my instruction to Morgan, I made my way inside the house and placed the new lock on the basement door to protect him from falling down and injuring himself.

As you might imagine it did not take long for Morgan to test the limits. He first would ride his tricycle right up to that line and stop inches from it. Then he would look back at me to see if I was watching. When he saw my eyes were focused on him, he would grin and make a hard right turn just missing the boundary line. But soon, he crossed the line. He didn't blast by it, he just made sure one wheel crossed the line be-

99

Notes and Quotes:

cause he wanted to see if this really was the boundary line. I did what I had told him that I would do. I took him from that tricycle and told him because he had done what he was told not to do, he was going to receive a spanking. He began crying long before the discipline was administered. But in the end, to my knowledge, Morgan never crossed that boundary again. He was protected from the dangers of that highway.

A few weeks later, we were in the house, and Morgan had wandered away into the kitchen as I was watching some TV. Little did I realize that I had been negligent in protecting him and had failed to close and lock that door that led to very steep steps. Of course he was taken by curiosity and tried to negotiate those steps only to lose his balance and go tumbling down them. I knew immediately what had happened. The screams began, and I rushed as fast as I could to his side. When I picked him up off the concrete floor at the bottom of the steps, I expected to see blood and have to rush him to the hospital for stitches. I saw no blood and felt some sense of relief that he did not appear injured. But I noticed that his face was bursting with anger not pain or fear. He was angry. As soon as he was able to compose himself a bit, I found out who he was angry at...me. "Why didn't you paint a red line at the top of those stairs?!" he roared. The message landed hard upon my heart. I had failed to protect him. I had great intentions. I had even bought and installed the protection. But I had not remained diligent in my responsibilities to protect my son. I also learned that day that Morgan had grown to be thankful for the boundaries that I implemented to protect him. He had even grown to be glad they were there.

We live in a day when we must protect our children from the worldliness that subtly erodes and invades our culture. Because of this, we must be extremely careful who we grant access to our children's minds as they grow up. We must not leave our children vulnerable to people whose character is questionable!

As I mentioned earlier, both of my children played sports growing up. Often I coached them. I did this for three reasons: 1) I loved being connected to them as a mentor. 2) The field of competition was a great training ground to impart character. 3) I did not want to entrust them to someone else who I did not know for certain had a Godly character.

As they grew older, I allowed them to play for other people and coaches. Partly because I was not always gifted to teach them in their area of sport. And also, because I wanted them to learn to deal with the authority of a person other than myself. However, I was the father that could almost always be seen standing in the shadows watching from a distance to assure they were safe. I thank God that when I could not be present, God offered His care. I tried not to be one of those busybody parents who made coaches cringe when I walked up. I loved the games and the competition, but the reason I was there had little to do with the sport. It had everything to do with their protection.

When my children reached high school, the rules changed dramatically. Parents were not allowed at practices. Coaches tried to make sure that parents were not allowed in a position to undermine their authority or promote anything other than the team. I understood these challenges and abided by the rules. But I still kept a close eye on my kids. Often I would drive by a practice field praying for my son or daughter and ask God's protection for them. What I did most of all during those days was what I would call debriefing. I asked lots of questions to find out what practice was like and how the coaches went about their jobs. When I felt that something was out of line and my children were in harm's way, I acted. Often this was not popular with their coaches. But I found that if I handled the conflict in an appropriate and Godly manner, and did not attack them, they came to trust my heart and responded to my concerns with compassion. Note that my concerns were never about their coaching decisions. It would have been totally inappropriate for me to question my son's playing time or the number of sprints my daughter was required to run in practice. No, when I went to a coach, it was all about a character issue that concerned me.

I won't soon forget a meeting that I had with two football coaches at midfield one afternoon at the end of practice. I was greatly concerned over some of the profane language that they spewed as the team would practice and play. I suspected from some of the things I heard from my son and his friends that coaches were trying to use foul language and name calling to motivate players to play harder. I immediately began praying for wisdom as to how or if to say anything. I began to sit closer and closer to the field in order to be able to hear what the coaches were saying to the boys during the game. I did not want to go and make things harder for my son by saying, "My son said you said..." I wanted firsthand knowledge and then to address what I saw and heard. The evidence was easy to gather.

Before I went and confronted the coaches, I sat down with Morgan and told him what I was going to do and why. I told him that I did not want

Notes and Quotes:

to put him in harm's way or perhaps be the reason that his playing time might be limited, but that this was more important than whether or not he got to play. In the end, I went with Morgan's blessing. "Dad," he said, "you have to do what you think is the right thing, regardless of what that might mean for me." I was blown away by his maturity.

That afternoon, I prayed in my car before I made the long walk out to the field. I had called in advance and asked for the meeting. And when everyone else was gone and I could speak freely, I shared my concern. Now I should interject that both of the coaches that I met with publically professed their Christianity. As I began to state my case, I asked them if they would do one of two things: 1) I asked them to change their language to both honor God and to offer a Godly example to all of the sons that were on the team. Or 2) if they would not change their language, I asked if they would consider stopping their publically confessing Christ because their language was creating a stumbling block for others. At first they were somewhat taken aback. But the Holy Spirit quickly invaded their hearts and they showed themselves to be men who desired to live for God but, were stuck in their worldly ways. In the end both men confessed and asked for forgiveness. They also asked me to pray for them as they were feeling tremendous pressure from parents and school administration. They had little time for their families during the season, and they were walking time bombs. When we finally said goodbye, we were all three praising God for His faithfulness in spite of our sinfulness.

One of those coaches died a very early death. But I can tell you that our encounter on the field that afternoon positively helped prepare him for eternity. God sent me that day for His glory and for this man's good. And the other coach is still my friend to this day. I prayed for both these men daily for the remainder of that season. And God did some amazing things.

There are so many things a father needs to protect his children from that come attacking from the outside. I have mentioned but a few. In this culture, here are a few obvious things to consider as you protect your children into their future. We must protect them from: laziness (slothfulness), all sorts of media - this includes the content of things they allow into their minds, and the amount of time they spend being entertained, video games, cell phone usage, movies, music and much more. Peers who influence them to move away from God rather than towards Him. Irresponsible activity that is founded in the faulty philosophy of adolescence. The list goes on and on.

Protect Them From Their Selfishness

Fathers, you must realize that your children will know what they want, but they will not understand what they need. Therefore, you must assert your leadership and make certain they are protected from themselves.

Early in my ministry, I had the privilege of serving as a youth pastor in a large church. It was a great opportunity to learn and grow as I was given a place at the table of a church staff with great mentors and gifted leaders. I was in my final days of college and had taken classes in youth ministry and knew the theory behind what to do to lead them. But some of that theory was flawed. In order to create ownership, the books taught that the youth should be a part of the planning process. Allow them to plan the direction of the ministry and they would be more apt to invest.

Early on I fell for this deceptive plan. I would gather the students and would plan the ministry with their input. They loved having a place at the table. "We need more all-nighters," was the number one theme that came from their mouths. More fun!!! More games!!! More parties!!! Structuring around what they wanted was easy, and it was fun. But I came to learn one thing: these youth knew what they wanted but not what they needed. Their natural bent towards selfishness drove them to pursue fun and games continually. But none of them were mature enough to see or to say, "We need more Bible study." In time I came to realize that I was called to lead them. And that meant that I needed to determine what they needed to lay a foundation that would give them a future. I developed a slogan, "Fun should be the byproduct of this ministry but never the reason." In leading your children, you must determine what they need and not be driven by simply what they want. Don't try to be their friend or superhero. Be their father. There will be time enough when they grow to adulthood to be their friend, but in those early days, they need your protection from their selfish desires. Be the Man! Lead and Protect!

Note of caution: Fathers, we live in a world that is dominated by child-centered homes. This leads to great heartache. When the children rule the home, they can easily become entrenched in selfishness. They want what they want, and if they don't get it, they will attempt to manipulate until they do. They will cry or rage or refuse to follow the rules until you give in to their demands. You must "Be Strong and Show Yourself a Man" in times like these. If your child learns they are in charge, it will create a deep anxiety within them. For they will know inside that

Notes and Quotes:

Notes and Quotes:

they call the shots. But they will also know that they are not capable of being the leader. Do not shirk your responsibility to be the leader of your home. Being a strong leader means you must draw boundary lines. Make an assessment of the places your children are vulnerable to failure and then draw a boundary line to protect them. Stand firm and do not waiver. Be consistent but do it in a loving way. Your children will one day thank you for it. But don't do it for their eventual "thank you." Do it so that they will walk in righteousness and God will receive glory.

Protect Them from Worldly Philosophies that Conflict with the Word of God

Let me remind you again...

> *We destroy arguments and every lofty opinion raised against the knowledge of God, and take every thought captive to obey Christ, being ready to punish every disobedience, when your obedience is complete.*

(2 Corinthians 10:5-6 ESV)

Men, we must engage ourselves in our children's education and make certain that the things they are being taught are in line with God's Word. When my children were small, my wife and I made a conscious decision to place them in a public school where they would not live in a sterilized bubble. We did this because we wanted them to learn how to live as a Christian in a world that was broken and far from Godly. We sought out a wonderful community that had old-fashioned values that aligned in many ways with what we believed. The school system was one where many of the teachers were Christian, and they were seldom bridled with regards to speaking of their faith in God. But we learned quickly that the state often required that they teach some things that directly contradicted God's Word. So we had to be diligent in knowing what our children were learning and make sure that we addressed any area that contradicted Scripture.

To be honest, we did not do a very good job of this as we parented. Life became busy and seldom did we spend the time we should have protecting their minds from the exposure to ungodly philosophies. It is by God's grace and protection that they turned out to have hearts and minds that could see Truth and embrace it even in the midst of false doctrines and theories.

Many of the things that are taught as factual in our schools today are not founded upon a Biblical worldview. Just a few examples here include: evolution, psychology, astronomy, the quest for self-worth, and ethics. Men, we should scrutinize the things that are being taught to our children and make sure that they are not being exposed to teachings that fly directly opposed to the Word of God. Worldview matters!

Now, don't misunderstand what I am saying here. I am not suggesting that you build a bubble and place your children in it so that they are never exposed to thoughts and teachings that are a part of a different worldview. I am saying that you need to be engaged, and when something is taught that contradict God's Word and way, you must expose it to your children for what it is and then help them to stand on Truth. We will never influence the world if we remain completely apart from it. We are called to "go into the world and make disciples." But this requires that our children know where the philosophies of this world fall flat in light of God's teaching and we must prepare them to stand against worldly philosophies.

Protect them From Becoming Simply Religious

Remember as we started this study, I stated that authentic behavior is founded upon identity in Christ. We must not fall for the trap of legalism that leads only to our children acting like Christians. No, we must engage their hearts. It is out of the overflow of their hearts that they act. Do not boil your parenting down to simply forcing a certain behavior. Call them to character and protect them from religion that has no foundation. Your rules can become a weight around their necks that sink them deeply into rebellion against you and against God unless they are able to see your heart. At times I found that my children needed to be protected from me. Not that I would ever hurt them intentionally, but sometimes I was more concerned with my image in the community and what others would think of me than my children's character and love for the Lord.

I know that pastor's kids are known for their rebellion and for not having a desire for God. That is so sad. Dwell on relationship! Relationship with God and relationship with each other. I believe it was James Dobson who said, "Rules without relationship leads to rebellion."

Remember the Three "P's"

Earlier as we looked at a man's responsibility to protect his wife, I offered three words that begin with "P" which can help us create a tangible plan of how to begin. Those words are Prayer, Presence and Perspective. Let's apply them to our children as well.

Notes and Quotes:

Notes and Quotes:

Men, we must pray continually for our children. Bring them daily before the Lord in prayers that seek the Lord's favor, blessing and protection for them. Pray that God's sovereign path would help them to grow into Godly men and women. Pray for God to deliver them from temptation. Pray they might come to understand Him better. And pray that God would place a hedge of protection around them. Never underestimate the power of prayer!

Secondly, men, we cannot afford to be so busy chasing after our own agenda that we fail to offer our presence to our children. They need you involved in their lives. You are to be the model of faith that leads them into understanding. You cannot protect them from your desk chair. You must be both available and interactive with them and their lives. Stand in the gap, especially when they are young, and do what a good shepherd does - protect your sheep!

Finally, exercise perspective. Remember that this means to order your life and the life of your family upon the Rock of God's Word. Do not allow for a worldview that is based on worldly philosophies but rather build a home on the foundation of Scripture. You will not be sorry you invested in this way. Your children will be both protected and blessed.

Be Willing to Sacrifice

I mentioned earlier Paul David Tripp's definition of love: "Love is willing self-sacrifice that does not require reciprocation and is not based upon whether the person being loved deserves it or not." Love always requires sacrifice.

If you are going to protect your children and prepare them for a future, it will cost you. It will require a huge amount of time, energy, prayer and investment. A REAL Man of God sacrifices for his children.

Discussion Questions for Chapters 9-12:

1. What responsibility does a Christian man have to defend God's reputation? Is this a biblical calling?

2. Do even single men have a responsibility to defend the institution of marriage?

3. Many wives are quite independent and seem to need no protection at all from their husbands. Do you see the author's challenge to protect and defend your wife to be inconsistent with the world's view of women today?

Notes and Quotes:

4. Does culture have anything to say about a man's responsibility to be the protector of his wife and children? Should it?

5. Have you ever been put in a position that you felt a burden to defend the gospel? Did you?

6. What are some ways that men can protect their children even when they may not be physically present in the home with them?

7. What, if anything, did you learn from the section explaining marriage God's way? And what in this section might be seen as countercultural?

A Portrait of a REAL Man...Paul Hand, a Man of Sacrifice

Paul Hand was born on April 20th, 1915 as a part of what Tom Brokaw would eventually name "The Greatest Generation." To put it simply, this generation was perhaps the last to hold fast to the values that made America great. "The WWII generation shares so many common values: duty, honor, country, personal responsibility and the marriage vow - For better or for worse--it was the last generation in which, broadly speaking, marriage was a commitment and divorce was not an option" The values Brokaw spoke about defined Paul Hand.

In many ways, one could call Paul a simple man. He did not finish high school, but eventually passed his G.E.D. As a teenager he lived through the Great Depression in West Virginia. He worked at Wheeling Machine Products until he felt a call to ministry at age 27. Then he moved his wife, Pearl, and their two children, Lois and Jerry, to Anderson, IN, to pursue a call to ministry. The year was 1942 and the United States was at war. It was not long after that move that Paul felt conviction in his heart that he was to serve his country. As a married man with children, and as a student, he had every excuse to stay home and stay safe. Yet, in spite of his government given deferment, Paul decided to go to war and serve his country. It was a great sacrifice, but Paul was a man of sacrifice.

When the war was finally over and Paul's commitment to the army was done, he came home and went back to finish his degree. He was ordained as a minister of the Church of God in 1947 and graduated in 1949. Life was good. He served as pastor of the First Church of God in Arcadia, IN during the final year and a half of his schooling and resigned upon his graduation to take the full-time position as pastor of a church in Petersburg, IN. It was there that his greatest sacrifice would be lived out.

Tuesday, August 9th, 1949- It was a hot August day in Petersburg. Paul was busy preparing for his sermon when his daughter, Lois, begged him to take her and her little brother to the White River so they could swim. Paul agreed and packed up his children along with his Bible and notebook and a folding chair, and he and the children set off for an afternoon adventure. They soon arrived at a place called "Stark's Ferry." Paul set up his chair on the edge of the riverbank. Soon Lois and Jerry were playing with great joy on a sandbar in the river and Paul was sitting with his Bible open on his lap, reading God's Word and preparing his sermon.

"The next thing I remember is that I had gotten into water way over my head and I could not touch bottom," Lois writes. "I yelled like crazy for help. My dad ran in the water fully clothed to save me. I cannot tell you how awful that experience was...I became aware that my dad had me on his shoulders and thinking that could not be a good thing. Somehow he managed to throw me to shallow water." (Cite: Lois Hand in her personal memoirs). Paul Hand saved his daughter's life that day. But in so doing, he lost his own. Or perhaps better said, he gave his own.

A local paper reported the news saying, "The Reverend Mr. Hand jumped into the water to recuse the child and succeeded in grabbing her and throwing her into shallow water. The current pulled him under and he failed to come to the surface. The body was recovered about 30 minutes later from seven feet of water by Dave Cardinal and Duane Abell of Petersburg, who were working on a sand barge a short distance away. The minister failed to respond to artificial respiration." (Cite: The Petersburg Times).

Three days later in their Church and Social News section they wrote: "One of the clergy of our city has climaxed his life of service to God with a heroic act of service to humanity. Reverend Paul Russell Hand gave his life unhesitatingly to save that of his 10 year old daughter. He did not question the safety of his move, but considered only that of his daughter, so that she might live the same good life in his footsteps."

Paul Russell Hand was a REAL Man who ran "unhesitatingly" into danger to protect and save one entrusted to his care. That's what a REAL Man does.

Last week I received a letter from Lois, the daughter Paul rescued. "It's been 63 years since that day my father saved my life. Seldom does a day go by that I don't think back to what he did for me and the gift he gave me. I have had a song running through my mind all week, perhaps you have heard it, You Raise Me Up."

You raise me up, so I can stand on mountains;

You raise me up, to walk on stormy seas;

I am strong, when I am on your shoulders;

You raise me up... To more than I can be.

(Cite: http://www.elyrics.net/read/j/josh-groban-lyrics/you-raise-me-up-lyrics.html).

Dennis Rainey, the national director of FamilyLife Today, relates this story. In the mid-1980s a missionary family serving overseas came home on furlough, needing a little R & R. Through the graciousness of friends, they'd been provided the use of a summer home on a beautiful lake. For these tired, front-line warriors, it was like a little piece of Eden.

One bright summer morning, Mom was in the kitchen fussing with the baby and preparing lunch for the family. Dad was in the boathouse puttering with something that needed some puttering. And the three children present were out on the lawn between the home and the edge of the lake. Three-year-old "little Billy" was under the care of a five-year-old sister and a twelve-year-old cousin.

When Sister and Cousin became distracted with some mutual interest, little Billy decided it would be an opportune time to wander down to the water and check out that shiny aluminum boat that had been bobbing so temptingly beside the dock. The trouble is, three-year-olds have limited experience in getting from a stable dock to a bobbing boat. With one foot on the dock and the other stretching toward the boat, Little Billy lost his balance and fell into five or six feet of water beside the little dock.

The splash alerted the twelve-year-old, who let out a piercing scream. That brought Dad on the run. After scoping out the situation for a second or two, he dove into the murky water and began a desperate search for his little boy. But the lake water was murky, and Dad couldn't see a thing. With lungs desperate for air, he resurfaced, grabbed another ragged gasp, and plunged back under. Sick with panic, the only thing he could think to do was to extend his arms and legs as far as he could and try to feel little Billy's whereabouts. Having nearly exhausted his oxygen supply a second time, he began to ascend once again for another breath.

On his way up, he felt little Billy, arms locked in a death grip to the pier post some four feet under the water. Prying the little boy's fingers loose, they burst together through the surface to fill their lungs with life-giving air.

Adrenaline continued to surge. Conversation would not return to normal for a long time. Dad just carried little Billy around, holding him close, unable to put him down for some time. Finally, when heart rates had returned to normal and nerves calmed a bit, this missionary dad turned to his little boy with a question.

'Billy, what on earth were you doing down there, hanging onto that post so far underwater?'

Little Billy's reply, laced with all the wisdom of a tot, reaches out and grabs us all by the throat.

'Just waitin' for you, Dad. Just waitin' for you!' (Cite: Dennis Rainey as told by Stu Weber in Four Pillars Of a Man's Heart. Pages 57-58).

A REAL Man is willing to sacrifice for his children. And in so doing, he changes their world.

"Our culture is hurting. Too many dreams are four feet under water, buried in the mud and muck of the last thirty years of cultural storms. This country is suffering. Its dreams lay dashed in the dust of decay. Let's get about rebuilding this place we call 'home.'" (Ibid. Page 58).

Chapter 13– A REAL Man is a Provider

Where have all the real men gone? Recently an ad by Dockers has given us a glimpse at the crisis among us today in the area of manhood.

"Once upon a time, men wore the pants, and wore them well. Women had to rarely open doors and little old ladies never had to cross the street alone. Men took charge because that is what they did. But somewhere along the way the world decided it no longer needed men. Disco by Disco, latte by foamy non-fat latte, men were stripped of their khakis and left stranded on the road between boyhood and androgyny. But today there are questions our genderless society has no answers for. The world sits idly by as cities crumble, children misbehave and little old ladies remain on one side of the street. For the first time since bad guys, we need heroes. We need grown-ups. We need men to put down the plastic fork, step away from the salad bar, and untie the world from tracts of complacency. It's time to get your hands dirty. It's time to answer the call to manhood. It's time to wear the pants."

But if anyone does not provide for his relatives, and especially for members of his household, he has denied the faith and is worse than an unbeliever.

(1 Timothy 5:8 ESV)

Perhaps the most mentioned role of a man is that of provider. We learn from Paul's writing to Timothy that a man is to provide for his family, and if he does not provide for them, he is worse than an unbeliever. That is pretty strong language. While the ESV says "if anyone does not provide for his relatives," the King James Version, along with others, says, "if any provide not for his own…" Certainly this speaks about a person's immediate family, but it also includes those who God has placed close to you for your care. The context actually is calling each person to care for their own circle of influence. This was very practical teaching because this protected the church from being consumed with the care of widows who still had family close enough to care for them. Therefore, the church was called to care for widows who had no one else to take

Notes and Quotes:

Who are the people God

has placed in your care

so that you might provide?

care of them. But for those who had people close, God expected them to provide for the ones that were entrusted to their care.

Who are the people God has placed in your life to care and provide for? Certainly if you are married and/or have children then they are to be in this ring of influence. But in our day when many are disconnected from a traditional family, all of us have people close to us that we are to provide for in a Godly way.

From the beginning, God intended that men play the primary role in providing for the family. This does not mean that a woman cannot participate, and in this day when there are so many families where the man is not present, women play a vital part in this area. But God intended for men to carry this responsibility.

After Adam and Eve's fall in the Garden of Eden, God spoke of the curses that would fall upon mankind. To the woman he addressed the difficulty of her role as child-bearer. Why? Because this would be a primary role in her life. To Adam, God placed His discipline upon the man's role as bread-bearer. From that day forward, it has been a challenging responsibility to provide for one's family. God said that because of sin, we as men would struggle to be the primary provider.

"Evidently God had in mind from the beginning that the man would take special responsibility for sustaining the family through bread-winning labor, while the wife would take special responsibility for sustaining the family through childbearing and nurturing labor. Both are life-sustaining and essential." (Cite: John Piper in Recovering Biblical Manhood and Womanhood. Pages 42-43).

"...when there is no bread on the table it is the man who should feel the main pressure to do something to get it there." (Ibid. Page 42).

Two Cautions Regarding This Role: The first caution regarding the man as the bread-winner in the home is that man should not become slothful or lazy in this responsibility. In this culture, men have become more and more comfortable with the idea of being less and less productive. I am not saying that a wife cannot help bring home the finances that are necessary to run the family. But never should a husband place this responsibility upon his wife so that he might enjoy a less encumbered life. God has placed the responsibility upon your shoulders. Take this calling seriously and show yourself to be a man.

Recently I have had the privilege of counseling a young couple who is struggling in their marriage. One of their struggles is a result of tremendous financial pressures. The wife is a stay at home mom with their two year old little boy. When the financial struggles began, she said with tears in her eyes, "I guess I am going to have to put my baby in daycare and go to work so we can have food on the table." It was obvious that the prospect of this broke her heart. But then a REAL Man, her husband, stepped up and said, "No, you don't have to go to work and make money so we can have the things we need because that is my role and calling. We will pray about our situation, and God will provide. I will work a second job so you can stay home and do that which you were made to do and called to do - to raise our son." My friend, that is a REAL Man's response. There would have been nothing wrong had she gone to work to help provide. But it is the man who is called to provide, and he should bear the primary responsibility. Why? Because he was made to carry it and she was not. Many a wife has broken because of the stress of carrying a burden and trying to fulfill the role her husband was called to carry and fulfill. We cannot become lazy in this calling.

The second caution regarding being the bread-winner in our home is to not see your role as provider to simply be the one who brings home a paycheck. This is just one aspect of being the provider. Many men take seriously this role and work to bring home a paycheck and yet do nothing to fulfill the other areas of provision. A REAL Man provides not only physically, he provides emotionally and spiritually as well. We will look at these areas shortly.

Notes and Quotes:
How are you doing as a
provider in the areas that
are most important?
Spiritually?
Emotionally?

Chapter 14– A Man's Provision for His Wife

It happens in an instant. One minute you're but a boy and the next minute you walk into manhood with a great responsibility. They are two of the smallest words in the English language, "I Do," but they are two words that forever change your life, your role and your responsibility.

October 13, 1979 is a day that will forever mark my passage from boyhood to manhood. On that day I said those two little words. In an instant I was given the title and calling to be a leader. I had just turned twenty years old. My bride was even younger. We thought we were mature. We thought we were ready. But ready or not, the responsibility was all mine. I would either rise to meet the challenges, or we together would struggle and the pain of my failure would hurt more than just me. It would be placed upon the shoulders of my wife as well.

For nineteen years, Angela had lived under the umbrella of her father's love, protection and provision. Now, post "I Do," she stood under my umbrella, relying upon me for the things she needed most in this physical world. Thankfully, she had a Heavenly Father, who cared for her when I walked in selfishness or unaware of my responsibilities to care and provide for her. Without Him there would have been a tragic ending to our story. But because of Christ's work in her life, my wife patiently waited and persevered while I grew into my Biblical calling to be a man, a husband, and eventually a father. I wish I could say she did not have to wait long, but that would be a lie. I have not come to the place that I stand today quickly. No, I have struggled to grasp my responsibility to be a Godly man. There have been many tears as she has waited and prayed. And though many of those tears are found in the past, I am still far from the man that I seek to become for God's glory and for her blessing.

The Obvious- There is nothing earth-shattering about a man needing to provide for his family in a physical way. REAL Men get a job, earn a wage and find a way to provide the essentials for their families. Just what are the physical essentials? In centuries past they were simply shelter, food and clothing. In this day and age they have expanded to include two more important staples: transportation and medical coverage.

Notes and Quotes:

Why the addition of transportation and medical insurance? The first is simply pragmatic. In order to effectively provide for your family, you need to be mobile and able to get to and from work. We are living in a day of great financial peril. Many families live from paycheck to paycheck unable to get ahead. Sometimes this is a result of poor stewardship on their part. Sometimes it is simply a result of the harsh economic climate of our day. I have seen too many families that were getting by, but just barely, when their vehicle broke down, and they did not have the resources to fix it. The downward spiral of poverty took over quickly and led them to the place of despair, even homelessness. Part of our practical provision as men is to see to it that our families have transportation.

Another area that is vital today is that of healthcare coverage. Many families are unable to address the physical needs of their family members simply because they cannot afford it. Men, consider this a challenge. Do the things you need to do to assure that your wife and children are not left unprotected. If you are unable to provide these things, (shelter, food, clothing, transportation and healthcare,) then pray daily and ask God to help you to address the deficiencies in your home. Perhaps He will give you opportunity to take a new job with better benefits. Or maybe you will receive wisdom instructing you to pursue more education so you can get a job that provides the essentials. Seek the heart of God and provide the necessities for your family.

In his book, Four Pillars of a Man's Heart, Stu Weber states that the heart of a man is a "provisionary" heart. Just what does this mean? I believe the answer to that question is found in Genesis.

Then God said, "Let us make man in our image, after our likeness. And let them have dominion over the fish of the sea and over the birds of the heavens and over the livestock and over all the earth and over every creeping thing that creeps on the earth.

So God created man in his own image,

in the image of God he created him;

male and female he created them.

And God blessed them. And God said to them, "Be fruitful and multiply and fill the earth and subdue it, and have dominion over the fish of the sea and over the birds of the heavens and over every living thing that moves on the earth.

(Genesis 1:26-28 ESV)

Dominion brings together two important elements: Authority and Responsibility. God gave man authority over certain things on this earth. But perhaps just as important, God gave man responsibility to care for the things placed in his world. This responsibility requires a man to step up and be a provider. Certainly one place that God requires a man to exercise dominion is in his home with both his wife and his children. Where does a man begin?

Therefore a man shall leave his father and his mother and hold fast to his wife, and they shall become one flesh.

(Genesis 2:24 ESV)

Notice here that a man is called to leave his family of origin. While some will say that the word man in this verse should be thought of as mankind, thus including both men and women, I believe that this is a directive specifically for men. It was the man who was to leave his parents behind and go out into the world and prepare a place to take his bride to start a new life. Even in cultures where the son would stay on a family estate, he would either build a new house to take his wife to live or, at the very least, build a new room. Then when he had established himself, apart from his parents, he would come for his bride and take her to the place he had created for her.

Not too long ago, my wife and I were blessed to have our son-in-law, Mike, come and asked for our daughter's hand in marriage. We knew this day was coming and had over several years prepared for it. It was after 9:00 PM when there was a knock at the door. I went downstairs and found Mike alone. This was the first time he had ever visited us without Amye, our daughter. I knew immediately why he had come. Amye was away at college and a spring break trip to Disney World with Mike's family was on her calendar for the following week. Mike sat with me while Angela made herself busy downstairs so Mike and I could have a man-to-man conversation upstairs.

It took a little while before Mike got the courage built to bring up the purpose for his visit. I did not make it easy for him. Finally, he began to form the sentence. "Well, I guess it's about that time." Playing dumb, which I can do quite well, I said, "Time for what?" "Well, I think it is time for Amye and I to get married, and I wanted to come and officially ask for your permission to marry your daughter." I do not know what he thought my response would be, but I had for a long time prepared my response. I said to him, "I will give you my daughter to marry on two conditions." I am sure his heart plummeted at that point. "What in the world was I talking about?" he must have thought. Then I went on to ex-

Notes and Quotes:
Is there anything that you
need to leave behind in
order to be a Godly
husband?

Notes and Quotes:

Is there anything in your

life that might be seen as

childish? Have you put

away childish things?

plain that in order for me to give him my daughter in marriage he had to 1) go and create a home for her apart from his parents and show that he could provide a place for them to become a family; and 2) he had to love and cherish her in the same way that I had loved and cherished her, seeing her as God's gift to him. Mike readily agreed to my conditions. On July 3rd of the following year, my son Morgan stood in the place of the pastor and said to me, "As the father of the bride, is there anything you want or need to say before we begin this ceremony of marriage?" I said that there were two things that I needed to know. 1) Had Mike established a home to take my daughter to where they could together begin a new life and family? And 2) did he promise to love and treat her with the same love that I felt for her and to always see her as the treasure of his heart for as long as they both would live? Mike said he had and he would, and the wedding was on! And we have celebrated ever since.

In order to become the provider for your wife, it is necessary for you to leave some things behind. The Apostle Paul said,

> *When I was a child, I spoke like a child, I thought like a child, I reasoned like a child. When I became a man, I gave up childish ways.*

(1 Corinthians 13:11 ESV)

We now live in a society where men refuse to grow up. We value play so much that some men never put their toys away and take upon themselves the responsibilities of adulthood. Men, don't fall for Satan's scheme that cements your feet in a fairytale world of childhood with no understanding of responsibility. Gaming is fun. I have enjoyed many moments with my children playing with them. But for an adult male, I refuse to use the word man here, to spend hours playing video games rather than to walk responsibly as the provider of his family is sin. Extended adolescence is crippling America and the church. We can do better, men. We must do better.

"Adolescence cannot last from 11 years old to 29 years old. Our society will crumble economically & socially under the pressure." (Cite: Adam McLane. http://www.youthworkers.net/index.cfm/fuseaction/ blog.view/BlogID/408).

Men, we must leave in order to establish a relationship with our wives. And this leaving is not simply a departure from our family of origin, it is a departure from childhood that we might walk into manhood. It is time for a new declaration of independence.

The not-so-obvious- Some of the things a man must provide are not-so-obvious in our culture today. They include: leadership, emotional support and stability, spiritual teaching and direction, and loyalty.

As the title states, these areas of your provision are not nearly so obvious. But they are vital to the welfare of your wife and children. Let's look at them one area at a time.

Leadership- Leadership in the home is not a special gift only given to some. Rather, it is something that every man is called to exercise in his relationship with his wife and with his children. A man should see leadership to be an essential element of his provision.

We must become intimately aware of what leadership looks like if we are going to honor God in this role. Leadership is not domineering or abusive towards the ones we lead. It is not exercised in a vacuum apart from the thoughts, ideas and concerns of those we lead. It is not dictatorship nor is it to be forced upon your wife. Your wife's call and responsibility to submit to your leadership is not something that you are to force upon her. Never in Scripture are you called to make your wife submit. Rather, it is the voluntary action of a Godly woman who is fulfilling her role as a Godly wife. Men, we must avoid the two extremes of

> **Leadership is not domineering or abusive towards the ones we lead. It is not exercised in a vacuum apart from the thoughts, ideas and concerns of those we lead.**

this particular calling. If we become passive and provide no leadership at all, then our loved ones will pay a great price. But if we become aggressive and overbearing in this role, then too will our loved ones suffer. We must find an appropriate way to live out this calling so that our wives and children flourish and experience security.

John Piper offers these suggestions as to how a man can provide Godly leadership in his home.

1. **Realize that leadership is found not in the demand to be served, but in the strength to serve and to sacrifice.**

Jesus said, "Let the greatest among you become as the youngest and the leader as one who serves." (Luke 22:26). "Leadership is not a demanding demeanor. It is moving things forward to a goal. If the goal is holiness and Heaven, the leading will have the Holy aroma of Heaven about it – the demeanor of Christ." (Recovering Biblical Manhood and Womanhood. Page 38).

Notes and Quotes:

Are you humble in the way that you lead?

Notes and Quotes:
How open are you to the
input of your wife?

2. Leadership does not assume the authority of Christ over women, it advocates it.

We are not to act as if we are our wife's savior. We are not. Only Christ can save. The role of leadership is simply leading our wives forward to depend on Christ.

3. Leadership does not presume superiority, but mobilizes the strength of others.

"No human leader is infallible…a good leader will always take into account the ideas of those he leads, and may often adopt those ideas as better than his own…A leader of peers may be surrounded by much brighter people than himself. He will listen and respond… Christ does not lead the church as his daughter but as his wife. He is preparing her to be a 'fellow-heir' (Romans 8:17), not a servant girl." (Cite: Ibid. Pages 38-39). We are not superior to our wives in any way. We must see them a co-heirs in Christ. Our responsibility is to mobilize and cultivate the strengths God gave them for His glory and for the good of our family.

4. Leadership does not have to initiate every action, but feels the responsibility to provide a general pattern of initiative.

"In a family the husband does not do all the thinking and planning. His leadership is to take responsibility in general to initiate and carry through the spiritual and moral planning for family life." (Cite: Ibid. Page 39).

5. Leadership accepts the burden of the final say in disagreements between husband and wife, but does not presume to use it in every instance.

"In a good marriage, decision-making is focused on the husband, but it is not unilateral. He seeks input from his wife and often adopts her ideas. This is implied in the love that governs the relationship (Ephesians 5:25), in the equality of personhood implied in being created in the image of God (Genesis 1:27), and in the status of being fellow-heirs of the grace of life (1 Peter 3:7). Unilateral decision-making is not usually a mark of good leadership. It generally comes from laziness or insecurity or inconsiderate disregard."

6. Leadership shows itself in romantic sexual relations by communicating an aura of strong and tender pursuit.

"It is the mingling of tenderness with strength that makes the unique masculine quality of leadership in sexual relations. There is an aura of masculine leadership which rises from the mingling of power and tenderness, forcefulness and affection, potency and sensitivity, virility and delicateness. It finds expression in the firmness of his grasp, the strength of taking her in his arms, the sustaining of verbal adoration, etc."

7. Leadership expresses itself in a family by taking the initiative in disciplining the children when both parents are present and a family standard has been broken.

"No woman should have to take the initiative to set a disobedient child right while her husband sits obliviously by, as though nothing were at stake. Few things will help children understand the meaning of loving, responsible masculinity better than watching who takes the responsibility to set them right when mom and dad are both present." Remember, leadership is never passive.

8. Leadership is sensitive to cultural expressions of masculinity and adapts to them (where no sin is involved) in order to communicate to a woman that a man would like to relate not in any aggressive or perverted way, but with maturity and dignity as a man.

While we are not to be defined by culture, there are some norms from culture that a man should understand and be willing to embrace as long as there is no sin involved. Some cultures show respect by bowing and others by the shaking of hands. These cultural traditions are not right or wrong. But culture has at times communicated that an appropriate way to honor your wife is by being considerate, opening a door for her, or allowing her to walk in front of you. These cultural traditions are man's way of showing love and respect. As long as they do not call you to sin, honor them as a vehicle by which you show love and respect to your wife.

Notes and Quotes:

Are you active in the disciplining of your children?

Notes and Quotes:

9. **Realize that leadership is a call to repentance, humility and risk-taking.**

"We are all sinners. Masculinity and femininity have both been distorted by sin. Taking up the responsibility to lead must therefore be a careful and humble task. We must admit as men that historically there have been grave abuses. In each of our lives we have ample cause for contrition for our passivity or our domination...The call to leadership is a call to humble oneself and take the responsibility to be a servant-leader in ways that are appropriate...It is a call to risk getting egg on our faces; to pray as we have never prayed before; to be constantly in the Word; to be more given to planning, more intentional, more thoughtful, less carried along by the mood of the moment; to be disciplined and ordered in our lives; to be tenderhearted and sensitive; to take the initiative to make sure there is a time and a place to talk to her about what needs to be talked about; and to be ready to lay down our lives the way Christ did if necessary." Wow! This is quite the calling! (Cite: The above nine statements about leadership were adapted from John Piper's work and found in Recovering Biblical Manhood and Womanhood. Pages 38-42).

Men, our homes are desperate for leadership. We must take our Biblical calling to lead seriously. But we must do so with love as our guiding principle. We cannot afford to live out this calling as a rancher, driving our wives and children in the way they should go. No, we must become shepherds in our homes, leading with love. If you lead in this way, your family will gladly follow.

What Must a Man Be to Be a Leader in His Marriage?

How are we to lead? A look at Ephesians 5

A husband must lead in love. Voddie Baucham defines "love" as "an act of the will (choice) accompanied by emotion (not lead or determined by) that leads to action on behalf of the object."

A husband must lead in the word. "Sanctify her by the water of the word." "Until you find a man who can disciple and lead you biblically, you haven't found a man you can marry."

A husband must lead in righteousness. "... making her holy and blameless...." "If you have found a man constantly pressuring you to do things that are unrighteous, you have not found a man ready to be your husband." A husband should pull you up to his level of righteousness.

A husband must lead in selflessness. "...nourishes and cherish-es...." The husband should be the first one in the family to go with-out, sacrifice, or lay it down for the family. "If he's not, then he's shortsighted. He doesn't realize what you're building for the future."

I particularly appreciated...connecting daily sacrifice for our wives with a longer-term sense of leaving a legacy and building a future. I'm far too prone to measure sacrifice in more mundane, self-seeking terms. I felt convicted about not having given enough consideration of the (future generations) that, Lord willing and Jesus tarries, will come after me. I need to understand sacrifice in light of a longer chain of relationships and events than just the immediate and often fleshly considerations of a given action.

A husband must lead in intimacy. Good practical exhortations here. Don't confuse sex with intimacy. Prioritize the marriage over the children. He makes two excellent observations regarding priori-tizing the marriage over the children. (a) Prioritizing the marriage helps protect the marriage from divorce by ensuring there's a rela-tionship there when the children leave. And (b) the security of our children depends upon the strength of the marriage. So, as we strengthen our marriages and prioritize them, our children know the stability and security necessary for spiritual growth. (Cite: Thabiti Anyabwile from http://thegospelcoalition.org/blogs/ thabitianyabwile/category/voddie-baucham/).

Emotional Provision- One of the glaring deficiencies in a hus-band's provision for his wife is in the area of emotional provision and support. As a marriage counselor I hear often, "He's just not there for me. And when he is there, he is only there in body. He just sits there." Wives are desperate for emotional interaction with their hus-bands. She is wired differently with different desires and needs. One of the strongest God-given desires is to be connected with you, her husband, on an emotional level. As we grow to be Strong Men, we must learn to operate in the realm of the emotional. We must not be-come feminine males who blubber about with no sense of composure or strength. But we must become vulnerable and transparent with our wives for that is the place that intimacy is found.

In Genesis 2 after God says that a man is to leave his mother and fa-ther and to cleave to his wife, becoming one flesh, the very next verse says that "the man and woman were both naked and felt no

Notes and Quotes:

Why do you think it is difficult for you to be there emotionally for your wife?

Notes and Quotes:

shame" (Genesis 2:25). Men, that is more than simply a physical nakedness. It is an emotional nakedness as well. When you chose to marry, you signed up to share your soul with another. Not just any other, but with your wife. She is to be your confidant, your closest ally and friend. There are to be no secrets between husband and wife. After all, we are to pattern our relationship after Jesus Christ's relationship with his church. And how many secrets do you think exist between Christ and his church?

One of your responsibilities in the area of provision is to provide for your wife on an emotional level. This will take an intentional approach. This will require that you learn to initiate emotionally.

"Why is it that some men can initiate great tasks and conquer overwhelming obstacles at work, yet remain passive in relationships or leading at home? It's as if there is a disease that infects the male species. None of us is exempt from the passivity virus." (Cite: Dennis Rainey in Stepping Up: A Call to Biblical Manhood. Page 105).

10 Ways to Provide Emotionally for Your Wife

1. Make it a point to communicate one private thought that you have each day and entrust that thought to her and her alone. We often give our best to others. Save the gems of your thought life for her and tell her that she is the only one to receive this part of you. As a pastor, I have a tendency to communicate in rather intimate ways from the pulpit. Often I have come home to hear my wife say, "I learn more about what is really going on inside of you when you preach to the masses." She is right to feel robbed. I should be saving the best of my thoughts and life for her. Now, I know what some of you are thinking. This would mean that you have to think something deep and profound every day and that is hard work. We need to put in the hard work so that others around us are provided for.

2. Make it a point to touch your wife with a non-sexual touch every day. In his book, Love Life for Every Married Couple, the late Dr. Ed Wheat offered 25 ways to insert non-sexual touch into your relationship. These are worth the price of the book. Often men only touch when sexual intimacy is sought. Our wives sometimes feel used if we do not show them love and attention outside of the marriage bed. This can open doors to emotional connection.

3. Make a brief phone call from work to simply let her know you are thinking about her. This is not rocket science. A woman wants to know that you love and desire her company. This is a great way to provide emotionally for your wife.

4. Take a few moments and sit beside her every day to show that you have a desire to be close to her. I am terrible at this. My wife has her chair and I have mine. We often camp out in them separated by space. We would be better off to move to the couch and sit side by side for at least a few moments each day. Most women would love to hear their husbands say, "Come sit with me for a few moments before we go our separate ways."

5. Plan special times away for just you and her, and then sacrifice what you would most like to do and choose to do something you know she will enjoy. When you go home and tell your wife that you have made plans to spend some time with her, and those plans include doing things you want to do, knowing she will find the plans boring or even worse, repulsive, then you are not providing well for your spouse. Make sure you arrange this in a way that will most stimulate her. You will come to know whether or not she loves surprises or not. My wife would much rather be in on the planning so she can anticipate times like this rather than be surprised. Some wives take joy in knowing that their husbands cared enough to plan this without any manipulation or input from them. It is important to study and come to know your wife so that you maximize your impact by investing in ways she will receive the greatest blessing.

6. Be willing to talk about yourself with her. Often as men we are so task oriented that we only talk about the things we do. I often hear the question from my wife, "What do you think about...?" My ungodly response is a short and brash, "Nothing." I know that many of us spend our time at work with our minds engaged and racing at 100 miles an hour. The challenge here is to engage your mind in the same way at home and in your relationship with your wife. Don't be afraid to make "I" statements. She wants to know you, not simply about your day.

7. Ask her lots of questions about herself and what she thinks. She will be shocked that you care about such things. Seek her out on an emo-

Notes and Quotes:

How long has it been since you initiated conversation with your wife?

Notes and Quotes:
Which is harder for you?
Caring for her emotionally
or spiritually?

tional level using questions to grant her opportunity to respond to your leadership. Remember, you are to be a leader. She was made to respond to you. Show you care for her by giving her license to talk about what she is interested in, passionate about and be attentive as she answers. Emotional provision is something you can give. But in order to do so, it will require a sacrifice of your time and attention.

8. Engage her in conversation about the foundational philosophies that should guide your family. Initiate discussions regarding what things you both want to impart to your children or how you want to structure your time around holidays. Life has a way of happening, and we seldom have taken the time on the important choices to assure that we are making the most of this gift of life and family. Talk about family priorities and values. She will see your provision as you engage her in these discussions.

9. Invite her into your private places of passion. This sounds sexual, and it certainly might include something of this nature. But this goes way beyond sex. What in life brings you to the place of positive emotion? I have a friend who went on mission trips to Africa, and his heart was exhilarated by the opportunity to serve such needy people. He would come home and tell his wife how wonderful it was to be used by God in this ministry. She listened, but simply could not relate. Until one day he invited her to go along. Her heart saw firsthand why he was so passionate about these precious people. An emotional point of connection was established that blessed their marriage.

Are you participating in
creating a Sacred History
in your marriage?
How?

10. Talk about spiritual things with her. Men are often very private when it comes to matters of faith. Be willing to talk to her about what you are learning about God and about yourself in relationship to who God is in your life. One of the things that Satan uses to destroy relationship is our constant focus on the superficial. Get beneath the surface and deal with issues of the heart. Faith is very personal and when you talk about your faith with your wife, you give her a gift. Not only does she enjoy the emotional connection, she is doubly blessed because of the spiritual connection that is forged. A byproduct of this is that she will come to trust you more when she sees your constant pursuit of God.

Spiritual Teaching and Direction- I will touch on this briefly here, but in the chapters that follow on a man's role to live as a prophet, a mentor, and a priest in his home, you will learn much more about this calling.

Loyalty- In a world that has walked away from vows, commitment and marriage God's way, there is perhaps nothing greater that you can provide for your wife than that of loyalty. A REAL Man of God is loyal all the way to the very end of life. There are so many stories out there about the brokenhearted. Men and women who have been traumatized by the selfishness of their spouse who at one point stood at an altar, in the presence of God, and pledged to love and to cherish until death. But then months or years later, came to the horrible place of saying, "just kidding." Men, we must throw ourselves upon the mercies of God and ask for the courage and the character to fulfill our promises and to provide over the long haul.

In his book entitled Sacred Marriage, Gary Thomas shares data that indicates that the more blessed days of marriage do not arrive or materialize until a couple has been married for at least thirty-five years. Statistics say that over time a couple develops what he calls a "sacred history" that is all their own and if they will persevere and endure the challenges of life together, they will eventually come to the place of great satisfaction. I shared that with a man in my office not long ago who had experienced two failed marriages and now at the age of fifty-five he was feeling as if he would never get to enjoy what God intended for him in life. He wept as he said to me, "I am fifty-five years old with no prospect for a wife. I will never get to experience that blessed season. Divorce and the lack of loyalty on the part of my first wife has robbed me of that opportunity."

We must be careful here to tell God what he cannot do in our marriages or to limit Him from giving us the joy and blessing he desires for us. But we must realize that "disposable marriage" and the lack of character and commitment of both men and women is costing us some very precious benefits. Men, we must make a choice to stay and invest for better and worse; in the good times and the bad, in sickness and in health. Without this commitment, we will never have a credible impact on our children or grandchildren. Be loyal...no matter what she does or how you feel. Stand firm and finish the race!

Notes and Quotes:

A Portrait of a REAL Man...Robertson McQuilkin:
A Loyal Man

Robertson McQuilkin is a REAL man. We have spent a lot of time in this book looking at the qualities of a REAL man. One quality that affords a man this title is that of being loyal to the right things and people. Robertson, now in his 70's, displayed remarkable loyalty toward the woman he called "my beloved, Muriel." The story began when Muriel was fifty-five years of age. At first it seemed innocent enough. But in time her forgetfulness began to concern Robertson.

Robertson and Muriel had given their lives to ministry. In fact, early in their ministry, they had served as missionaries to Japan. The final twenty-two years of his public ministry were spent serving as the President of Columbia Bible College and Seminary in Columbia, South Carolina. It was a ministry he loved.

In the first ten years or so of Muriel's disease, Robertson managed to care for her and to continue to serve the students of Columbia Bible College. That does not mean that it was easy to accomplish both tasks. Muriel grew more and more dependent upon Robertson with each passing year. It seemed that she was only secure if she was in his presence. Many served as caregiver to Muriel in those years that Robertson tried to manage both worlds. But Muriel would often escape from home and walk the half-mile or so that had to be traveled to the campus in search of Robertson. Many a day he would be sharing in a classroom or a meeting only to have Muriel slip in to just watch him.

In his book, <u>A Promise Kept</u>, Robertson gives us a glimpse into those difficult days of their journey. "During the latter years of my presidency at Columbia, it became increasingly difficult to keep her at home. As soon as I left for the office, she would take out after me. With me, she was content; without me she was distressed, sometimes terror-stricken. The walk to school is a mile round trip. She would make that trip as many as ten times a day – ten miles, speed walking. Sometimes at night when I helped her undress, I found bloody feet. When I told our family doctor, he choked up. 'Such love,' he said simply." (Robertson McQuilkin in <u>A Promise Kept</u>, Tyndale House Publishers, 1998, 2006. Pages 26 & 27).

In 1990, after ten years of trying to manage two worlds, Robertson was faced with a difficult decision. Either he had to place Muriel in an institution to manage her care, or he had to quit his job as president and stay home and care for Muriel full-time. The following is his letter of resignation to the people associated with Columbia Bible College:

"Twenty-two years is a long time. But then again it can be shorter than one anticipates. And how do you say goodbye to friends you do not wish to leave?

The decision to come to Columbia was the most difficult I have had to make; the decision to leave 22 years later, though painful, was one of the easiest. It was almost as if God engineered the circumstances so that I had no alternatives. Let me explain.

My dear wife, Muriel, has been in failing mental health for about 12 years. So far I have been able to carry both her ever-growing needs and my leadership responsibility at Columbia. But recently it has become apparent that Muriel is contented most of the time she is with me and almost none of the time I am away from her. It is not just 'discontent.' She is filled with fear – even terror – that she has lost me and always goes in search of me when I leave home. So it is clear to me that she needs me now, full-time.

Perhaps it would help you to understand if I shared with you what I shared in chapel at the time of the announcement of my resignation. The decision was made, in a way, 42 years ago when I promised to care for Muriel "in sickness and in health...till death do us part." So as I told the students and the faculty, as a man of my word, integrity has something to do with it. But so does fairness. She has cared for me fully and sacrificially all these years; if I cared for her for the next 40 years I would not be out of her debt. Duty, however, can be grim and stoic. But there is more: I love Muriel. She is a delight to me – her childlike dependence and confidence in me, her warm love, occasional flashes of that wit I used to relish so, her happy spirit and tough resilience in the face of her continual distressing frustration. I don't have to care for her. I get to! It's a high honor to care for so wonderful a person." (Ibid. Pages 21-23).

Robertson's resignation came in 1990. Muriel lived for nine more years before finally going to be with her Lord. Those nine years were not easy for Robertson. Listen to a few more quotes that speak of his brokenheartedness.

"As Alzheimer's slowly locked away one part of my Muriel, then another, every loss for her shut down a part of me. Ministry was changing, of course, from less public to more private. There was another sense of loss, however, an ache deep inside, as I watched my vivacious companion of the years slip from me.

Even in this loss, however, I made a wonderful discovery. As Muriel became even more dependent on me, our love seeped to deeper, unknown crevices of the heart. Though she never knew what was happening to her, as I cared for her she responded with gratitude and cheerful contentment.

It was no great effort to do the loving thing for one who was altogether lovable. My imprisonment turned out to be a delightful liberation to love more fully than I had ever known. We found the chains of confining circumstance to be, not instruments of torture, but bonds to hold us closer.

But there were even greater liberations. It has to do with God's love. No one ever needed me like Muriel, and no one ever responded to my efforts so totally as she. It's the nearest thing I've experienced on a human plane to what my relationship with God was designed to be: God's unfailing love poured out in constant care of helpless me.

Surely he planned that relationship to draw from me the kind of love and gratitude Muriel had for her man. Her insatiable —even desperate —longing to be with me, her quiet confidence in my ability and desire to care for her, a mirror reflection of what my love for God should be." (Ibid. Pages 32-35).

Now that, my friend, is a portrait of a REAL man. A real man is loyal to his God, to his wife and to his word.

Chapter 15– Providing for Your Children

"Behold, I will send you Elijah the prophet before the great and awesome day of the LORD comes. And he will turn the hearts of fathers to their children and the hearts of children to their fathers, lest I come and strike the land with a decree of utter destruction."

(Malachi 4:5-6 ESV)

Oh men, how we need our hearts to be turned towards our children. We should be alarmed today in America. A crisis rages, and yet as a culture many walk unaware. I am speaking of a crisis in the home, a crisis in the area of fatherhood. Our children are growing up without fathers. To be honest, we do not yet know the depth of the trauma that will be brought into the lives of those who are exposed to this terrible plight. But almost universal agreement exists from those who have studied this breakdown in our culture. The price will be devastating, and generations will be affected.

"I humbly but firmly submit that the soul of our nation is in crisis in large part because American men have – from ignorance and for various and sometimes even subconscious reasons – abandoned their God-given role of fatherhood. They have discarded the notion of being responsible for the physical and spiritual wellbeing of those around them." (Weldon Hardenbrook in <u>Recovering Biblical Manhood and Womanhood</u>. Page 378).

"...for the first time in the history of humankind the overwhelming majority of little boys and little girls continue in the direct domination and supervision of ladies until they reach maturity. This has never happened before in history. Crusades, wars, migrations, pestilence – nothing for a people as a whole ever before took so large a percentage of young adult and older adult males out of the family context for so much of the waking time of the children." (Cite: Marion J. Levy in <u>Modernization: Latecomers and Survivors</u> in <u>Recovering Biblical Manhood and Womanhood</u>. Page 379).

Notes and Quotes:

How did this happen? Subtly over a period of perhaps thirty years. Satan lulled us to sleep and then stormed in while we were chasing after the idol of self-fulfillment and robbed us blind. There are many contributing factors, but I will only mention three.

Marriage fell into disrepair- Earlier I used a term that I believe is accurate when we talk about how marriage is treated today: disposable marriage. When marriage became disposable and lost its luster and traction, the role of fatherhood quickly came under attack as well. Forever the backbone of this nation has been its family structure and family values. When those crumbled, it was easy for decline to happen. Yet, many men and women alike have become so hard-hearted towards God and His ways. They have spit in the face of the Almighty and sprinted into presumptuous sin. And in so doing, they have willingly sacrificed their sons and daughters on the altar of their own selfishness.

> Subtly over a period of perhaps thirty years. Satan lulled us to sleep and then stormed in while we were chasing after the idol of self-fulfillment and robbed us blind.

Keep back your servant also from presumptuous sins; let them not have dominion over me!

Then I shall be blameless, and innocent of great transgression.

Let the words of my mouth and the meditation of my heart be acceptable in your sight,

O LORD, my rock and my redeemer. (Psalm 19:13-14 ESV)

The feminist agenda in this country has devastated the family and has led to role and gender confusion. First this began to affect the adults, but over time there has been a trickle down effect that has attacked our children as well.

"...feminist ideology has profound implications for the family, business, the economy, politics, the military, marriage, sexual preference and identity, childrearing, and education. The mechanisms by which society has prepared, placed and sustained each generation are being called into question." (Cite: David J. Ayers in <u>Recovering Biblical Manhood and Womanhood</u>. Page 313).

Sadly, the sacrifice of the marriage and children was not shocking to the architects of the feminist movement. They understood all along that pursing this agenda would lead to exactly what we have gotten.

"We can predict a higher divorce rate when the criteria of success in marriage change from family, integrity, security, and contentment to happiness in which people are to grasp opportunity to feel vital; when compromise is judged to be a sign of inadequacy; when 'doing your own thing' and 'getting yours' are legitimized...when divorce is easy to obtain...when the negative costs of commitment are emphasized... when selfishness is idealized as autonomy...and moral responsibility is to self rather than to the relationship, divorce increases...Commitment involves not only mutual feeling but also interdependent obligation." (Cite: Judith Bardwick, <u>In Transition</u>. Pages 120-121).

How sad that this intentional attack on the family would take place and the masses in this country would sit by idle and complacent. We are where we are because we have done what we have done. The time to take back that which Satan has stolen, is now.

Finally, we are experiencing this crisis because we as men have stopped patterning our fatherhood after our Heavenly Father. Instead, we have begun to allow worldly philosophies such as sociology, anthropology and psychology to shape our methodology as fathers.

"American society has divorced itself from Heaven because American fathers have ceased to pattern their fatherhood after the Fatherhood of God. There is no hope for the children of America unless their fathers return from the exile of self-serving behavior and offer their souls to the mercy of the Father who created them." (Cite: Weldon Hardenbrook in <u>Recovering Biblical Manhood and Womanhood</u>. Page 383).

What Must We Provide For Our Children?

In light of the climate and culture we have just addressed, a man's calling to provide for his children is vitally important. What we do now matters! I do not believe that it is too late. God is more than able. But it will not happen by accident, and it will not happen if REAL Men do not step up and lead the way. I want to add here that this challenge is not just for the married men who are still at home with their children. No, this challenge must be taken on by every man.

Notes and Quotes:

Notes and Quotes:

How are you promoting

marriage God's way to

your children?

We Must Provide a Healthy View of Marriage- Marriage is under attack on almost every front in America. Our children must begin to see that we love the institution that God designed and that we are passionate about its future. How do we do this? We must, in a general sense, begin to fight against the philosophies that speak against the authority and knowledge of God. We must unashamedly speak against the sins of selfishness, the pursuit of personal happiness at all cost, sex outside of marriage, cohabitation, no fault divorce, and the spirit of individualism that leads to twoness rather than oneness. Men, we must fight in a public arena and do so in full view of our children so they see our passion and our heart for God's blessed institution of marriage.

In a practical way, we can promote marriage in our homes by showing our children that we are committed to live out marriage God's way. Plan regularly to take your wife out and lavish her with love and attention. And do so in full view of your children. They will see your love for your wife and their mother, and they will also come to know your commitment and dedication to the high calling of marriage. Plan regularly to attend marriage enrichment events to help continue to grow your marriage and show your ongoing investment in your spouse.

The next thing is vitally important. Never speak poorly of or against the institution God created to be the most sacred of human relationships. In this day when so many have been burned, marriage has a bad connotation. Christian men and women who have been hurt by ungodly spouses have often fallen to the place of speaking poorly about the institution. "Oh, I have been twice burned," a man said to me recently. "I won't ever marry again. I will just live with the woman." The saddest part of this statement is that it was spoken by a man who claimed to be in Christ. The message he was sending to his children was the wrong message. Marriage has always been, and will always be, God's design. It is good because God created it. Promote it as you do life. Men, if you are divorced and your marriage did not turn out the way you hoped or prayed it would, your testimony to your children must shout, with great clarity and vigor, that marriage God's way is a glorious thing; that it was meant by God to be a blessed thing, and yet too often we allow sin to destroy what God intends for good. Your testimony must lift up marriage to be an honorable and challenging calling that is to be fought for even when life is difficult. Do not let your personal heartbreak drive you to skepticism. Our problem is not with God's design. Our problem is that we are sinners who fail to honor God and walk in His ways. But when we practice confession and repentance, marriage is, and can be, a wonderful journey.

We Must Provide them Security by Loving Our Wives

There is no quicker way to produce insecurity in your child than to live before them a fractured marital relationship. Every child wants to live with both a mother and a father. And when it becomes obvious that there are struggles in your marriage, your children suffer. However, the most important thing to understand here is that the thing our children need most of all is to see our love and commitment. Satan has deceived many a man or woman that the children would be better off living apart from their father than to have to endure the tragedy of a mother and father living out a loveless marriage. This is simply not true. It is an excuse. And it is an excuse that is bringing terrible pain to our children. Do not use this excuse to exit a difficult marriage. God is not finished yet.

What children need to see in our marriages is commitment! We do not live perfect lives or have perfect marriages because we are sinful people. Every husband sins against his wife and every wife sins against her husband. It is a given. But the marriage is to be maintained and invested in even as we struggle with sin. In fact, marriage is designed by God to deal with sinful hearts so that we can be redeemed and sanctified for His glory. Marriage is to be the sandpaper that rounds off the rough edges of our character in order to make us look more like Jesus Christ.

If you want to provide security for your children then communicate to them that you love their mother so very much and that you made a vow before God that you will stay married to her for better and for worse, in sickness and in heath, in joy and in sorrow, until death do you part. Some may say, "Well I can't promise that because I have no control over her." And that would be true. But you must approach marriage from the place of YOUR commitment. She could opt out at any time and you might not even get a vote. But you should always communicate that you will not give up and you will not leave. This will give great security to your children.

Realize too that this kind of commitment is contagious. Sit with your wife and discuss the need for your children to see this type of love and commitment lived out and expressed on a daily basis. Cultivate love in such a way that your wife has no reason to want or need to exit the marriage.

Finally, teach your children to approach marriage from the permanence view. They are to look to marry a person of Godly character who they believe will live to God's standard. Often we create problems for our-

Notes and Quotes:

What do your children

think about your

marriage?

Is your marriage a good

example of a Godly

marriage?

Does the word father

have a good or bad

connotation in your

children's lives?

selves because we are not careful enough about the type of person we date and ultimately, marry. We are also too flippant with regards to our sons and daughters dating lives. We allow our children to become involved in dating relationships that expose them, and their hearts, to people who do not have the character or foundation to carry out the vows that they make. I believe you, as a father, should never allow your daughter to date anyone who you believe lacks the character for her to marry. Dating should be one's search for a spouse. You are called to provide wisdom to your daughter regarding the man she will someday marry. You also must teach your sons what it means to be a Godly man and help them to cultivate Godly character so that other Christian fathers will be happy to give them their daughters hand in marriage. Your son's future father-in-law should know that your son has been raised in such a way that he has the character to live to his vows and fulfill his commitments.

We Must Provide an Accurate View of God- It is not by accident that we bear the very same name that the Almighty does when it comes to familial relationships. The title is father. Our role is to provide for our children in much the same way that God provides for us, His children. He is our Heavenly Father. Therefore, we are to look like Him, especially in our role as fathers.

Years ago I was asked to write curriculum for teenagers. When I was given my assignment, something troubling jumped off the page of my instructions. The note read something like this: "Because we live in a world today where fatherhood has fallen into disrepair, we ask that you do not refer to God as Father." How sad that we have desecrated the name father. I did not mean any disrespect, but I did not adhere to their request. Why? Because Scripture refers to God as our Heavenly Father. We as fathers can either live out our calling in ways that reflect an accurate view of the Almighty to our children or, we can live is a way that brings about terrible conflict in how they see and understand God.

In order to give them an accurate view of God, we must teach them the things found in God's Word; we must model for them what a Godly man looks like and how he lives humbly before God and man; we must quickly confess and repent when we sin; we must join them in worshipping His majesty; and we must practice Romans 12:1. We must live sacrificially for His glory.

I appeal to you therefore, brothers, by the mercies of God, to present your bodies as a living sacrifice, holy and acceptable to God, which is your spiritual worship.

(Romans 12:1 ESV)

Much more regarding this will be presented in future chapters focusing on a man's role as prophet and as priest. For now, realize that you carry the responsibility to point your children to God and His amazing love.

We Must Provide Our Presence

We live in a world today where time is more valuable than money. In fact, time is our most hoarded valuable. I believe one of Satan's many weapons attacking the family is that of busyness. We just simply don't have time.

Our children need our time, both in quantity and in quality. "On average, American fathers give each of their children a mere three minutes of undivided attention each day." (Cite: Ibid. Page 379).

It is bad enough that many fathers are not in their homes to raise their children and to instill values in them. But often, even those fathers who are in the home are absent in many respects.

In his study entitled The Quest for Authentic Manhood, Robert Lewis speaks about what he calls the absent father wound. As you listen to him speak about it, you can see the emotion well up in his face. He tells of his personal pain created by the simple fact that his father was not engaged in his life. Now, I want to caution that this can never become an excuse for us to try to justify a "that's just the way I am" type of attitude. Too many adults blame their father or mother for the way they have turned out. The reason that I share this today is that I believe this is an easy thing to remedy. If fathers will simply realize that their children are desperate for their time investment then we have the ability to quickly reprioritize our lives to include them in our schedules and lives. It is not that we can't do it. Rather it is that we have not made the choice to do it. We *can and must do better.*

> *Look carefully then how you walk, not as unwise but as wise, making the best use of the time, because the days are evil.*

(Ephesians 5:15-16 ESV)

"The use of time is one of the most difficult subjects to broach with Christian men. We've grown so accustomed to burning the candle at both ends that we tend to bristle at any suggestion that we need to 'dial it back' a bit to make time for that which most matters. Nevertheless, we cannot equip family shepherds effectively without ad-

Notes and Quotes:

What area of your life most shapes your identity? Home or work?

Notes and Quotes:
Has your recreation or
entertainment become an
idol for you?

dressing the issue of our schedules." (Cite: Voddie Baucham in <u>Family Shepherds</u>. Page 155).

Men, how many of us have sacrificed our children on the altar of our careers? We often rationalize and say we are doing all this work for them. But if we truly examine our hearts, our motives are founded in the fact that our identity is seldom found in our home and most often found in our work. This means that when you leave the office at the end of the day, you drive away from your purpose and you drive towards a responsibility that seems to take us away from the "sweet spot" of our lives. Our wives and children are to be our "sweet spot." In order the reprioritize your time, you must reprioritize your heart. Your identity must change. It cannot be drawn from what you do for a living, rather it must be found in 1) who you are in Christ; and 2) the most important roles of your earthly life, that of husband and father.

I must also address one other factor that comes into play here as well, our leisure. How many of our children have to stand in line behind our love for hunting, or golf, or football?

"Our entertainment driven culture has provided us with laptops, iPods, iPads, iPhones, Droids, Wi-Fi, XM, Tivo, and a whole host of other devises and mechanisms to keep us plugged into the matrix. If we are not purposeful, the cultural inertia will make it possible to live meaningful lives. We will look up one day and our kids will be gone – and all we will be able to say is, "I wish I'd taken better advantage of the time." (Cite: Ibid. Page 161).

Earlier this year, I had the chance to play a round of golf with my son, Morgan. We have often played together and enjoy the time to talk more than time of hitting the little white ball. But as we played this time, something seemed different. He seemed a bit distracted. If I didn't know better, I would have thought that he would have rather been somewhere else with someone else. Then I realized that was true. And in that moment, I became so very proud of the REAL Man he has become. Harper, his daughter and my granddaughter, was born near the end of last year's golf season. And since her birth, he had seldom played golf. We happened to be playing on a Wednesday afternoon, which was his day off. All the Wednesdays of Harper's young life she had spent in the company of her daddy. And now he finally had a chance to get back out on the course and enjoy his leisure and recreation. But guess who was missing who. I am sure Harper was missing him, but it was awesome to see that he was missing her. And that golf no longer held that place of priority in his heart. It isn't that our recreation is sinful in and of itself. But if it holds a priority above our families, we must realize that we have given it too large a role in our lives. The key to time management is to set proper priorities based upon God's order. Family is important in God's eyes. Don't shirk your responsibility to be present and invested!

We Must Provide Direction

Let me remind you that your role in your home is to be the leader. And leaders are called to set the agenda and to determine direction. Many of our families are wandering aimlessly with no purpose. I suggest that you and your wife begin to pray and determine goals for your family and for your children, especially spiritual goals.

Not long ago I was sitting in the barber's chair listening to a woman ramble about all kinds of nonsense as she cut my hair. She was actually ranting about faith. She was also unaware of my calling to be a pastor. It was just before Easter and she spoke of how "stupid" (her word and not mine) it was for people to celebrate a man's death on a cross and her skepticism about the claim that he rose again. She then revealed her ignorance regarding her role of raising her children when she spoke about her philosophy of parenting. She said, "I want to raise my children with no faith so that when they grow up they can choose for themselves a religion that is right for them without any influence from me." Okay, so I had heard enough and I declared my calling and began to preach that God had called every parent to give direction to their children. That was exactly what parenting was about! I have to tell you, I got the fastest haircut you can imagine as she began to move at breakneck speed to get me out of her chair and out the door.

And these words that I command you today shall be on your heart. You shall teach them diligently to your children, and shall talk of them when you sit in your house, and when you walk by the way, and when you lie down, and when you rise. You shall bind them as a sign on your hand, and they shall be as frontlets between your eyes. You shall write them on the doorposts of your house and on your gates.

(Deuteronomy 6:6-9 ESV)

Fathers, do not provoke your children to anger, but bring them up in the discipline and instruction of the Lord.

(Ephesians 6:4 ESV)

Fathers we must provide direction for our children. This is a significant element in our calling to be fathers. Set goals for your family and for

Notes and Quotes:

Are you guilty of provoking your children to anger?

Notes and Quotes:

each of your children. Watch them as they grow and assess how God has gifted them and then invest in helping them to develop their gifts so that they will be able to be effective for God as they grow up. Choose for them the things that will make them grow and give them a foundation of faith. There is no such thing as neutral. You have been entrusted with a precious gift. Don't miss this opportunity to develop them for God's glory and for their own benefit and blessing.

Men, sit with your wives and begin to pray for God's direction for your family and for each of your children. Write out specific goals for what you want to accomplish over the next year. Be diligent, as the Scripture above states. Our children need direction. Our families need direction. Our nation needs direction. And we as fathers have the God-given responsibility to provide it!

Conclusion

As you can easily see, this section could go on and on because the things we need to provide for our children is expansive. The list above is far from an exhaustive list. As you contemplate how to be a good provider for your wife and children, make certain that you are addressing three significant categories: 1) their physical wellbeing; 2) their emotional wellbeing; and 3) their spiritual wellbeing. Don't fall for the belief that your responsibility is found primarily in bringing home a paycheck. Your role is designed to be far more involved than that. You will learn more about what you are to provide as we unpack the next two areas of responsibility: to be a prophet in your home and to become a priest in your home.

Father God, I want to pause at this point and ask for Your wisdom for every man that will read this book. I acknowledge that we have a huge challenge before us as we attempt to stop the decay of our society that is rapidly leading our children into harm's way. I ask, O God, that you would place within the hearts and minds of every man, a vision for their family. Instill in each one a pure motive so that this great calling will be lived out for Your glory and for the blessing of their children. Equip us that we might be capable. Inspire us that we might be willing. Direct us that we might lead in the right direction. And grant us the courage to be REAL Men of God. I ask all this in Jesus' name. Amen.

Discussion Questions:

1. The author spoke of three areas that a man must provide for his wife and children: 1) Physically, 2) Emotionally and 3) Spiritually. Which of these areas is most difficult for you to provide and why?

2. In the first part of this book the author mentioned that man was given dominion over certain things by God. What does this fact have to do with a man being a provider for his wife and children?

3. The author writes: "One of the glaring deficiencies in a husband's provision for his wife is in the area of emotional provision and support. " Do you agree or disagree? Why?

4. In this section the author offers ten ways to practically provide emotionally for your wife. Which are you most likely to implement into your marriage? Why?

5. Had you ever thought about the importance of loyalty to your spouse and children. If asked, "How loyal do you see your husband to be, what do you think your wife would answer?

Notes and Quotes:

Chapter 16- Prophet, Mentor, Teacher, and Coach

Follow my example, as I follow the example of Christ. (1 Corinthians 11:1 NIV)

As we learned in the first section of this book, every man needs a mature man who is further along in the journey of faith to follow after; a man who is a leader among men; a man who is a credible witness for Christ; a man I call a spiritual director. But not only does every man need someone who can help lead them into maturity, every man needs to see himself as a leader; one who can say to his wife, his children, his neighbors and his friends, "follow me as I follow Christ."

In my life, I have two very different mentors. The first man who has mentored me is a quiet and gentle man who is full of a "common sense" type of wisdom. His name is Ted Back. Ted hails from Kentucky, is a place he calls "God's Country." I love the quiet, unassuming way Ted lives his life. I smile when he speaks of himself as "Teddy," even as he has lived well into his sixties. For more than a dozen years, Ted and I have met for lunch weekly. Our relationship is simply based on friendship and being connected as brothers in Christ. Seldom do I ask him specific questions as if he was an answer man. Our relationship is not based on an expert giving his wisdom to his student. No, it just looks like friendship. Seldom do I ask Ted to pray for me about specific things or to encourage me when I am down. But I know for sure that Ted does pray for me, and sitting at lunch weekly and just talking about life is almost always encouraging to me. One of the things that I love about Ted is his humility. When people speak of his wisdom, he laughs and says he has no idea where they get an idea like that. I chose Ted to be my mentor for that very reason. I sought out this man because he displayed the character of Christ by choosing to humble himself. Why? Because I am a man who struggles to be humble. And I was drawn to his authentic humility. And as I have sat across the table from him for many years now, I believe God has used Ted to mentor me in this area especially. Ted is my mentor in the everyday things of life. I am blessed to have such a man in my life.

Be Strong and Show Yourself a Man

Notes and Quotes:

Do you have men in your

life who can say to you:

"Follow me as I follow

Christ?"

Who are they?

Dr. Woodrow Church is a much different man than Ted Back. Woody and I met many years ago when I sat under his teaching to become a certified Biblical Counselor. I was attracted to his intellect. Woody has earned his doctorate. He is the most well-read person I know. When you sit with Woody, you learn things you would have never even thought you needed to know. And the learning comes naturally as he addresses you with compassion and grace. Not only is Woody a learned man, he is a kind and gentle man in spirit. But his kindness and gentleness do not make him wimpy. No, Woody is one of the boldest men I know. He is the kind of person who can tell you that you are a terrible sinner and yet make you feel so incredibly loved. I asked Woody how he managed to do that one night at dinner and he responded, "Well, some people have called me a velvet brick." Most learned men that I have met have been pretty full of themselves. Woody is full of God. He is quick to give God glory in every situation. Woody is my "go-to answer man." When I don't know how to interpret a Scripture, I call Woody. When I need a deeper understanding of a doctrine or theology that I am studying, I call Woody. And what I love most about him is that he never just gives me the short version of the answer I desire. No, he always says, "Let's do coffee next week and we can talk this thing through." Woody is a very busy man, but he gives me his precious time. Everyone needs a Woody in their life!

The modern day title for this man who leads is mentor. A mentor is one who understands his place and responsibility in a generational flow of life and faith. He realizes that he bears a responsibility to pass on what he has been entrusted with to those who come after him. He recognizes that he has been blessed with the investments of others and begins to live out the verse, *"Everyone to whom much was given, of him much will be required, and from him to whom they entrusted much, they will demand the more." (Luke 12:48 ESV).*

What does a mentor do? "A mentor must pass on his values; lessons learned by his mistakes, successes and defeats; the essence of his life. He intentionally passes on wisdom to the next generation and casts a vision on how they can do the same." (Cite: Dennis Rainey in Stepping Up: A Call to Courageous Manhood. Page 143).

The biblical name for a mentor is prophet. We need more prophets in this world. It is funny how two words can have the very same pronunciation. It is even more interesting that two words that sound the same can have very different meaning. I am talking about the difference between prophet and profit. We live in a world that is consumed with profit, a world that pursues profit at all costs. But we also live in a world that is in desperate need of a prophet.

In the Old Testament the word prophet had two particular meanings. First, it meant to foretell. This is a look into the future to tell what is to come. Of course the Prophets of the Old Testament often told of the coming King, Jesus Christ. They told of what was going to happen because of the people's sinful pursuit of self. This definition is not the one that I want to focus on in this study. The second definition of prophet is on who forth-tells. This is the area of our study. One who forth-tells speaks for God. Voddie Baucham simply defines a prophet as "one who instructs his people in God's truth." (Cite: What He Must Be. Page 153). We need men who will speak for God. We need men who are bold and can accurately deliver a message to the world today. We need prophets who will take seriously the call of God upon their lives.

> *He established a testimony in Jacob*
>
> > *and appointed a law in Israel,*
>
> *which he commanded our fathers*
>
> > *to teach to their children,*
>
> *that the next generation might know them,*
>
> > *the children yet unborn,*
>
> *and arise and tell them to their children,*
>
> > *so that they should set their hope in God*
>
> *and not forget the works of God,*
>
> > *but keep his commandments;*

(Psalm 78:5-7 ESV)

Why do we need Prophets in our lives? We need prophets to teach us what we do not yet know. We need prophets to inspire and encourage us to fight the good fight of faith. We need prophets to challenge our thinking. We need prophets to hold us accountable. We need prophets to help us become.

Notes and Quotes:

Chapter 17- We Need a Joshua 24:15 Moment

"...choose this day whom you will serve...But as for me and my house, we will serve the Lord..." (Joshua 24:15 ESV excerpts).

Every man needs a Joshua 24:15 moment. What does that mean? Every man needs a time when he sits down with his wife and kids and declares his intent to become a prophet in his home.

Some men have been Christians for years but have never taken a stand for Christ in their marriages and in their homes. They have been nominal Christians who have just kind of gone with the flow and have never taken their responsibilities as a Christian man seriously. This is the moment that a man becomes "all in" in his responsibility to be a Godly leader in his home. This is a powerful and yet humbling moment. I suggest that you plan for this defining moment and take it seriously. Mark it with a special gift to your wife; take her out to dinner and tell her you have something important to talk to her about. Give her a book on Biblical roles in marriage and tell her you want to rise up and be the kind of leader in your marriage that God has called you to in His Word. I suggest you get companion editions of The Excellent Wife by Martha Peace and The Exemplary Husband by Stuart Scott and invite her to study with you what it means to follow God's plan in your marriage. Ask for her support and help. Don't minimize this calling. This is something that can and will change the rest of your life together.

This is the time and place that you drive a stake in the ground and say to your wife and to the world, "From this day forward things are going to change!"

Men, note that it is important to seek the support of your wife in this endeavor, but do not base your future on her response. It would be awesome if every wife embraced this immediately, but some won't. Some will have become calloused and hard-hearted over the years of neglect they have felt and experienced because you were less than a man in this area. Some of us paint ourselves into a corner and make it really hard to get out. If your wife does not immediately respond in a favorable way, take that as your challenge to show her over time that you mean business; that you are here for the long haul; that life from this day forward is going to be dif-

Notes and Quotes:

Would your wife say that

your leadership would be

best described as:

A. A Shepherd

B. A Rancher

C. Non-existent

ferent. If she responds with skepticism, simply humble yourself and ask for her forgiveness for having failed to lead her and your family effectively in the past. Tell her that with God's help, you are going to rise up and show yourself to be a REAL Man.

It is important that you deal primarily with your role and responsibility as a Godly husband and father. Your role is defined as being the leader in your marriage and family. And your responsibility is to lead in the same way that Christ showed leadership of his bride, the church...with a lavish, selfless, sacrificial love. It is also important that you have some understanding of what your wife's role and responsibilities are so that you are able to encourage her to become the woman, wife and mother that God created her to be. Her role is to be your helper, and her responsibility is to submit to your leadership. You are to partner with her, each fulfilling your roles and responsibilities so that your home functions in a Godly manner.

There is one major caution that I want to place before you at this point. It is not your job as the leader in your marriage and home to make your wife submit to your leadership! This is extremely important. God's way has always been for the wife to voluntarily submit to her husband. The word for submit in Scripture is the Greek word, Hupotasso. Hupotasso, according to the New Testament Greek Lexicon, is a Greek military term meaning "to arrange [troop divisions] in a military fashion under the command of a leader". In non-military use, it was "a voluntary attitude of giving in, cooperating, assuming responsibility, and carrying a burden". This is actually the combination of two words. Hupo which means under and tasso which means to arrange. Literally it means that a wife is to arrange her life under her husband's leadership. But an interesting note for those who know and study the Greek language, Hupotasso is what is called the Greek middle. This means that the wife is to choose voluntarily to submit to her husband. If she fails to submit to your leadership, men, be gentle and not demanding. Show patience and pray for her for she is first and foremost out of step with God, and secondly, she is not standing in her place of blessing, benefit and protection. Hold the umbrella of love and protection steady, and allow God in His time and in His way to direct her to the place she is to stand.

Next, after having a "Joshua 24:15 moment" with your wife, ask your wife to join you as you communicate this defining moment to your children. If they are old enough to understand, then sit with them and speak about the good news that something special has happened to their father and that from this day forward there are going to be some new priorities. Years ago Bill Gaither wrote a song entitled "Something's Happened to Daddy."

Something's happened to daddy
He's not the same anymore
Things are different at our house
Like never before
Mommy says he met Jesus
And it washed him white as snow
Something's happened to daddy I know

What a powerful message to share with your children. As you have this "Joshua 24:15 moment," communicate with your children about any areas that you want to ask for their forgiveness. Some fathers need to ask their children to forgive them for not having been a good protector or provider. If God lays it on your heart to ask your children for forgiveness, humble yourself and do it! Some have the failed philosophy that says that we can never be that vulnerable with our children, that it will show weakness and lead to insecurity. I completely disagree. It is always a Godly thing to ask for forgiveness when we have sinned against another person. This is a great opportunity to do the business of reconciliation.

As you begin this new chapter in your family life, it will be important that you concentrate on what God is calling you to do and not focus on what God is calling your wife to do. As I have outlined in this book, your role as a Godly husband is to be the leader of your wife. This leadership should show itself in every area of your marriage; but your role as prophet in your marriage and home should have a spiritual expression. Spiritually you need to take responsibility. It is amazing to me that we often never intentionally consider what it means to live lives of spiritual purpose. Now is the time to make some important decisions and changes regarding spiritual formation in your home.

What does spiritual responsibility look like in your home? First of all, make sure your family has a foundation. Make sure that your family is immersed in a church fellowship where the Bible is preached. If you are not involved in a church fellowship, then you need to take as stand and find a church home and invest yourself and your family in regular church attendance.

Secondly, you must make sure that you don't fall into compartmentalization regarding your faith. Insert faith into your marriage and home. Your wife and children need to see that your faith is important to you every day of the week and not just on Sunday.

Notes and Quotes:

Are there sins that you have committed injuring your children that need to be confessed?

What kind of role model are you?

Notes and Quotes:

Read your Bible every day and make it known to your family that this is important. I am convinced that the reading of God's Word gives strength and meaning to life. It is our "daily bread." It gives us the spiritual nourishment that we need in order to grow and be spiritually healthy. Don't just read it to yourself, but read it to your family as well. This does not have to be a lengthy time commitment every day. It can be as simple as sharing one verse with your wife and children every time you sit down for dinner. When I was a little boy, my grandmother and grandfather had a box of Scripture cards that sat on their dining room table. When I was blessed to spend time with them, we would draw a card from that box at every meal and would read it aloud. The message I received as a little boy was a significant one. What God says in His Word is important!

Once you have gotten these two basics of choosing a church home and integrating faith into your every day, you are ready to begin the journey. Take some time to ask God to teach you how to lead your wife and children into a deeper understanding of God. Ask for wisdom so that you know how to lead.

Chapter 18- Developing Oneness with Your Wife

Therefore a man shall leave his father and his mother and hold fast to his wife, and they shall become one flesh.

(Genesis 2:24 ESV)

Just what does it mean to be "one flesh?" Some have interpreted this verse to simply speak of sexual union in marriage. And that certainly is part of its meaning. But to be one flesh goes beyond the act of sex. Oneness with our wives is something that we must strive for spiritually and emotionally as well as physically. I believe that there is a natural order to Oneness and it grows out of the following order: When a husband and wife work together and develop a spiritual oneness, the door swings wide open for their relationship to grow and bear the fruit of intimacy which leads them to a place of emotional oneness. Spiritual oneness is the foundation and key. If they can seek the Lord together and worship Him in all their ways, then they will begin to see their intimate communication grow stronger and develop a heart-to-heart connection that will eventually lead to a greater physical oneness as well.

The sad part about this understanding of oneness is that very few ever pursue this kind of spiritual oneness with their spouse. Being a prophet in your marriage means that you take the initiative to grow spiritually with your wife.

There are a number of things that you can do to develop this jewel in your marriage. The place I suggest you begin is by learning to pray together. Years ago, my wife, Angela and I wrote a study entitled <u>Developing Spiritual Oneness ...Through Prayer</u>. In it, I relate my struggle to pray with my wife. The following is my testimony:

It was a crisp, fall day in Indiana, as Angela, my wife, and I both arrived home from our different jobs and decided to take advantage of the few moments before the sun would go down to enjoy a bit of God's glorious creation. Fall in Indiana is beautiful. So we each grabbed a light jacket and after a quick supper, we set out on a walk that would ultimately change our lives and

Notes and Quotes:
Leading spiritually is
difficult for most men.
Which is most difficult for
You? Leading physically?
Emotionally?
Or spiritually?

marriage. Over our thirty plus years of marriage, we have found that walking together is one way that we deepen our conversations. At home, I often get distracted. I must confess to you that I am easily knocked off track. Angela will be sharing the most challenging moments of her day and suddenly I hear that ESPN jingle in the background and my eyes wander to the TV to see just who made today's plays of the game. Or the little icon on my computer screen screams "You've got mail!" Over the years, we have come to enjoy walking together, and as we walk, we talk. We talk about everything: our jobs, our kids, the stresses of life, the joys of life. Almost always, these conversations wind themselves around to talking about faith and life and how they intertwine themselves.

On this particular afternoon, as we began to round the final turn of our journey, the conversation turned to an uncomfortable subject for me. For years and years, Angela had longed to pray together as a couple. Not only had she longed for us to pray together, she had asked for us to pray together, begged for us to pray together, and even pleaded for me to pray with her. It wasn't entirely that I didn't want to pray together. In fact I believed praying together would be a godly thing. But the fact was that every time we did pray together, it was uncomfortable for me. The bottom line is that all the reasons I struggled to pray with her fall into two categories: 1. Excuses and 2. Satan loves division. He is the deceiver. And he placed all kinds of fear and distortions in my mind to keep me from responding as a godly man.

Excuses, Excuses, Excuses

In the fast-paced world in which we live, time has become a valuable commodity. From the moment we get out of bed until the final moment that we lay our head on the pillow, we are a busy people. Or so we say. Angela has a full-time job and so do I. She is an accountant and has to drive forty-five minutes every day to work. I am a pastor. My schedule is such that I am at the church several nights a week teaching, counseling, and meeting with people who work all day and volunteer for ministry in the evenings. Both Angela and I are biblical counselors, so we both have a wide variety of rather weighty responsibilities. My first excuse not to pray with her was that I just didn't have time.

Several years ago, a counselor in our church who specializes in counseling children became frustrated when one of the children she was counseling was not doing his homework. Biblical counseling uses Bible-based homework assignments to help the counselee learn and grow. The counselor asked the child why he had not done his homework. The child's response was "I didn't have time." Then the counselor asked, "Did you have time this week to play your video games?" The answer was a very definite "Oh, yes." Then she had to tell that child, "Then you did have time, you simply chose not to do it." I wonder where that small child learned that excuse. I can tell you my children learned it from me. We have promoted leisure to the point of idolatry. We desire to be entertained far more than any generation past. And the result of this quest for leisure and entertainment has devastated the church and family. Spiritual disciplines have become all but extinct. In all honesty, I was saying, "I don't have time to pray with you." But truthfully, I found it to be inconvenient. My hard heart wanted my way regardless of what Angela wanted or needed.

Some may say the Bible does not communicate about husbands and wives praying together. And they would be partially right. There is no command that I find in Scripture demanding couples pray together. But there is biblical guidance that I believe provides a foundation upon which to build a godly marriage. Two of those passages are:

24 Therefore a man shall leave his father and his mother and hold fast to his wife, and they shall become one flesh. Genesis 2:24 (ESV)

25 Husbands, love your wives, as Christ loved the church and gave himself up for her... Ephesians 5:25 (ESV)

Husbands, I want you to know that God has called you to be a leader in your home. (Ephesians 5:23) The Genesis passage above says that marriage should be a relationship where two people leave their past and sacrifice their individuality in order to pursue the biblical calling of oneness. You will never accomplish this without a commitment of your time. But more importantly, you will never accomplish this without a commitment of your heart!

The Ephesians passage calls a husband to love his wife in the same way that Christ loved the church. How did Christ love the church? He sacrificed himself even to the place of dying for her. I know many men who say they would die for their wives and children. But they have no desire to live for them - to fulfill their biblical responsibilities and calling in the marriage and in the home. Romans 12:1 says that we are to be "living sacrifices" for the Lord. I want to challenge the men who read this to "man up" and take seriously God's call for them to lead their wives sacrificially. I wish I could tell you that this responsibility comes naturally, but in our sinful nature godly sacrifice is never easy. It requires an act of our will. We must decide to do this. Make a choice to lead your wife and children and see if God doesn't open the floodgates

Notes and Quotes:
How do you think that
daily prayer with your
wife would affect you?
Your wife?
Your marriage?

Notes and Quotes:

of heaven upon your marriage and family.

My second excuse for not pursuing a prayer life with my wife was founded in both my insecurities and in my ego. Over years of marriage, I had come to expect certain things from my wife. Sometimes past history becomes a coffin that renders the living dead. I had put my wife in a coffin of her own past mistakes and decided she would never change or grow, and that was sinful on my part. In writing this, I am attempting to be honest and vulnerable with you so that you can learn from my mistakes. Perhaps you will have the courage to open that coffin you have placed your spouse inside and let them out to grow beyond his or her own past failures. I have come to realize that my placing Angela in this coffin did not mean that she was unable to grow. Rather it means that I was unwilling or unable to see and acknowledge the growth that God had done in her because I had defined her by her past behaviors. This is important for us to realize whether we are in the position of husband or wife. I know of some men who long for spiritual oneness more than their wives do. And I believe that both husbands and wives have, at times, fashioned living coffins for their spouses. Another way of understanding this living coffin is that we often hold our spouse hostage to his or her past failures. Let's forgive each other and pursue oneness in Christ. Unlock the lid and begin a journey together!

Angela has been passionate about marriage for much longer than I have been. As I mentioned before, she has longed and longed for years and years to develop a spiritual oneness in our marriage. She has prayed for it! She has asked for me to consider numerous ways to cultivate it. My second excuse for not praying with her was my misguided belief that nothing would ever please her or be good enough. I have always felt that I am "playing catch up." In the words of another, "I married way over my head." Once I got a notion to lead, I went on the Internet and found a seven sermon series on marriage that I brought to her for us to listen to and discuss. She was overjoyed. The first night, we listened to the sermon online and had a deep discussion. I failed to tell her that my plan of leading her into this deeper marriage included us listening together to a sermon a week and discussing it. The next morning, she awoke exhilarated by our study and discussion from the night before. Not knowing my intentions of studying a sermon a week together, she went online and downloaded the remaining six sermons of the series in written form and consumed them as fast as her eyes could read and her mind could digest them. She was so excited. But when she told me what she had done, I was far from overjoyed. I felt she had run ahead and that I would never be able to catch up with her.

So, I put her in that coffin and locked it, believing she would never let me lead. And I used that as an excuse whenever I needed it, to not push myself or challenge myself. In my mind, nothing would ever please her, so why try.

Satan's Distortions

I did not realize for a long time that my excuse that I could never please Angela was based upon Satan's lies. I want you to know that Satan is the deceiver. His desire is to lead you astray. When couples begin to grow toward oneness, I believe Satan begins to quake in his boots. And he begins a spiritual battle based on deception. Satan, for a long time, was winning the battle and convincing me that I would never be able to accomplish this calling to be a leader in my marriage and home. I always thought that I was not disciplined enough, not smart enough, not capable enough to answer God's call to become a spiritual leader in my home.

Now I want to interject here that, for a long time, I had the wrong goal in mind. I was simply trying to please Angela. Or probably more accurately, I was trying to appease her. Husbands and wives, I want you to realize that because of our human sinful nature, this is an impossible task. It was not until I came to the place of realizing that my goal must be to please God that I saw a breakthrough. 2 Corinthians 5:9 calls us to make it our goal to please Him. Please don't enter into this study and journey to simply try to appease your spouse. Make your goal a higher, more noble goal: to please the Lord Jesus Christ and honor Him in your marriage!

As I have begun to grow as a leader in my marriage, God has accomplished in me what I have never been able to accomplish in myself. He has given me a discipline that I have desperately needed and longed for over the years of my life. He has answered my prayers to make me hungry and thirsty for Him and His righteousness.

Another way that Satan has attacked me along this journey is a result of a conversation that Angela and I had shortly after I first began to pray with her. Because I am a pastor, I pray publicly often. Most of these prayers are corporate in nature. As a result, when I would bow my head and voice a prayer with her, they often sounded pastoral and not personal. When she brought that to my attention, I became immediately defensive. How dare she judge my prayers! Again, I opened her coffin and said this is just too hard for me to deal with. Even though I continued to

Notes and Quotes:
Has Satan distorted your
thinking about your wife?

pray with her on a more and more regular basis, I did so from a more guarded position. It was out of duty that I was praying with her. And I was far from transparent or real. But due to all the above mentioned excuses and distortions, I avoided praying with her when I could. Satan worked hard to convince me that her desire was to control and to manipulate. I realize now that my perceptions of her were not true. And I have had to rethink things according to Philippians 4:8 which calls us to "set (our) minds on that which is true, noble, right, pure, excellent and praiseworthy." I have come to realize that Satan's distortions and lies almost destroyed what God desired for us. But thanks be to God that He was not finished. And I am thankful that Angela did not give up on me or the "God in me." That afternoon, as we walked toward home, the subject of prayer came up again. I was defensive as usual. She was determined as usual. It was actually one sentence that broke my hard heart. "Why won't you just pray with me every day?!"

I had heard those words years before. And I can honestly say I was not a godly enough husband to honor her request. At that point, I began by committing to God (without telling her I should add) to pray with her once a week. It was a discipline that I willed to accomplish. I did not tell her of this commitment for fear that if I failed, she would lose hope, or even worse, see me as a hypocrite. Looking back, this was a beginning point in our praying together. It was still not comfortable. But out of duty I committed to God to try. I daily asked Him to give me the desire and courage to honor that commitment. As months passed, I became more comfortable praying with her. And as I became more comfortable, we prayed more than once a week.

I am not talking about a prayer thanking God for our food. We have always done that from our first day of marriage on. But I am talking about an intimate prayer as a couple.

I don't know what happened that afternoon as we walked and she once again passionately asked that I would pray with her every day. But this time, God had prepared my heart. I was not defensive in the way I usually was towards the idea. Instead, I told her I would pray about the idea and seek God's direction. As I prayed in my own prayer time, I came to realize that God had been preparing me over time to rise to this place of leadership in my marriage and my home. And beginning the next morning, I was committed to pray daily with Angela.

I can honestly say that over time, I have become more and more comfortable praying with her and now it seems very natural. It has become a part of our everyday life. We pray for each other, for our children and friends. We lift up those in need. The overflow of our journey has led us to the place of promoting prayer among other married couples who might be able to learn from our experience. We do not consider ourselves experts – just fellow pilgrims on this journey. It is my prayer that as you begin this study, God will grant you His passion and that you will experience a sense of urgency, a hunger and thirst for Him and His righteousness. I pray you will find it within yourself to tear down the walls that have been built between you and your spouse...to let them out of the coffin of their past. And as you learn to pray together, may God richly bless your union and make you One!

Seek God Together in the Everyday of Life

As you become a prophet in your marriage, it is important to realize that faith is grown in the everyday of life. In his book, What Did You Expect?, Paul David Tripp says that we need to realize that God is active in the little moments of our lives, for those are the places that our lives are lived. We must insert faith into the everyday moments of our lives. It is not enough to simply have a formal plan to teach and study. There is absolutely nothing wrong with the formal. But the informal is just as critical in the development of spiritual oneness.

In Deuteronomy 6, we are instructed about how to teach our children the things of God. In it we are told to "talk about them (the things of God) when you sit in your house, or when you walk by the way, and when you lie down, and when you rise." This is a great example of what I am speaking about. Angela and I spend every Sunday afternoon going to Starbucks for a reading date and then on to our favorite restaurant to sit and discuss what is happening in our lives. This discussion almost always finds its way to the things we are studying and learning about God. As these discussions take place, spiritual oneness simply happens. We don't go looking for it to happen, it just naturally is born as faith becomes woven into our everyday experiences of life.

Let me conclude this section by saying, we should not throw stones at the formal processes of learning together as couples. One way that I long to grow in oneness with my wife is intentional study together. At times Angela and I have been blessed to study together. One particular season was when we sat together and studied a catholic "Couples Prayer Series" that we found and went through as we developed the Developing Spiritual Oneness...Through Prayer study. These formal times offer great opportunity to grow in oneness. Unfortunately, we have allowed the busyness of our schedules to limit the times that we have studied together. I pray that spiritual oneness will become a wonderful

Notes and Quotes:

Would you say your faith is more interwoven in your life or more compartmentalized?

Notes and Quotes:

spiritual adventure for those who read this book. From our brief times of studying together, I see great potential for oneness. We have found that doing a book study together, especially when we travel, has led to greater spiritual oneness. I drive and she reads and then we discuss. It is a great way to productively travel for hours to a favorite destination. On our annual trip from Indiana to Florida each fall, we usually complete at least one book. Last year that book was <u>Family Driven Faith</u> by Voddie Baucham. It was a great study and many of the concepts have been woven into this book. The concepts of this book are not nearly so impressive as the passion behind the author. His passion for faith and family have landed him a spot in this next Portrait of a REAL Man.

A Portrait of a REAL Man- Voddie Baucham
...A Man Committed to Change

Voddie Baucham, Jr. is a man who is all about changing the fabric of his family. Born to an unwed teenage mother in the heart of downtown Los Angeles, CA, Voddie grew up in tremendous poverty. That poverty was much more than an economical poverty. His life was shaped by a spiritual poverty that left him vulnerable to great tragedy and harm. As Voddie speaks of his upbringing and the struggles that were created by his environment, he does so with great compassion for his family of origin who he loves and wants to see come to a saving knowledge of Jesus Christ. But what matters most to him, are the people God has entrusted to his care here on this earth. Those who matter most to him are his wife and their children.

In the DVD series The Art of Marriage by FamilyLife Ministries, Baucham speaks about the broken family system that both he and his wife come from. "In the last two generations of our families combined," Voddie says, "there have been twenty-five marriages and twenty-two divorces." As you look into his eyes as he speaks those words, you see his pain. But as he continues to speak, you also see the fire of passion that lights up his eyes when he talks about the future. "It's time for my wife and I to drive a stake in the ground and say, NO MORE! Not on my watch!!!" His passion for the call upon his life to change his family tree is both challenging and contagious. Voddie is on a mission to change his family forever. And I for one believe he, with God's generous help, will accomplish what he has set out to do.

Voddie is a popular speaker, pastor, and writer with lots of opportunities to build his career and reputation. But he has kept his eyes on the most important goals, that of being a husband and father and changing his family tree.

"The most important side of my life is the one where I bear my most cherished titles – husband and father. There is nothing in this world that means more to me than the fact that I am Bridget's husband and Asher, Jasmine, Trey and Elijah's father...my family is the primary place where my walk with Christ takes on flesh...It is my relationship with my wife and children that gives my walk with Christ legitimacy." (Cite: Family Driven Faith. Page 15).

The final chapter of Voddie's quest to change his family for the glory of God has not been written. We do not know if he will be successful or not. We do not know if his children will grow up to marry and to serve the Lord. We don't know if they will remain married for a lifetime. But what we do know is that the world needs more Voddie Bauchams; men who will sacrifice for the future of faith and family; men who will stand firm on the foundational principles of God's Word and fight the battle for faith and family. His story is inspiring. The battle rages on before us. Every family is the battleground. We will either win the war one family at a time, or we will lose it one family at a time.

Chapter 19- Teach Your Children

In the Hebrew culture, it is called the Shema - the most defining passage of Scripture regarding parenting in the Good Book. Jewish families spoke these words often. In fact, when a family would return to their home after an outing, they would recite these verses prior to entering. They were important then, and they are important verses today for us as we provide for our children as well.

"Hear, O Israel: The LORD our God, the LORD is one. You shall love the LORD your God with all your heart and with all your soul and with all your might. And these words that I command you today shall be on your heart. You shall teach them diligently to your children, and shall talk of them when you sit in your house, and when you walk by the way, and when you lie down, and when you rise. You shall bind them as a sign on your hand, and they shall be as frontlets between your eyes. You shall write them on the doorposts of your house and on your gates.

(Deuteronomy 6:4-9 ESV)

When it comes to being a prophet to our children, the most obvious responsibility we bear is to teach our children about the Lord and to help them come to understand how to live in a way that pleases Him. The verse above says that we must "teach them diligently." Just what does that mean?

dil·i·gent [dil-i-juhnt] adjective

1.constant in effort to accomplish something; attentive and persistent in doing anything: a diligent student.

2.done or pursued with persevering attention; painstaking: a diligent search of the files. (Cite: www.dictionary.com).

The part of this definition that jumps out at me is the small but powerful phrase "persevering attention." This is an adjective that calls us to practice the spiritual fruit of long-suffering. It is not easy to raise children and to provide the things that they need as they grow up. But it is a

Do you agree that parents

are to be the most

responsible party when it

comes to teaching their

children?

What do you find most

difficult about being their

primary teacher?

vital, God-given responsibility for every father. We must teach them, and we must be diligent in our approach!

Don't Be So Quick to Delegate

We live in a world where men often delegate their responsibility to others. We delegate the responsibility of daily discipline to our wives because they are often more connected and present with our children than we are. We delegate their education to the school system, and in so doing we lose control of what their minds are exposed to and what is taught as truth and what is taught as theory. And we often delegate their spiritual development to the church thinking that these pastors are the "professionals" who have trained to be experts in faith and character development. Men, we need to realize that the responsibility to teach our children the things that they will need to mature and have a life that honors God is our responsibility. We can and should at times delegate certain pieces. If we are not very capable in a particular subject then it seems logical to find someone who is knowledgeable and seek out their help to teach our children. But when it comes to faith, I believe we must call men to be the prophet of their home; to become capable and active in the faith development of their children. This is not a job that can be done by professionals in your church in fifty hours a year. Your pastor and the people on the church staff are to be helpers and equippers in this process. But you are the primary one responsible. You are to teach them diligently. You are to raise them in the instruction of the Lord.

One of the great things about the Shema is that it gives us a very practical model as to how to impart this knowledge to our children. It says that we should "talk of them (the things of God) when you sit in your house, and when you walk by the way, and when you lie down, and when you rise. You shall bind them as a sign on your hand, and they shall be as frontlets between your eyes. You shall write them on the doorposts of your house and on your gates." I love the fact that the Bible is very practical here. Weaving faith into everyday life is vital.

Model Faith Everyday

Where have all the role models gone? When I was a boy there were people who I looked up to as role models. These were people who displayed qualities that made me want to be like them. Some of those role models were on T.V. Some were teachers who showed great character. But most of the role models in my life came from the area of church and family.

My father was a great role model for me when it came to an understanding that REAL Men work hard and come home at the end of each day. My father was a hard-working man with an important job that he took very seriously. He was a chemical engineer that gave almost all of his career life to Dow Chemical. I still remember those nights when the telephone would ring and he would talk with great intensity and concern to his coworkers about things that were happening in the plant. Often after one of those calls he would drop everything and jump in his car and return to make sure that things at the plant were going well. He was obviously dedicated. And his dedication rubbed off on me. Why? Because I saw him as a role model and when I got my first job at fifteen, I modeled my work ethic after my father who taught me how important it was to be a good and dedicated employee. One thing I took for granted in those years of growing up was that at the end of each day, a man went home to care for his family. Many never saw that principle lived out. I was blessed that I grew up in a two-parent home and that I could count on my dad coming home when his work was done.

I also had a great role model growing up in the area of faith. My grandfather was instrumental in my spiritual development. This is not surprising. God often uses grandparents to insert faith into the lives of their grandchildren. When I was nine years old, I went to spend the summer with my grandparents in Neshoba County, Mississippi. It was a summer that would change my life. I write about it extensively in Lessons Learned on Papa's Pond. For now, suffice it to say that the investment and teaching of my Papa that summer changed my life forever. In the months that followed, I came to know Jesus Christ personally, in large part because my Papa spoke God's Word into my life. He modeled for me a love that was beyond himself. And the results of his modeling ushered me right into the kingdom of God. I was blessed to have this prophet in my life.

You can be a prophet in the life of your child. You should be a role model to your children. In order to provide this you must walk in faith and be able to credibly turn to your children and say "Follow me as I follow Christ." Lead the way, O man of God. Show them how to walk in a way that honors God.

Content Matters

Like it or not, as a father you are a role model in your child's life. And they will learn from you many things, whether you intentionally teach

Notes and Quotes:

Can you say, "Follow me as I follow Christ" with credibility?

them or not. The content of what you teach them matters. Teaching them with diligence falls short if there is no content or substance in what you teach them.

As I have done often throughout the pages of this book, I must call you to be very intentional in this area. What is it that God would have you teach your children regarding faith? Another way to voice this question is this: What things should my children know about God and His Word when they leave my home and supervision and walk out into adulthood? I suggest you take some time and make a list.

A while back I had the great opportunity to sit with a wonderful couple, Bryce and Beth Fox. Bryce and Beth have spent countless hours developing a plan for what they want to teach their children before they leave home and walk out into the world. Their list is the most exhaustive list that I have come in contact with. They have taken their roles and responsibilities seriously when it comes to providing good and sound teaching about God, faith and His Word. Here is their list. Perhaps it will help you begin your own in the days to come.

The Fox Spiritual Plan

Our Desired Outcomes for Each Child

* Experience the heart's cleansing through Salvation through Jesus Christ

* Experience the power of the Holy Spirit in their lives on a daily basis

* Serve Jesus completely with their life -- whatever their career or talent

* Strong understanding of Scripture

* Strong understanding of Bible mechanics

* Develop the Spiritual Discipline of consistent, daily reading of God's Word

* Understand the Power of Prayer and be an Intercessor

* Memorize many, many Scriptures (in order to combat temptation, as well as to know how to pray and to understand God's heart)

* Develop a heart for Missions, Evangelism, and the Lost

* Ability to defend the Gospel of Jesus Christ by understanding Apologetics

* Ability to teach others

* Ability to articulate their own personal testimony

* Ability to lead/assist in Worship (instruments/singing)

* Possess a Biblical world view

* Ability to be a Strong Leader (confidence to make Godly choices)

* Tithe & practice wise financial concepts

* Live by Faith (willing to step out of their comfort zone when God instructs)

* Possess & Express a Cooperative Spirit (humble and submissive when needed)

* Make wise choices for caring for their temples of the Holy Spirit (bodies) -- eating and exercise

PRACTICAL SCHEDULE

Morning/Daily Personal Devotion time: (Younger ones listen to the Bible on cd/ipod)

* MON - Restudy scriptures and Bible points from Sunday's sermon. At the evening meal, explain how they can practically apply the message from the pastor's Sunday sermon to their lives

* TUES - Restudy scriptures and Bible points from Monday's family devotion time led by Dad

* WED - Put to memory the Bible verse of the week (earlier presented in family devotion time)

* THURS - Restudy scriptures and Bible points from Wednesday's sermon

* FRI - Restudy scriptures and Bible points from Thursday's family devotion time led by Dad

Family Devotion Nights: Monday & Thursday

Prayer

* Learn to be still before God, to listen, and to praise God before we present our requests

* Use Prayer sheet that Mom gave that has scriptures to pray for many different circumstances (there's power in God's Word)

* List top three people that they're praying for salvation

* Keep a list of prayer requests...and check them off when God answers that prayer

Notes and Quotes:

Notes and Quotes:
Do you believe there are
certain things about God
and faith that you ought
to teach your children?
If so, name a few:

* Pray the Psalms

While traveling

* Always commit our trip to the Lord and pray for protection

* If we travel over 100 miles, then we'll listen to an Apologetic teaching

TO DO:

* Help them discover their Spiritual Gifts

* Use them in practical ministry situations that match their giftings and yet help stretch them as well

* Allow them to participate in adult world situations to see how it functions and how to appropriately interact.

* Encourage servanthood as a way of life

Remember!! In order to develop Strong Leaders...As the parents, we must give out responsibly, allow our children to naturally live with their consequences, reinforce what they are doing well, which will dispel fear and encourage/inspire them!!

We strongly agree with the mission: TO KNOW GOD, AND MAKE HIM KNOWN!!

Catechism, an Old Method that Offers New Opportunity

When I was a small boy, I remember other children mentioning having to attend catechism classes in their churches. I had no idea what this entailed. Many of these friends involved in catechism classes were from a catholic background and I just figured it was something that was founded in a different system of faith than my own. But in recent days, I have studied more and more about this type of education and want to lift up some of the merits of this systematic approach. Bryce and Beth's list above can very easily qualify as a system of catechizing.

"The system of catechizing...includes a short, simple, and plain exposition and rehearsal of the Christian doctrine deduced from the writings of the prophets and apostles, arranged in the form of questions and answers, adapted to the capacity and comprehension of the ignorant and unlearned; or it is a belief summary of the doctrine of the prophets and apostles, communicated orally to such as are unlearned, which they again are required to repeat." (Cite: Zacharias Ursinus in <u>What is Catechism?</u> Quoted by Baucham in <u>Family Sherherds</u>. Page 64).

In his book, <u>Family Shepherds</u>, Voddie Baucham shares three benefits of using a catechism in your home teaching. First, catechism promotes theological literacy. "I cannot think of a more effective tool to put into the hands of a young father (or an older one, for that matter) who's a new convert or has never been discipled. This presents the perfect opportunity for him to grow and learn while beginning to lead his family. (Cite: Family Shepherds. Page 660.

The second benefit to using a catechism is that it trains one in the important area of apologetics. Apologetics simply means a way to defend the truth of God's Word. "What better way to prepare a Christian to answer questions about his or her theological beliefs than by teaching those beliefs through a series of questions and answers? Catechism serves thus a pivotal apologetics tool." (Ibid. Page 66).

The third and final benefit that Baucham lifts up is that catechism brings about a sense of doctrinal unity in the church. While it is not essential that we agree on every little thing regarding our understanding and interpretation of Scripture, it is vital that we have agreement on the foundational things regarding our faith and belief. Some things must be non-negotiable. We must lift up Jesus Christ as the only way to God the Father. Too many in the church have watered this down and believe that Jesus is but one way to God. This, in my opinion, is a non-negotiable. If you are a part of a church that teaches that Jesus is not the only way to God, I suggest you find a new church. Another non-negotiable in my view is that Scripture is the inspired, authoritative Word of the Lord. A catechism can and should bring about a sense of unity in the church, and the congregation you attend should be like-minded regarding the non-negotiables of faith.

A Caution When it Comes to a Catechistic Approach: Realize that this approach is information driven. It is looking at Scripture and at God from a knowledge based approach. While knowledge about God and His Word are important to establish as a foundation to build belief upon, the heart must become engaged if your child is to truly have an experience of faith. I again come back to a quote I made earlier. "Authentic behavior is always a result of identity in Christ." It is NOT enough for your son or daughter to know lots of things about God. You want them to have a personal relationship with His majesty. But Biblical illiteracy is running rampant in the church and a catechistic approach will help to fill in Biblical understanding. I suggest you proceed by teaching in this way, but do so by bathing the entire process in prayer and asking God to break the heart of your child in His time and in His way so that faith might be more than facts. God bless you as you do this for His glory and for the future of your children.

Notes and Quotes:

Are your children too tied to this world?

Notes and Quotes:

Teach Your Children to Live "In the World" But Not Be "Of the World"

The final area I want to cover with regards to being a prophet in your children's lives is in the area of preparing them well to live "in this world" and yet not be "of this world."

> *"If the world hates you, know that it has hated me before it hated you. If you were of the world, the world would love you as its own; but because you are not of the world, but I chose you out of the world, therefore the world hates you.*

(John 15:18-19 ESV)

> *I have given them your word, and the world has hated them because they are not of the world, just as I am not of the world. I do not ask that you take them out of the world, but that you keep them from the evil one. They are not of the world, just as I am not of the world. Sanctify them in the truth; your word is truth. As you sent me into the world, so I have sent them into the world. And for their sake I consecrate myself, that they also may be sanctified in truth.*

(John 17:14-19 ESV)

> *Do not love the world or the things in the world. If anyone loves the world, the love of the Father is not in him. For all that is in the world—the desires of the flesh and the desires of the eyes and pride of life—is not from the Father but is from the world. And the world is passing away along with its desires, but whoever does the will of God abides forever.*

(1 John 2:15-17 ESV)

Is it important that boys become masculine and girls become feminine?

John has much to teach us here about this concept of being "in the world" and yet not "of the world." Throughout this book I have called you to look with perspective at the world you live in. This perspective must be found with our understanding firmly established in the spiritual rather than in the physical. We must have an eternal perspective rather than a physical perspective. We are an alien people traveling in a foreign land. This world is not our home. No, our citizenship is found in heaven (Philippians 3:20). Don't become so captured by this world that you miss what is true. We must help our children to come to understand this concept and to teach them how to accomplish it as well.

Teach Sons to Be Masculine and Girls to Be Feminine

As you have already seen and gathered from this book, I am greatly concerned over the loss of biblical gender roles in society today. We

PRE-DEFINED IMAGE

have even allowed this to creep into the church. Initially it appeared that the battle for a woman's rights was about equal value. But soon that battle deteriorated from seeking equality to seeking sameness. This has caused great harm and has blurred the lines between masculine and feminine greatly. We are NOT the same. God intentionally made men and women differently. We cannot sit idly by as the world tries to erase God's intentional design for creation. God made men masculine and women feminine, and we must teach our children what this means.

"The tendency today is to stress the equality of men and women by minimizing the unique significance of maleness and femaleness. It is taking a tremendous toll on generations of young men and women by minimizing the unique significance of maleness and femaleness. It is taking a tremendous toll on generations of young men and women who do not know what it means to be a man or a woman. Confusion over the meaning of sexual personhood...is more divorce, more homosexuality, more sexual abuse, more promiscuity, more social awkwardness, and more emotional distress and suicide that comes with the loss of God-given identity." (Cite: John Piper in <u>What's the Difference?</u> Page 9.)

Some will look from a worldly perspective and say, "What is wrong with fighting for sameness?" And most seem to believe that a man can do anything a woman can do and a woman can do anything a man can do. There are no differences between the sexes. At the heart of many of our struggles with regards to family is a loss of the gender roles that have, in my opinion, been ordained by God and taught in Scripture. If we turn away from this teaching and discount it because culture calls for something different in this age, we open ourselves up to some tragic consequences.

If everyone is the same and there are no differences; if a man can do anything a woman can do, and a woman can do anything a man can do; and if we are interchangeable parts, then if we walk backwards from this faulty philosophy we will logically arrive at the place of homosexuality and same sex marriage. If you can interchange parts and genders with no concern over male or female roles, then it is only logical to conclude that a man can marry a man and a woman can marry a woman because there is no difference between men and women. This undermines all of the principles regarding marriage in Scripture. We must not fall for this false doctrine of sameness. We must teach our boys to be masculine and our girls to be feminine. The future of family depends on it.

For more information on this topic, I suggest you read an article enti-

Notes and Quotes:

tled <u>Psychological Foundations for Rearing Masculine Boys and Feminine Girls</u> by George Alan Rekers. Time and space simply prohibit a longer discourse on this subject. But I conclude this section with this final quote from Reker:

"The Bible asserts: 'So God created man in His own image, in the image of God He created him; male and female He created them' (Genesis 1:27). This means that sexuality in men and women reflects the 'image of God.' When the unisex mentality denies the human 'distinctions based on sex,' it is denying the image of God in human personality. But what else would we expect from the godless worldview of relativistic humanism? The unisex mentality denies the existence of God and His Word's authority, and in the same sweep, denies one mark of God in the human personality – the distinctions of male and female." (Cite: <u>Recovering Biblical Manhood and Womanhood</u>. Page 311).

"In gender role development, the evidence points to fathers having the more important influence, not only in fostering a male self-concept in boys, but femininity in girls. Mothers do contribute to their daughter's adoption of the feminine role, but have little influence on the masculinity of their sons." (Cite: Sueann Robinson Ambrom in <u>Child Development</u>. Drawn from <u>Point Man</u> by Steve Farrar. Page 186.)

The final word I want to say on this topic is that your children's view of their sexuality is important! It is important to God and it must be important to you. Don't leave your children without good sound biblical direction regarding their sexuality. The consequences of that will be devastating to them.

Data indicate that homosexuals commit suicide five or six times more than (studies on this number vary between five and six times) those who are heterosexual. It also indicates that homosexuals have a higher rate of alcoholism.

One recent study gathered self-report data from nearly 32,000 grade 11 students in Oregon. The findings revealed that 21.5 percent of the gay teens surveyed reported suicidal tendencies, while only 4.2 percent of straight teens did the same.

Gay rights activists blame those numbers on the church. Why? Because they believe the churches teaching against homosexuality is persecution and makes the homosexual feel badly about themselves. A biblical view says that sin brings guilt to the human heart. And unconfessed sin leads to suffering and brokenness. Eventually, unconfessed and unrepented sin leads to hell. The stakes are high. Teach your sons to be masculine and your daughters to be feminine! (Cite: The study, published in <u>The Journal Pediatrics</u> online on April 18, 2011).

What Must We Teach Them In Order to Accomplish This?

The following is a list of Scriptures and teachings that we must insert into the spiritual content that we provide for our children:

Teach them Genesis 1:27-28. *So God created man in his own image,*

> *in the image of God he created him;*
>
> *male and female he created them.*

And God blessed them. And God said to them, "Be fruitful and multiply and fill the earth and subdue it, and have dominion over the fish of the sea and over the birds of the heavens and over every living thing that moves on the earth." (Genesis 1:27-28 ESV)

We learn from this passage that God made man and woman equal in value. The differences between man and woman are obvious. We are physically and emotionally different. But our souls are the same. We simply have been given differences for God's purposes.

One of these purposes is that we might be "fruitful and multiply." Same sex partners cannot carry out this commandment.

Teach them Genesis 2:18-25. *"Then the LORD God said, "It is not good that the man should be alone; I will make him a helper fit for him." Now out of the ground the LORD God had formed every beast of the field and every bird of the heavens and brought them to the man to see what he would call them. And whatever the man called every living creature, that was its name. The man gave names to all livestock and to the birds of the heavens and to every beast of the field. But for Adam there was not found a helper fit for him. So the LORD God caused a deep sleep to fall upon the man, and while he slept took one of his ribs and closed up its place with flesh. And the rib that the LORD God had taken from the man he made into a woman and brought her to the man. Then the man said,*

> *"This at last is bone of my bones*
>
> *and flesh of my flesh;*
>
> *she shall be called Woman,*
>
> *because she was taken out of Man."*

Therefore a man shall leave his father and his mother and hold fast to his wife, and they shall become one flesh. And the man and his wife

Notes and Quotes:

If you are uncomfortable talking about sexuality with your children, pray and ask God to give you the ability to talk matter-of-factly with them about this important subject.

Notes and Quotes:
Use both formal and
informal teaching
methods to impart
important truths.

were both naked and were not ashamed." (Genesis 2:18-25 ESV)

Out of this passage you must help your child understand that God designed marriage to be between a man and a woman. It was, is and always will be God's design and intent that marriage be between a man and a woman. Culture desires to change the rules, but they cannot change God's intent.

Adam was made intentionally incomplete. God was more than capable of making Adam complete and able to fend for himself. But God's plan was that man would need a helper. Therefore He fashioned Eve. A few people are given a gift of celibacy that is for the purpose of being unencumbered so that they might devote themselves fully to the ministry of Christ. But unless your son or daughter is given this gift, it appears that God has designed them to marry and then to pursue "oneness."

We learn from verse 24 that a man will leave his father and mother and then cleave to his wife. This teaches that a man's responsibility is to rise up and leave his family of origin and prepare himself to take a wife. This is a call to masculinity. It does not say that a woman is to leave. She is to wait under the umbrella of her father's love and protection until her future husband comes for her and then she is given from a loving father to a loving husband.

We also learn from this passage that two people, a husband and a wife, are to become one flesh. Together they equal one. A man without a wife is less than one. And a wife without a husband is less than one. We need each other. Oneness is physical for sure. Sexual union brings about a physical oneness that God intended. It is for more than just procreation. It is also for pleasure and blessing to the married partners who celebrate God's gift of sex. But it is also an emotional oneness, and certainly it is a spiritual oneness.

In verse 25 we learn that there should be transparency and honesty between husbands and wives. This is a picture of intimacy.

How Do We Go About Teaching These Things?

Again I call your attention to the Shema where we read earlier that we are to teach the commandments of Scripture, "You shall teach them diligently to your children, and shall talk of them when you sit in your house, and when you walk by the way, and when you lie down, and when you rise. You shall bind them as a sign on your hand, and they shall be as frontlets between your eyes. You shall write them on the doorposts of your house and on your gates." (Deuteronomy 6:7-9

ESV) This teaching is informal in many ways, and yet it is very intentional. Study the material above and be prepared to teach it over and over during the everyday of life.

Notes and Quotes:

Chapter 20- Becoming a Priest (Don't Freak at this Title) in Your Home

It is the responsibility of every REAL Man, to be a family shepherd; to be the lead pastor in your home; to bind up the broken hearted and to care for the souls of those entrusted to your leadership and care. I have come to call this responsibility "soul care." If you are married and have children and have been born again into the kingdom of God, then you have been called to the ministry. And your mission is to be a priest to the ones you love - to administer the love, mercy and grace of God to those in your family.

To put this simply, it is the call of every husband and father to care about and for the souls of their wives, and sons and daughters. Nothing should be of more concern to you than the soul and eternity of those entrusted to your care. Your role as a priest in your home is directly related to the care of the souls of your flock.

"The greatest malady of the twentieth century (was) its loss of soul. When the soul is neglected, we experience obsessions, addictions, violence, loss of meaning, and emotional pain." (Cite: T. Moore as quoted in Competent Christian Counseling by Clinton and Ohlschlager. Page 122). "No one has made a better assessment of the last century. As our society has become more complex and technological, it has also become more superficial. The emptiness of our times is revealed in a spiritual vacuum that cries out to be filled by the Divine. We are no longer a predominantly Christian society. The heart and soul of the Western world have been polluted by the secular pursuit of life without God." (Ibid. Page 122). Men, if we are to make a stand for the future faith of generations that come behind us, then we must rise up and carry out the responsibilities of the priesthood. We must represent God and do it well.

Today there is controversy in the church over this idea of acting as a priest in the home. There are two basic objections to referring to a husband and father as the priest of his home. The first objection is that we no longer need a priest to intercede since Jesus Christ died on the cross. We will look at that shortly. Secondly, some equate priesthood with male headship and fight against any thought of male headship in the home quoting verses like Galatians 3:28 which says, "There is neither Jew nor Greek, there is neither slave nor free, there is no male and female, for you are all one in Christ Jesus." This verse certainly says that God looks at any and everyone who is "in Christ" the same way. We are all, regardless of gender, equal in the site of God and have equal value. But there is a difference between equal and sameness as I have argued earlier. This is not a question of value, but of function. There are specified rolls throughout Scripture that are reflected even in the way that the Godhead functions. God the Father, God the Son and God the Holy Spirit are all God. But each Entity functions in different roles: Jesus functions as Savior and mediator; the Holy Spirit as our comforter. There are different roles that are ordained within even the Godhead.

Now I commend you because you remember me in everything and maintain the traditions even as I delivered them to you. But I want you to understand that the head of every man is Christ, the head of a wife is her husband, and the head of Christ is God.

(1 Corinthians 11:2-3 ESV)

In this passage we can plainly see that God is the head of Christ. And we also see that a husband is to be the head of his wife.

What do I mean when I say Priest?

I must begin by stating that when Jesus died on the cross, the concept of priesthood did not die with him. We desperately need a priest. We still function under a priest who intercedes on our behalf. His name is Jesus Christ. Without Jesus Christ, who according to Scripture is our "high priest," we cannot have access to the father. All access to the Almighty must go through him. Jesus taught this as he walked the earth. John 14:6 we read, "Jesus said to him, "I am the way, and the truth, and the life. No one comes to the Father except through me." Again I say, the need for a priest is not dead. We need Jesus as our priest in order to have access to God.

The writer of Hebrews helps us to understand more about this when he writes, *"Since then we have a great high priest who has passed through the heavens, Jesus, the Son of God, let us hold fast our confession. For we do not have a high priest who is unable to sympathize with our weaknesses, bu*

(Hebrews 4:14-16 ESV)

Now take a moment and follow this logic. We still have a priest and his name is Jesus Christ. He is not only our "high priest," but he is also the head of the church. In Ephesians 5 we read, "Wives, submit to your own husbands, as to the Lord. For the husband is the head of the wife even as Christ is the head of the church, his body, and is himself its Savior. Now as the church submits to Christ, so also wives should submit in everything to their husbands." (Ephesians 5:22-24 ESV).

This verse teaches that the husband's role in the marriage is to be patterned after Christ's role in the church. One of the roles that Jesus fulfills in his relationship with the church is that he is her priest. Therefore, it is not unbiblical to call every husband to play this role in his marriage; rather it fulfills the call found in Ephesians 5.

Men, I want to caution you regarding the dismissal of large amounts of Scripture with just the pronouncement that this particular passage is no longer relevant because the culture is different now than it was then. This is a slippery slope that leads to the undermining of the authority of God's Word. 1 Corinthians 11:2-3 and Ephesians 5:22-24 both undeniably say that the husband is to be the head of the wife. This cannot be disputed. The question then becomes, "Does God mean what he said?" Many scholars today argue that God said it but you need to be a deep thinker and scholar to be able to go back into the Greek and unpack what this really means. In their unpacking this, they jump through mental hoops on their way to their predetermined outcome that the Bible says this but God did not mean it. For years I bought their arguments. They were based upon a culture that I was rooted in. The person who uses the argument that you must go back into the Greek in order to truly understand what God meant will often try to make you feel inadequate and inferior if you do not align with his/her interpretation. The message sent seems to be, "If you were as smart as me, you would see that this is really deep and complicated and perhaps you just aren't smart enough to get it." Don't buy this tactic and allow it to silence you. God's Word says what it says because God meant to say it. As I tried to rationalize a different understanding of what these passages taught, I soon came to realize that doing so demanded that I walk away from one of the core values that I held regarding God and Scripture: that God's Word was and still is authoritative. To have to jump through so many mental hoops to explain away what the Bible literally says became too much for me to bear. Therefore, when the Scriptures say one thing and culture or scholarship teach another, I must always side with Scripture. There are things that are a part of God's Word that I must confess I do not understand. But when I come across those things, I simply have to place them under the words of Isaiah 55. *"For my thoughts are not your thoughts, neither are your ways my ways, declares the LORD.*

Notes and Quotes:

Notes and Quotes:
Do you have a special
place in your home
designated to be a
sacred space?

For as the heavens are higher than the earth, so are my ways higher than your ways and my thoughts than your thoughts." (Isaiah 55:8-9 ESV).

What Does it Mean to Be a Priest in Your Home?

Very simply put, "a priest is an intercessor who represents his people before God." (Cite: Baucham in <u>What He Must Be.</u> Page 153.) We should see this as a call to prayer. Intercession means that we come before the Lord carrying the burdens and needs of those we love and ask God to provide for them all that they need. In his role as priest, Jesus did this often. He prayed for those entrusted to his care.

> *I am praying for them. I am not praying for the world but for those whom you have given me, for they are yours. All mine are yours, and yours are mine, and I am glorified in them. And I am no longer in the world, but they are in the world, and I am coming to you. Holy Father, keep them in your name, which you have given me, that they may be one, even as we are one. While I was with them, I kept them in your name, which you have given me. I have guarded them, and not one of them has been lost except the son of destruction, that the Scripture might be fulfilled. But now I am coming to you, and these things I speak in the world, that they may have my joy fulfilled in themselves. I have given them your word, and the world has hated them because they are not of the world, just as I am not of the world. I do not ask that you take them out of the world, but that you keep them from the evil one. They are not of the world, just as I am not of the world. Sanctify them in the truth; your word is truth. As you sent me into the world, so I have sent them into the world. And for their sake I consecrate myself, that they also may be sanctified in truth.*

(John 17:9-19 ESV)

As Jesus' prayer continues, not only did he pray for his disciples, but he also prayed for us. I find this amazing.

> *"I do not ask for these only, but also for those who will believe in me through their word, that they may all be one, just as you, Father, are in me, and I in you, that they also may be in us, so that the world may believe that you have sent me. The glory that you have given me I have given to them, that they may be one even as we are one, I in them and you in me, that they may become perfectly one, so that the world may know that you sent me and loved them even as you loved me. Father, I desire that they also, whom you have given*

me, may be with me where I am, to see my glory that you have given me because you loved me before the foundation of the world. O righteous Father, even though the world does not know you, I know you, and these know that you have sent me. I made known to them your name, and I will continue to make it known, that the love with which you have loved me may be in them, and I in them."

(John 17:20-26 ESV)

I am so blessed every time I read verse 20 and realize that Jesus prayed for me. If we follow Jesus' example, we should be praying for our wives and children. This is a responsibility we carry as we live out our role as priest in the home.

Black Monday

Have you ever had one of "THOSE" days? You know… the one that is so terrible and horrible that you won't ever forget it, a day that will live in infamy. Those days often are given a title and placed into history as a defining moment. As a nation we have those days marked by titles such as 9/11, Pearl Harbor, or Columbine. Just a brief title goes into your memory bank and resides there as a marker that quickly paints in one's mind a dark and tragic hour. Families have days like that as well. Perhaps they have no national significance, but they mark life-changing experiences that are wrapped in pain and disappointment. One of those days in my family was what has simply become entitled "Black Monday."

It all happened on a Monday afternoon. My daughter Amye had spent her afternoon at cross country practice as she did every afternoon after school in the fall. She was dedicated to her sport and had excelled in ways we never imagined that she would. For most of her high school career, Amye had led her team and was one of the top runners in the state. She loved her teammates and her coaches. But on this particular Monday afternoon, something happened and the scene deteriorated quickly. I do not know what her coach was thinking, but he apparently thought that Amye needed to be humbled and broken down. Some coaches use that principle of breaking the athlete down so you can then build them up and they are supposed to be stronger as a result. Whatever his reasoning, the coach on this particular afternoon began to verbally attack Amye. The whole team seemed shocked and began to take up for her, and before it was over, the attack became personal and abusive. Amye began to cry and when she did her tears seemed like blood in shark infested waters. Before the coach's tantrum ended, Amye lay in emotional ruin, broken-hearted and perplexed.

How long has it been since you served your loved ones?

Notes and Quotes:

I arrived at the house just moments before she did and was preparing for an evening at home. When Amye arrived, it was obvious that something had happened. Her eyes were red and swollen. It looked as if someone she loved had died. Pain was etched all over her face. When I asked about her day, tears welled up in her eyes and she said she didn't want to talk about it. I knew that she needed to but realized she needed some time. I began then and there, praying for God to begin a healing process in her, even though I did not know what had happened.

After an hour or so, Amye was ready and able to talk about what had happened. She cried a bucket of tears as she spoke of all that had happened and all that was said. As I listened, I became angry with the coach. He had stepped way beyond the lines of what was appropriate. My first reaction was that I needed to be my daughter's protector. I thought about calling that coach and giving him a piece of my mind. Then I thought that perhaps the best thing was to set up a meeting with the school's principal and ask for them to discipline the coach. But as I pondered what I should do, it became crystal clear that what needed to happen first was that I needed to play the role of a priest for my daughter. I needed to hold her and embrace her as she cried. I needed to generously provide my presence in her life. I do not remember what was on our schedules for that evening. But I do remember that Angela and I cancelled everything so that we could be there for her in this time of tragedy. Her body was not injured, but her soul grieved. We both prayed for her that night. And prayer was the only thing we knew to do to help her get up the next morning and go to school. As fathers, we must practice the three "P's" that have been mentioned often in this book. We must Pray, provide our Presence and offer Perspective. When we do these three things, we are administering the love, mercy and grace of God in ways that are both pastoral and personal. For the Adcock family, we won't ever forget the pain of that evening. But what we will remember even more vividly than the pain, was the healing that God provided. The severed relationship with that coach was eventually restored. In fact, the coach and Amye eventually found common ground, and together, with the support of a great team of girls, they went all the way to the state finals. Years later when Amye married, the coach and his wife sat in that sanctuary. God did an awesome thing.

Perspective means that we are to step back and find a place of emotional distance in order to make good and godly choices. It is important that you ask the Lord which of these four roles you are to re-spend from. In this situation, I felt immediately that warrior/protector spirit rise up within me. I wanted to go and get in the face of that coach and to stand between him and my daughter. But perspective brought about a different response. Rather than spend my time protecting her, I felt led by the Spirit to enter into a priestly role and simply care for her. In the years that have followed I come to realize that choosing to be a priest that afternoon rather than a protector prepared her well for her future. As hard as it was for me to not go after that coach and rip him into little shreds, it was important that I allowed the experience to be a teaching moment about life. I learned that I could not be there 24/7, and as she became a woman I would have to trust God and eventually her husband for her protection. Standing with her in a time of pain and lovingly caring for her and praying for her rather than rescuing her was vital in her growing up. The lesson taught was important. Sometimes people sin against you and it hurts. But God is able to bring healing and hope even in the aftermath of pain. She also learned that sometimes we cannot control circumstances and we must trust God to see us through. And in those times, we must walk in faith. Those lessons learned paved the way for future battles to be fought and won. Like the afternoon Amye's boyfriend, Mike, who eventually became her husband, was diagnosed with cancer. As much as I would have loved to protect her from that painful chapter, there was nothing I could do. I wanted to kick cancer's butt, but I was powerless. Husbands and fathers, when you can do nothing else in the midst of the harsh realities of your wife's and your son's and daughter's lives, you can always do one thing; you can always pray. Be a priest! Intercede on behalf of those you love and see just what God will do.

Over the years there have been countless opportunities to be a priest in my home. There was a similar instance when my son Morgan was severely reprimanded for missing a tackle and the coach publicly attacked him and embarrassed him. My heart broke for him and I went to my knees and asked God to provide for him. There are often days when Angela comes home from work having been chewed up and spit out by a world that devours the meek. I have learned over the years to practice those three "P's" of prayer, presence and perspective. A man's first reaction is often to try and fix things. But often God allows these challenges to teach us important lessons for our future. Become a prayer warrior in your home. Your wife and children will be blessed by your investment.

In a related area, I suggest that every priest have a bottle of anointing oil to use when they pray for the sick in their home. James says, "Is an-

Notes and Quotes:

yone among you sick? Let him call for the elders of the church, and let them pray over him, anointing him with oil in the name of the Lord." (James 5:14). This is an awesome opportunity. Just yesterday I had the opportunity to anoint and pray for several members of my congregation. This was a very intimate moment. The members of the congregation gathered around them and placed their hands upon them and we prayed. What if we would call the whole family together when one of our loved ones was ill and pray over them? God would be honored and that family would be blessed.

Other Priestly Acts to Be Administered in Your Home

While prayer is perhaps the most important thing you will ever do in your role as priest, there are a couple of additional opportunities that lie within this great calling that I want to touch on.

First, a priest is one who administers the sacraments of the church. It is the priest that offers the sacrifices on behalf of his community. This means that as husband and father you have been given a sacred responsibility. Lead them into the holy Presence of God. This means that every husband and father is a worship leader. You may say, "But I can't carry a tune in a bucket." The worship that I am speaking of is not founded upon a musical ability or expression. No, it is simply being a man who intentionally leads his family into the Presence of God to thank Him for the gifts and blessings and to listen to what He has to say to us. One way to accomplish this is by leading your family in intentional times of family worship.

In this role you must work to recapture and teach a view of that which is sacred. Some of my earlier writing has unpacked this extensively. Here is just an overview.

If we are to have a lasting impact on our children's lives, we must teach them the concept of sacred. We have lost track of the sacred things of life. Marriage is no longer sacred; life is no longer sacred. The church has even lost track of that which is sacred. Sacred by definition means that something has been set apart for God's purpose. If we are going to rebuild sacred structures for generations to come, then we must carve out "sacred spaces" for the purpose of teaching those we love about the majesty and glory of God.

Sacred Space- As you begin this journey to shape the future faith of your children and grandchildren, consider developing a sacred place. Perhaps you have ample property to fashion a prayer garden. Or perhaps you will be confined to simply preparing a small corner in your home. Choose a place that you will dedicate to be your sanctuary and choose carefully the things that you will build into this sacred space. Perhaps you may want to physically build an altar where you can kneel and pray and eventually share special moments of worship with your children and grandchildren. Some will include written passages of Scripture. Others will incorporate candles and things that tangibly bring about remembrances of God's faithfulness. In the Old Testament, when God had shown His faithfulness towards Israel, He often instructed them to build an altar and worship there. For generations, those altars stood as physical places to remember God's faithfulness. Let us build modern day altars to remember and to share with future generations the personal faithfulness that God has shown to our families.

Sacred Time- In the world in which we live today, Satan has used busyness to draw us away from God. In order to develop a deeper relationship with the Lord, it will be important for you to set aside a sacred time to meet with Him. We as priests must teach this concept to our children and grandchildren and allow them to join us as we bow before the Lord on a daily basis. Remember that many things are better caught than taught. Lead by example. Simply invite your wife and children to participate in that which is set apart for God's glory.

Once you have established a sacred place in your home and carved out sacred time, then begin to look at the content of what you will insert into your time of family worship. This is not the same as the things taught in the area of being a prophet/teacher. This is not focused on teaching your children. No, it is focused on praising God and bringing Him a sacrifice of thanksgiving. Combining times of worship and times of biblical teaching often works well. But make certain that you are taking adequate time adoring God in moments of family worship and not simply teaching them about Him. Worship is one way to transfer information about faith in God to the heart. Some ways this can be accomplished are by listening to worship music together and talking about whether or not the songs you listen to appropriately lift praise to God. Pray together and help each person in the family learn to articulate their heart-felt prayer and praise to the Lord. Testimony is a powerful thing. Asking how did you experience or see God today is a great way to enter into a time of worship?

Another way you can serve as a priest in your home is by being a humble servant of those you are called to lead. No man should be above kneeling before his wife or his children and washing their feet. Jesus did it for his disciples and then said that we are to go and do likewise. A physical time of footwashing can be powerful. But an ongoing life of

Notes and Quotes:

How long has it been

since you served your

loved ones?

187

symbolic footwashing is vital to your leadership in your home. As you show compassionate love for your family, they will grow to trust you and will begin to follow you. A good priest kneels often before God and before those he is called to love and exercises humility.

Living as family is not easy. In the midst of rubbing shoulders on days filled with stress and busyness, sometimes things begin to unravel and people can become difficult to live with. Egos sometimes rear their head and bring hurt and challenge to relationships in the family. What if, on those most difficult days, you would get up from the table and quietly walk over to the sink and draw a basin of water and then literally kneel in front of your wife and children and wash their feet? It would be a powerful moment of leadership. And it would fulfill your priestly role and calling. Perhaps if you choose to do this you will follow it up with a teaching time from God's Word as you read to your family the story of the last supper.

Still another way to serve your family as a priest can include administering communion as a part of your family worship time. As a pastor, I find the opportunity of standing before the congregation entrusted to my care and leading them in Holy Communion to be a humbling and blessed experience. There is a part of communion that is private. When one bows their heart unto the Lord and experiences an intimate connection we say they are communing with God. Often on a Sunday morning as I arrive hours before everyone else to prepare my heart to preach, I will take communion. In these times, God ministers to my heart and prepares me for the day of worship.

While communion is sometimes a private experience of worship, more often than not, it is a corporate experience; it is something that we share together. As I look back at many of the high moments of my life as a worshipper, communion has somehow been a part of those moments. There was the time when Angela and I were on the final night of a trip with youth in Longbeach, CA. The night was getting late, and we knew that daylight would bring an end to a wonderful trip. Someone suggested that we should mark the end of the trip with a time of communion down by the bay. Agreeing that it was a good idea, the whole group loaded up in our rented van and set off to find communion elements. Midnight had already passed and we found bread, but no juice. Few places were open and those that were did not carry grape juice. Finally as the clock got closer and closer to 2 AM we decided that we had to improvise. We decided that under the circumstances God would forgive us if we used rootbeer instead of grape juice. We sat on the edge of the bay and every person served their prayer partner communion.

Notes and Quotes:

There were moments of laughter and there were tears of thanksgiving. That time of communion was like an altar that marked a special time in the lives of those friends. We would forever be connected from that day forward.

I wish I could say to you that I had administered family communion when my children were at home, but to be honest, I never even thought about doing it. But I have come to believe that this could be a wonderful thing for a family to share together. And this Thanksgiving, I plan to lead my family in our first family communion. It is part of my responsibility as their priest, to administer the ordinances of the church.

Being a Priest in your home is not an easy task. But if you will rise up and lead in this way, the people entrusted to your care will be blessed. Everyone needs compassion and love. What better way to experience this than in the safety of a loving relationship that mirrors the relationship that God has with His children. Provide this for your wife, children and those closest to you, and watch as Christ uses your investment of love to breathe blessing into their lives!

Discussion Questions:

1. Of the two roles discussed, which role is more difficult for you to show yourself a man in? Being a Prophet? Or being a Priest? Why?

2. In your role as prophet, what must you do to prepare yourself to be able to be the primary discipler of your wife and children?

3. Do you agree with the author that the primary responsibility of teaching faith should biblically be placed upon the children's parents rather than upon the church?

4. Review the Shema found in Deuteronomy 6:4-9. How are you doing teaching faith in the everyday of life? How might you do a better job?

5. What are the first things that come to mind when you hear the word catechism? Is this a new concept to you?

6. If you were designing your own catechism for your family, what do you feel strongly should be on that list of things that your children will learn before they leave your home and go out into the world?

7. Do you find praying with your wife and children easy or difficult? Why do you think most men struggle to be spiritually vulnerable with the people closest to them?

Notes and Quotes:

8. What do you think the challenges will be as you insert family worship into the life of your family? How might you go about doing this if you have never done it before?

9. Leading your family in a time of communion can be a wonderful experience. What should a man know about the ordinance of communion in order to be able to help his children understand the spiritual significance of this wonderful experience we call the Lord's Supper?

Concentric Circle #3- Samaria...

A Man's Relationship with His Church and Community

But you will receive power when the Holy Spirit has come upon you, and you will be my witnesses in Jerusalem and in all Judea and Samaria, and to the end of the earth."

(Acts 1:8 ESV)

As living water begins to flow out from your personal relationship with Jesus Christ, it will eventually begin to reach and affect his church and the community where he lives and works. Realize that when that water reaches these areas of your life, you must have been an effective minister to those closest to you in order for you to have credibility in the eyes of people in your church and community. If you have not fulfilled your calling to lead and love your wife, children and those closest to you, then why would you expect to have a positive impact on the people of your church and community? Impact and influence must begin at home before it can extend out to those in the next ring.

We live in a day and time when many people who claim to be Christians have no relationship with a community of faith. This is devastating on many levels. Lone ranger Christians are usually untaught and often undisciplined in their faith. I do know of a few exceptions when families are so deeply committed to their faith that they struggle to engage in churches that are not serious-minded about their relationship with God. But this is seldom the case. I believe that God intends for every Christian to be connected to the Body of Christ for the purpose of sound teaching, accountability, and fellowship.

And let us consider how to stir up one another to love and good works, not neglecting to meet together, as is the habit of some, but encouraging one another, and all the more as you see the Day drawing near.

(Hebrews 10:24-25 ESV)

The community you live in is desperate to see Christ revealed. And you may well be God's delivery system to bring His love and grace to a fallen and needy people. We often talk about missions around the world, and I will address that responsibility in ring #4 as we look at the calling of a man to carry the gospel to the ends of the earth. But one must affect his homeland before he can affect the world. May the challenge to love our neighbors as ourselves be lived out in the church and in the communities where we live every day.

Be Strong and Show Yourself a Man

Chapter 21- Understanding the Church of God

It happened in an instant. I didn't see it coming, but in hindsight, I am not surprised those words spewed out of my lips. Perhaps it happened because I was just immature in my faith, or perhaps it was because I was ignorant and simply didn't understand, but in either case, it still happened.

It was a season of frustration for me and many others who attended Chapelwood Church of God in Baton Rouge, Louisiana. The congregation seemed to have such potential and yet it had atrophied over several years of time. The reason, in my not so humble opinion, was the pastor. I was but eighteen years of age. Yet in this small congregation, I was serving on the church council. It had been a great joy to me to be included in the inner circle of leadership. From the time I was sixteen forward, I had been given the chance to plan and lead worship. I was blessed in so many ways. Yet, I was arrogant and full of myself.

Sitting here today, I cannot even remember what set me off. But what I do remember was my sinful response. I stormed into the pastor's office on a mission to speak my mind. I do remember he seemed startled by my abrupt arrival as I burst through the door. There were no pleasantries. I got right to the point. I had come to deliver a message and I wanted to be heard. Not only were my words harsh, but my body language showed no respect for the pastor as I wagged my finger in his face and said the now infamous words. "I will have you know that this was MY church before you got here and it will be MY church when you leave," I shouted. Oh, how far off base I had become.

A decade and a half later, I would hear those words again, but they would not come from my mouth. No, then the roles were reversed. I was in my early thirties and in my first senior pastorate in Clearwater, Florida. Again, my immaturity was haunting me and my leadership was lacking, but in that day I did not see that I was a big part of the problem. The congregation was gathered for a church business meeting. And a major part of the agenda was about me as their pastor. Many were for me, but many were against me as well. Emotions were running high when Fred finally stood to his feet. When the chairman of the church recognized him, he began

Notes and Quotes:
Why is it important not to
claim ownership of the
Church?
Are you a member of the
Church? What makes you
a member?

to spew. And before too long I heard that same statement that I had used years before. "This was MY church before you got here, and it will be MY church when you leave." The words cut to the bone. Never had I realized the pain that I had afflicted on my pastor that day in his office until hose very words were turned on me. In the aftermath of that failed ministry, I spent many a day hearing those words in my head play out over and over again. My mind told me that those words were wrong. He was wrong to say those hurtful words to me!

What made those words wrong was not the personal attack that was harsh and deliberate. No, what makes those words wrong is they are not true. The church does not belong to me. Nor did the church belong to Fred the day he shouted those words at me. And the church does not belong to you. What made those words wrong is the fact that the church is God's church. It belongs to Him and Him alone.

In Matthew 16:18 Jesus responds to Peter regarding the ownership of the church. Jesus has just asked his disciples, "Who do people say that I am?" Some of the disciples responded by saying that there were people who believed that he was Elijah who had returned from the dead. Other disciples said that there were some people who thought he was a great prophet or teacher. Then Jesus asked them directly, "Who do you say that I am?" Peter answered, "You are the Christ, the son of the living God." Jesus said to Peter, "And I tell you, you are Peter, and on this rock I will build my church, and the gates of hell shall not prevail against it."

As we look at the church, it is important that we understand whose church it is. Ownership belongs to God and Him alone. We are simply members of the body. Christ is the head of the church and we are the members of that body. Jesus is the cornerstone. That is, Jesus is the most important part of the church, and we are living stones. These concepts are vital to our understanding as we begin to ask ourselves how we might be used to bring living water into the church.

Let's define "the church." When I use the term "the church," I am not speaking of the congregation that you attend. I am not talking about a denomination or a group that meets for worship in a building somewhere. When I use the term "the church," I am speaking of every person who has a personal relationship with Jesus Christ. In this day, I probably need to be even more specific than that. When I use the term "the church," I am speaking of every person that believes that Jesus Christ is the Son of the Living God...that he came to earth for the expressed purpose to die for the sins of the world so that we might be saved; that he rose on the third day destroying death and is now seated at the right hand of God interceding on behalf of those he died for. And moving beyond simply believing this to be the case, "the church" is every believer who has bowed their heart to God and received and embraced the sacrifice of Calvary and now has the Son living within their heart as both Savior and as Lord. That is "the church."

Reasons the Church has Fallen Into Disrepair

Reason #1- We are Driven by the Ways of the World Rather than by the Ways of God

I needn't say much here to convince you that the church has fallen upon hard times and is in disrepair in America. I recently heard James MacDonald say that 6000 churches are closing their doors every year in America. Statistical data indicate that only six percent of the churches in America are growing.

Our response to this decline has been, in my opinion, exactly the opposite of what was needed. Rather than turn back toward a biblical understanding of the church, we began to bring more and more marketing strategies into the church. Instead of searching the Scriptures for a deeper understanding of how to be the church, we began to poll those who were outside the church and then build the church around principles they thought were important in their lives. The rationale seemed good. If we wanted to reach the unchurched then we must somehow connect with them and create a church where they would be willing to come. But this strategy has backfired. The Great Commission was not to bring all those who did not know Jesus into the church so they could be saved. No, it was and is to go into all the world and to preach, teach and baptize. We got it backwards.

In October of 1975, a well-intentioned pastor by the name of Bill Hybels started a new church on the south side of Chicago. Hybels had a desire to reach those who had not been reached with the gospel message. It made good sense strategically to go to those who he wanted to reach for Christ and ask them what kind of church they would be willing to attend. So he polled the unchurched in the community and asked that question. Then he built his ministry around the things that were most important to those in the world. He fashioned a church around entertainment that required little of the person in the pew. And before long he had a large congregation. But the real question is, "Were they a church?" The church has fallen into disrepair because we have brought the world, along with all of its idols, into the church. Because Hybels was so successful, scores of congregations have chased after the same

Notes and Quotes:
Write down five ways that you see the world's ways having infiltrated the Church.
Should the world have a voice in what the church does?

Notes and Quotes:

Do you agree that the

messages preached today

are more superficial than

in decades past?

Why or Why not?

methods. The results have been heartbreaking in many respects. Congregations gather weekly, but they learn more about themselves and how to use God to get what they want out of life than to learn more about God and what He desires of them.

I should state here that I believe Hybels had a well-intentioned desire to do great things for God. And I believe his ministry has had great impact on many. But the strategy has contributed to the downfall of the church. In recent years, Hybels has humbly come forward to say that some of these strategies have harmed the church. I appreciate his confession. But still today, many churches chase after man's way rather than God's way, and the result has been a loss of vision and a biblical purpose.

Reason #2- We Preach a Watered Down Version of Scripture

Our response to this decline of the church is alarming. Rather than boldly proclaiming the gospel message and teaching the timeless principles of Scripture that could and would bring about a new vitality, we are instead hearing preached a watered down version of the gospel that is founded more upon what people want to hear rather than what the world is desperate to hear.

I charge you in the presence of God and of Christ Jesus, who is to judge the living and the dead, and by his appearing and his kingdom: preach the word; be ready in season and out of season; reprove, rebuke, and exhort, with complete patience and teaching. For the time is coming when people will not endure sound teaching, but having itching ears they will accumulate for themselves teachers to suit their own passions, and will turn away from listening to the truth and wander off into myths. As for you, always be soberminded, endure suffering, do the work of an evangelist, fulfill your ministry.

(2 Timothy 4:1-5 ESV)

The Apostle Paul was right on target. We are living in a time when people migrate to listen to a gospel that their ears are itching to hear; it is an incomplete gospel message that is but a reflection of truth. And the church has embraced it with church growth schemes and mentalities that take advantage of a preaching that is based primarily upon what the people want to hear. This next statement may shock you, but I believe it to be true. It is not terribly hard to gather a large crowd and call it a church. If you tell the people what they want to hear and make them feel good about themselves and they will flock to your service. But in so doing you will not become the church. We must stop catering to the self-indulgent mentality of the American church and realize that the church has little to do with us and everything to do with Him!

Reason #3- We Have Become Too Broad in Our Teaching and Theology

As we have brought more and more of worldly philosophies into the church, we have broadened our teachings and theologies in order to become more attractive to the world. The result of this has been tragic. Many today have built upon the doctrines of tolerance and fairness and have elevated these doctrines to be guiding principles for the church. We have fallen for "cheap grace," and the price we are paying in the church is great.

"Cheap grace has served as an inoculation or more accurately, a vaccination. We have gotten just enough of Jesus to prevent us from catching the real thing. As a result we begin to feel secure even in the midst of godless living. We become aware of our disobedience, and cheap grace provides us with a deceptive sense of strength... Cheap grace is grace without discipleship, communion without confession, baptism without church disciple, absolution without personal confession, preaching forgiveness without requiring repentance. In addition, it is characterized by belief without obedience, hearing without doing, and intellectual assent without life commitment...it is grace without the cross...grace without Jesus." (Cite: Dietrich Bonhoeffer in The Cost of Discipleship).

I recently came across an article about a church in Michigan that has taken down their cross and elected to replace it with some culturally relevant symbols. The ideas expressed in this article are alarming.

SPRING LAKE — A prominent Spring Lake church removed its cross Tuesday and has changed its name as part of a series of moves intended to make it more inclusive. C3Exchange, 225 E. Exchange, Spring Lake, was formerly known as Christ Community Church. The Rev. Ian Lawton, the church's pastor, said the name change and removing the cross were designed to reflect the church's diverse members.

"Our community has been a really open-minded community for some years now," he said. "We've had a number of Muslim people, Jewish people, Buddhists, atheists. ... We're catching up (to) ourselves." . . .

Lawton said the church decided to change its name about a year ago and began taking ideas from members. He said the new name was

Notes and Quotes:

How have you noticed

"cheap grace" on display

in churches today?

Notes and Quotes:
Should the church be so
narrow as to think and
proclaim that Jesus is the
only way?

chosen because the church is on Exchange Street, and "our community is a place where people can come to exchange ideas."

He said the church is considering painting a heart, a globe and the word "exchange" on its exterior wall on the side where the cross stood, to symbolize "one love" for "all people."

"We honor the cross, but the cross is just one symbol of our community," Lawton said.

Lawton gave a sermon March 21 likening using the cross as a symbol of Christ's life to using a bullet to remember Martin Luther King Jr. He said that opinion is his and not the church's.

. . . "The cross has become a negative symbol for a lot of people." (Cite: http://www.mlive.com/news/muskegon/index.ssf/2010/06/spring_lakes_christ_community.html).

It has been more than a decade now since the Columbine massacre. Even then we could see the results of this tragic demise of the teaching and theology of the church. In the aftermath of the tragic loss of lives there were many religious services to help the grieving deal with their painful losses. One such service was televised, and I, along with millions of others, sat glued to the screen with tears in my eyes. Leaders from all different faiths came together and spoke of the need for morality to rise up and grow in America. But the diversity among the different faiths was too much. My heart was broken when a Christian pastor rose and offered a benediction. His prayer was heartfelt. But his final statement before the amen was blasphemy. He prayed, "...we pray these things in the name of Mohammed the prophet, in the name of Buddah, in the name of Jesus..." I could hardly believe my ears. In that dark hour when he had the chance to bring the light, he faltered and failed. The church of the living God lays in shambles today, partly because we have watered down the Truth of the gospel for the purpose of making it palatable to the masses. We must remember that Jesus said...

"Enter by the narrow gate. For the gate is wide and the way is easy that leads to destruction, and those who enter by it are many. For the gate is narrow and the way is hard that leads to life, and those who find it are few.

"Beware of false prophets, who come to you in sheep's clothing but inwardly are ravenous wolves. You will recognize them by their fruits. Are grapes gathered from thornbushes, or figs from thistles? So, every healthy tree bears good fruit, but the diseased tree bears

bad fruit. A healthy tree cannot bear bad fruit, nor can a diseased tree bear good fruit. Every tree that does not bear good fruit is cut down and thrown into the fire. Thus you will recognize them by their fruits.

(Matthew 7:13-20 ESV)

Reason #4- The People of God Have Lost Touch with His Word

Men, it is alarming to me that our congregations are filled with biblically illiterate people. Many have been raised in the church but have no commitment to or love for the Word of the Living God.

Recently I stopped at a garage sale to look for some cheap toys for my granddaughter to have to play with when she came for a visit. Walking amongst the hidden treasures of this household, I spotted a table of old books. As I got closer I recognized one particular old book that seemed to be in excellent condition. It was a 1901 edition of the Revised Standard Version of the New Testament. It was one I recognized because it was the exact edition that my Papa, my grandfather on my mother's side of the family, read to me from when I was a little boy. On the shelf in my library is that Bible, duct-taped and in disrepair due to the man hours of usage and study. This copy looked to be in much better condition. Hardly used at all. That is the problem with the Bibles on the shelves of our homes today; they are hardly used at all. As I picked up that old Bible and began to leaf through its pages, I came across handwritten notes. I first saw a reference about Mr. and Mrs. Alonzo Leak who were married in 1888. Then I noticed that just inside the front cover was a handwritten family history. It said, "To: Mother; Christmas 1952; Love Clyde and Geraldine." Underneath that it said: "Then presented to Ivy Tharp; December 20, 1955 by Mrs. Gertrud Leak." This was a family treasure. And yet it lay on a table in a garage sale with the hefty price tag of twenty-five cents on its cover. Realizing that it was a priceless treasure, I grabbed it and went to pay. The lady at the table taking the money appeared to be in her late 50's. I said to her, "Are you sure you want to sell this for just twenty-five cents?" She looked at me with a perplexed look on her face. I opened the front cover and asked her if the names located there were family of hers. She read them and then said, "Oh yes, those are the names of my husband's grandparents and great-grandparents." Again I asked, "And are you sure you want to sell this?" Her response floored me. "Well, it's just an old book that we have no use for anymore." How sad that we in the church have lost our love for the Holy Bible.

In the Old Testament there is a true story of a time when the people of

Notes and Quotes:
Have you lost touch with
God's Word?

Notes and Quotes:

God lost track of His Word. In that day God raised up a young man by the name of Josiah to be the King of Judah. He was only eight years old when he became king. Eight years into his reign as king he was convicted to clean up the kingdom and to bring restoration to the temple of God. The results of this were that Josiah called for the destruction of all the altars that had been used for the worship of false gods in the temple. He had all the idols broken into pieces and destroyed. And after the temple had been cleansed of the false gods, he order the complete renovation of the house of God. During this renovation something amazing was located...the word of the Lord was found in the rubble of a temple in disrepair. Those who found the book had faint memories of the stories of history that included the God of Moses who had led them out of captivity. The book was soon carried to Josiah who asked that it be read to him. When he heard the Word of the Lord, he was moved and called the people back to the law of the One true God.

"Go, inquire of the LORD for me and for those who are left in Israel and in Judah, concerning the words of the book that has been found. For great is the wrath of the LORD that is poured out on us, because our fathers have not kept the word of the LORD, to do according to all that is written in this book."

(2 Chronicles 34:21 ESV)

How sad that our children are experiencing the wrath of God because many fathers have not kept the word of the Lord. We must rise up and begin again to value the Word of the Lord.

Reason #5- We Have Taken an Individualistic Rather than Corporate Approach

Gary Thomas said it well when he said, "God intends for us to fight sin as an army, not as a soldier." (Cite: Thirsting for God. Page 91). Yet, for many, faith has become an individual sport rather than a team sport. God never intended for us to live separate lives of faith apart from a congregation of believers. But in America today, there are plenty who profess a relationship with God through Jesus Christ, but have no connection at all with His church. This is dangerous. Not only is the church helpful in teaching the timeless message of Truth, it is also to be a fellowship of interconnected believers who offer

"God intends for us to fight sin as an army, not as a sol-dier."

-Gary Thomas

encouragement and accountability to one another. It is God's way to keep us motivated and moving forward for His purposes and glory. Yet we seem to find it more comfortable to go it alone. Perhaps we don't care for the challenge of others who are seeking Truth. Or perhaps we don't like to be accountable to other men. Whatever the reason, an individualistic approach has been a part of the downward spiral that has placed today's church in disrepair.

Church attendance is as vital to a disciple as a transfusion of rich, healthy blood to a sick man. – (Cite: Dwight L. Moody at http://www.whatchristianswanttoknow.com/21-great-quotes-about-church/#ixzz27OCWsKoo).

And let us consider how to stir up one another to love and good works, not neglecting to meet together, as is the habit of some, but encouraging one another, and all the more as you see the Day drawing near.

(Hebrews 10:24-25 ESV)

According to the U.S. Census Bureau, America saw a decrease in church membership between 2001 and 2008 from 1.3 million members in 2001 to 736,000 members in 2008. The decline is happening rapidly and is cause for great concern.

Many have declared the church to be boring in a day when our senses are constantly enticed by the world of media, and entertainment has become a false god. Our gaze has turned to selfish desires rather than to the Holy One.

Others declare that church is no longer relevant because the world has changed. Therefore we have ceased to live out our call to be connected in faith for the purpose of growth and accountability.

Reason #6- We Have Taken a How-to Approach Rather Than a Who-to Approach

While many in the church are seeing the terrible downward spiral of faith, our response has been the wrong one. We have fallen for a how-to approach that is faddish and based upon programs rather than a who-to approach that is founded upon refocusing the gaze of the people upon the majesty of God. This who-to approach is based upon authentic worship.

"What the Church needs today is not more machinery or better, not new organizations or more and novel methods, but men whom the Holy Ghost can use — men of prayer, men mighty in prayer. The Holy Ghost does not flow through methods, but through men. He does not

Notes and Quotes:

In what ways do you see the How-to church emerging in our culture?

In what ways do you see the Who-to church?

Notes and Quotes:

come on machinery, but on men. He does not anoint plans, but men, men of prayer."- E. M. Bounds

For many years I fell into the trap of a how-to approach to ministry. Conferences happen all across America where "expert pastors" who have found success in the eyes of people tell their stories of what they did to change the trends of downward spiraling churches. Bookstores are filled with books that tell of "new" ways to do church. Struggling pastors flock to these conferences in hopes of finding something that will work in their floundering ministries and turn the tide in a positive direction. But this how-to approach seldom results in positive direction. Why? Because it is most often founded upon the ideas of man.

What is desperately needed is not a new how-to approach but an old fashioned who-to approach. The answer is not found in methods but in worship. Man was made with a heart that will worship. The question is, "What are you worshipping?"

Therefore God gave them up in the lusts of their hearts to impurity, to the dishonoring of their bodies among themselves, because they exchanged the truth about God for a lie and worshiped and served the creature rather than the Creator, who is blessed forever! Amen.

(Romans 1:24-25 ESV)

Yes, we have fallen for worshipping the creature rather than the Creator. We have fallen for worshipping our own ingenuity rather than the Majesty and Glory of God.

Chapter 22- Oh God, Revive Us from This Slumber

But when anything is exposed by the light, it becomes visible, for anything that becomes visible is light. Therefore it says,

> *"Awake, O sleeper,*
>
> > *and arise from the dead,*
>
> *and Christ will shine on you."*

(Ephesians 5:13-14 ESV)

Oh how we need an awakening to come to God's church. We are desperate to wake from the slumber that has closed our eyes and hearts to the call of God. We need a passion to begin to burn within our souls that cannot be extinguished. A terrible tragedy looms if we continue to sleep. Danger not only exists but it has found its way into our backyards and seeks to drive a death nail through our hearts. Satan has a plan and it is not pretty. Unless we act now, some we love will die in their sleep.

If the enemy was literally in your backyard and the ones you loved were in harm's way because they slept unaware, you would act and do so boldly. You wouldn't just lightly tap on their bedroom door and say in a soft voice, "Wake up honey because there is a problem that could lead to your death." No you would be more aggressive than that. You would rush into their room, out of love and concern for them and shake them with all your might so that they would wake up and prepare to defend themselves from the attack of evil. But the church has grown cold and unaware in many ways as this downward spiral has begun to pick up speed. I don't think I can overstate this: Peril looms unless we act now! But the good news is that it is not too late. What we need is a revival...a spiritual awakening. We need passion to consume our hearts. We need fire from heaven to fall upon the church and ignite a new day of spiritual vigor.

Some will say that the odds are against us and that it is too late. Nothing will turn the tide of culture back in a new direction. I agree that we stand against the odds. But so did Elijah, and I believe that God is more than able to bring His slumbering church back to life.

Notes and Quotes:

How hard is it for you to

stand against the world?

In 1 Kings 18, Elijah, the prophet of God, faces off against a mighty opponent. That opponent outnumbers him 450 to 1. 450 prophets of Baal versus 1 Man of God. Despite the facts, I like his chances. The contest is to see whose God is the real God. So both sides take a bull and cut it up and place it on an altar and begin to pray for fire to consume the sacrifice. For hours and hours the 450 prophets of Baal cry out to their god with no response. Finally it is Elijah's turn. Before he prays he digs a trench around the altar and then has water poured over the sacrifice so that there will be no question regarding what happened. When he prays, God answers with a raging fire that consumes not only the sacrifice but also the whole altar. Even the water is licked up by the flames. We do live in a dark hour. But God is still able. I love a quote from Stu Weber in his book entitled Spirit Warriors. "This is a magnificent time to be a Christian. The darker our culture grows, the brighter and more radiant our light becomes." (Cite: Spirit Warriors. Page 215).

> Besides this you know the time, that the hour has come for you to wake from sleep. For salvation is nearer to us now than when we first believed. The night is far gone; the day is at hand. So then let us cast off the works of darkness and put on the armor of light.

(Romans 13:11-12 ESV)

Realize that Revival is Conditional

In 2 Chronicles 7:14 we are given a great understanding of what it will take for revival to begin in God's church.

> ...if my people who are called by my name humble themselves, and pray and seek my face and turn from their wicked ways, then I will hear from heaven and will forgive their sin and heal their land.

(2 Chronicles 7:14 ESV)

> "This is a magnificent time to be a Christian. The darker our culture grows, the brighter and more radiant our light becomes."
>
> -Stu Weber

If we are going to see a spiritual awakening, we must follow the path laid out for us in this great verse.

We must humble ourselves- The place we must begin is by falling on our faces before the Lord and acknowledging our inability to save ourselves. We cannot do this without God bringing it about. How do you humble yourself? Look into the face of God. When you do so, you will begin to see yourself in an appropriate way. One of the most notable things of this spiritual decline in America is man's infatuation with himself. When we set our gaze on self we find destruction. When we set our Gaze on Him we find meaning and purpose. It was so in Isaiah's day and it is still so today. Look upon the majesty of God and you will naturally bow. Let us fix our eyes upon Him.

"The perfect church service, would be one we were almost unaware of. Our attention would have been on God." - C.S. Lewis

We must pray- Martin Luther said, "Prayer is a strong wall and fortress of the church; it is a goodly Christian weapon." Many in the church today act as if we are powerless in the midst of what is happening. Prayer is a powerful weapon. When Paul writes that, *"...the weapons of our warfare are not of the flesh but have divine power to destroy strongholds,"* (2 Corinthians 10:4 ESV) he is speaking of prayer. Certainly one of our weapons is prayer. We need to get on our knees and bombard the gates of heaven on behalf of the church and ask God to show himself to His church and to send revival!

We must seek Him- Several years ago I ran across the Greek word for seek, Zeteo. What a wonderful word. Zeteo is the word for seek when Scripture says, "Ask and it shall be given; Seek and you shall find." It is imperative that we begin to seek the Lord. Without this, we will never see a spiritual awakening. I love A.W. Tozer's work, The Pursuit of God. In the early parts of that book he speaks of a heart "athirst for God." What a beautiful picture. Men, a drought of faith has come to America. Water and nourishment have dried up. And yet where is our desperate thirst of Him?

Consider praying Tozer's prayer of longing: "O God, I have tasted Thy goodness, and it has both satisfied me and made me thirsty for more. I am painfully conscious of my need of further grace. I am ashamed of my lack of desire. O God, the Triune God, I want to want Thee; I long to be filled with longing; I thirst to be made more thirsty still. Show me Thy glory, I pray Thee, that so I may know Thee indeed. Begin in mercy a new work of love within me. Say to my soul, 'Rise up, my love, my fair one, and come away. Then give me grace to rise and follow Thee up from this misty lowland where I have wandered so long. In Jesus' Name, Amen." (Cite: The Pursuit of God. Page 9).

We must turn from our wicked ways- Every revival that has shown to have lasting impact on America has begun when people have taken seriously the call to confession and repentance. Perhaps the last great revival came to America back in 1970 as the students of Asbury College were overwhelmed by the Holy Spirit.

Notes and Quotes:

Have you ever been

a part of a true

experience of revival?

One morning in 1970, without warning, all heaven broke loose during Asbury College's 10 a.m. chapel service. "When you walked into the back of Hughes Auditorium ... there was a kind of an aura, kind of a glow about the chapel," said Dr. David Hunt, a Louisville physician who was then a student. "I always have been reminded of the verse 'Take off your shoes, for you are standing on holy ground.' You just walked in and sensed that God had indeed sent His Spirit."

The service, a routine meeting, was scheduled for fifty minutes. Instead, it lasted 185 hours non-stop, twenty-four hours a day. Intermittently, it continued for weeks. Ultimately, it spread across the United States and into foreign countries. Some say it is being felt even today.

On that Tuesday morning in 1970, Custer Reynolds, Asbury's academic dean and a Methodist layman, was in charge. President Dennis Kinlaw was traveling. Reynolds did not preach. Instead, he briefly gave his testimony then issued an invitation for students to talk about their own Christian experiences. There was nothing particularly unusual about that.

One student responded to his offer. Then another. Then another.

"Then they started pouring to the altar," Reynolds said. "it just broke."

Gradually, inexplicably, students and faculty members alike found themselves quietly praying, weeping, singing. They sought out others to whom they had done wrong deeds and asked for forgiveness. (Cite: A Revival Account. http://forerunner.com/forerunner/ X0585_Asbury_Revival_1970.html).

Did you see that last line? "They sought out others to whom they had done wrong deeds and asked for forgiveness." As I have studied the great revivals that have come to America, that seems to be one of the keys; in revival, people confess and repent. That should not come as a shock to us because that is what Scripture teaches. *"...if my people... will turn from their wicked ways, then shall I hear from heaven and forgive their sins and heal their land."*

If we are to see our hearts set on fire for God, then we must turn away from sin. Jim Elliot said, "I lack the fervency, vitality, life, in prayer which I long for. I know that many consider it fanaticism when they hear anything which does not conform to the conventional, sleep-inducing eulogies so often rising from Laodicean lips; but I know too that these same people can acquiescently tolerate sin in their lives and in the church without so much as tilting one hair of their eyebrows." Let us deal appropriately with sin so that we might experience a powerful change in the church. Let us crucify complacency and find an urgency within the church. I pray that God might be glorified.

Men, revival is possible. We cannot manufacture it nor should we try. But if we will follow after God's Word and do what it says, don't be shocked when the floodgates of heaven open up and an awakening comes to His church.

A final note on this: As I have noted often in this book, America is in a terrible place of moral and spiritual decline. Some politicize this and say, "If we just had a different president, a more Godly leader." But the answer to this problem facing our country is not found in the political arena. We can change the president or we can change the congress and still see America spiral into ruin. The answer to the problems that face this nation lie in the hearts of the people of the church. Not until the people of the church awaken from their slumber will we begin to see lasting change needed. Pray for revival to break out. Pray that we, the church of the living God, would become passionate in our pursuit of Him. Pray, O man of God, pray!

Notes and Quotes:
What can we do to
experience a revival
without manufacturing
one?

Chapter 23- A Man's Relationship with A Congregation of Believers

And they devoted themselves to the apostles' teaching and the fellowship, to the breaking of bread and the prayers. And awe came upon every soul, and many wonders and signs were being done through the apostles. And all who believed were together and had all things in common. And they were selling their possessions and belongings and distributing the proceeds to all, as any had need. And day by day, attending the temple together and breaking bread in their homes, they received their food with glad and generous hearts, praising God and having favor with all the people. And the Lord added to their number day by day those who were being saved.

(Acts 2:42-47 ESV)

This passage records the earliest moments of the church. Jesus has ascended to heaven and the Comforter has come. Power from on high has anointed the disciples, and the Word of God has been preached. Peter was the proclaimer, and at the conclusion of his first sermon, more than three thousand were saved and the church was born. Immediately following this radical beginning, the first congregation of the church was established. And from that day forward, congregations have been vital to the fulfillment of God's plan to care for the church.

If we only have a general view of the church, which is the spiritual connection of every person who has a personal relationship with Jesus Christ, and we have no specific context in which we live out being the church, then we fall short of God's plan of being the church.

We see in this passage that the people were devoted to two things: 1) To the Apostle's teaching which is learning about faith and 2) To the fellowship, which is the people who are to provide the context of how their faith begins to show itself in everyday life. Too often we see people claim to be a part of the church in a general sense. They proclaim a relationship with God through Jesus Christ but have no specific context to live out what it truly means to be the

Notes and Quotes:
If you are a part of the
Body, which part would
you say you are?
Why?

church. They lack an understanding of fellowship. We, the people of God, are to be connected to one another.

One of the best analogies of Scripture that expresses what the church is to look like is that of the body. Paul writes about this in 1 Corinthians 12.

For just as the body is one and has many members, and all the members of the body, though many, are one body, so it is with Christ. For in one Spirit we were all baptized into one body—Jews or Greeks, slaves or free—and all were made to drink of one Spirit.

For the body does not consist of one member but of many. If the foot should say, "Because I am not a hand, I do not belong to the body," that would not make it any less a part of the body. And if the ear should say, "Because I am not an eye, I do not belong to the body," that would not make it any less a part of the body. If the whole body were an eye, where would be the sense of hearing? If the whole body were an ear, where would be the sense of smell? But as it is, God arranged the members in the body, each one of them, as he chose. If all were a single member, where would the body be? As it is, there are many parts, yet one body.

The eye cannot say to the hand, "I have no need of you," nor again the head to the feet, "I have no need of you." On the contrary, the parts of the body that seem to be weaker are indispensable, and on those parts of the body that we think less honorable we bestow the greater honor, and our unpresentable parts are treated with greater modesty, which our more presentable parts do not require. But God has so composed the body, giving greater honor to the part that lacked it, that there may be no division in the body, but that the members may have the same care for one another. If one member suffers, all suffer together; if one member is honored, all rejoice together.

(1 Corinthians 12:12-26 ESV)

We Are Called to Unity

We are all called to come together in order to be one body...the Body of Christ. This means that we must, as the people of God, rally around that which we all share in common. The common link of the church is that of Jesus Christ. By definition, the church includes all those who have come to a personal relationship with Jesus Christ by receiving the free gift of salvation. If you do not know Christ, then you are not a part of his body, the church. Unity is not founded upon everyone coming to a consensus of opinion about issues of doctrine and theology. Unity is if found "in Christ."

Unity is important to God. That is quite evident when we see what Jesus prayed for in John 17.

> *And I am no longer in the world, but they are in the world, and I am coming to you. Holy Father, keep them in your name, which you have given me, that they may be one, even as we are one.*

(John 17:11 ESV)

Jesus prayed that we might be one, just as he and the Father are one. May it be so in the church today.

There is Diversity within Unity

Unity is founded upon two non-negotiable understandings in the church. First is the one mentioned above: that Jesus Christ is the only way to God. The second is interconnected to the first, and that is the Bible as the authoritative Word of God. They are interconnected because Scripture teaches that Jesus Christ is the only way to God (John 14:6). Upon the cornerstone established by these two doctrines, God has built His church. The substance of these two non-negotiable statements is like the mortar that holds together the people of the church who are the living stones that stand together in faith to represent God to the world.

While the whole church is "united in Christ," that does not mean that every stone is or looks the same. There is great diversity within unity. This means that we do not hold to a legalistic understanding regarding every expression of faith in Jesus Christ. I was born into a family with two brothers and a sister. All of us are related by blood. We have the same mother and father. But our personalities are vastly different. My older brother spends his time and career in the not-for-profit world of Habitat for Humanity. He has a passion for the homeless and fights injustice in this nation every day. When he seeks out a congregation to connect to, he naturally looks for people who share his passion, a congregation where a doctrine of social justice is integrated into the ministry of that congregation. My younger brother is much different. He has been involved in politics for all his adult life, serving as the national security advisor to the Senate Majority Leader at one point in his career. He is intense and focused. The congregation that he and his family choose to worship in reflects his passion to affect the world using a political platform. Living in Washington D.C., there are many like-minded Christians that worship together. My sister is vastly different than either of my brothers. She is a wife and mother who has a

Notes and Quotes:

What are the two

non-negotiables that

the author mentions?

Notes and Quotes:
What makes people in
the church blood kin?

passion to be present and available for her three children. She has worked hard in her field of library science but has made significant choices to limit her career so that her family receives her best. She and her husband attend a congregation of like-minded believers that believe family is worth sacrificing career for. I am related to all of them, but my life looks vastly different than theirs. And the congregation that I pastor is greatly different than all my brothers' and sister's congregations. Does the fact that we are different change the fact that we are related? No. We are related by blood. And in spite of the different ways we approach life, we are and will forever be related.

The church is a collection of people who are related by blood; not the blood of earthly parents, but the blood of Jesus Christ. When we each received the gift of salvation, we became brothers and sisters in a spiritual relationship. But we often live out our faith differently. Scripture teaches that we all approach the body from different places of perspective. We are different parts but all of us are part of one body. Some exercise the gifts of the Spirit differently than others. Some are more passionate about evangelism than others. Some have a different view of eschatology than others. But in spite of our differences we are still "one in Christ."

Every man should carefully choose a congregation of believers to invest in. This congregation should particularly express the values and traditions of the personality of himself and his family. He should not do this in a vacuum but with input from his wife. Together they must seek out a congregation of believers to participate in for the purpose of living out the corporate challenges of faith. Some things that we are called to do cannot be accomplished alone; they are much bigger than we are. Therefore we need to pursue the model of the early church in Acts 2. We need to come together for the purpose of learning the things of God, worshipping in a corporate setting, and connecting with like-minded brothers and sisters for the purpose of encouragement, challenge and accountability.

Realize again that the foundation of unity must be held with integrity. You cannot relax the requirements of the non-negotiables. If you are worshipping in a congregation where they believe that there are other ways to God than that of Jesus Christ, you must sever your relationship with that congregation. This principle cannot be challenged. And if you attend a congregation that does not believe and teach the Bible to be God's authoritative Word to be our standard for life, then you must walk away. To subject yourself, your wife and your children to philosophies that deny these two things is to wander into heresy. Pray and ask God for discernment. If you do not know what the congregation you attend teaches about these things then ask to meet with your pastor. Ask him questions that will require him to make 'I' statements regarding his personal devotion to these two principles. Also ask how the congregation teaches and lives these two principles.

Notes and Quotes:

Chapter 24- A Man's Relationship with His Community

The two greatest commandments according to Jesus' teaching are: 1) To love the Lord with all your heart, soul, mind and strength and 2) To love your neighbor as yourself. The immediate question that followed this statement was this: "But who is my neighbor?" In order to answer this question, Jesus told the parable of the Good Samaritan.

"A man was going down from Jerusalem to Jericho, and he fell among robbers, who stripped him and beat him and departed, leaving him half dead. Now by chance a priest was going down that road, and when he saw him he passed by on the other side. So likewise a Levite, when he came to the place and saw him, passed by on the other side. But a Samaritan, as he journeyed, came to where he was, and when he saw him, he had compassion. He went to him and bound up his wounds, pouring on oil and wine. Then he set him on his own animal and brought him to an inn and took care of him. And the next day he took out two denarii and gave them to the innkeeper, saying, 'Take care of him, and whatever more you spend, I will repay you when I come back.' Which of these three, do you think, proved to be a neighbor to the man who fell among the robbers?" He said, "The one who showed him mercy." And Jesus said to him, "You go, and do likewise."

(Luke 10:30-37 ESV)

In this parable we find the method by which we are to impact our community for Jesus Christ. If the Living Water is going to affect those who live around us, our neighbors, then it will be because we serve them.

The Gospel Must Be Lived

One of the awesome opportunities that we have is to be instruments in the hands of a gracious God. Another way to voice this is that we are the conduit God uses to deliver His love to the world. If you are a man of God, then God intends to use you as the delivery system of His amazing love to those who live around you. It is true that everyone we come into contact with

How well do you know

your neighbors?

Have you ever witnessed

about Christ to your

neighbors?

is our neighbor. But more often than not, you will rub shoulders with the people of the community in which you reside and call home.

We live in a world today where being neighbors is simply about geography and not relationship. There was a day when neighbors were intimately connected. My heritage goes back to the small, rural community of Neshoba County, Mississippi. My grandparents did not live in a neighborhood, but they certainly had neighbors. And to be someone's neighbor meant that you were connected to them. Seldom would a day go by when I was visiting them that a car or truck wouldn't turn into that driveway and out would climb a person from the community that lived down the road just beyond some holler. They would often have a homemade pie in their hand or a tub of freshly picked vegetables from their garden that had brought to share. It was a beautiful picture of community. Last year I had the opportunity to visit my aunt and uncle who now live in the house my grandparents once lived in. I was touched to realize that Neshoba County is still a neighborly place. It seems to me that there are not too many neighborly places left in our world today. In fact, shortly after I arrived, the phone rang. On the other end of the line my aunt talked to one of her neighbors from "just up the road a piece." At first there were the normal pleasantries spoken, and then the neighbor got to the purpose of her call. She knew that my aunt and uncle had company coming in to visit. And she wanted to make us a pie to enjoy while we visited. Aunt Nancy took the phone from her ear and looked at me. "What is your favorite kind of pie?" she asked. I decided on chocolate. And before the day was finished, a pie appeared in a neighbor's hand. It was a touch of God's love designed in a tangible and real way. If only there were more places like that today in America. Today neighbors are often only neighbors because they live next to each other. There is no intimate relationship.

Angela and I walk a lot in our neighborhood when the weather is nice. And it is not unusual at all to see one of our neighbors arriving home after a long day of work. They may or may not offer a wave as they drive by us. As they approach their home, they reach up to the sun visor in their car and push a button. Immediately their garage door begins to rise. They quickly pull into that garage and push the button a second time. The door closes. Many have been taught to even remain in their car until the door is completely closed affording them a safer and more controlled environment to manage as they make their way inside the house. Though they live close by scores of people, they do not know any of them in the way my grandparents knew their neighbors. I have come to realize that it is hard to serve a neighbor who draws his curtains shut to close out the world. But Jesus said we must serve our neighbors, and for that reason, we must move outside of our comfort zone and risk rejection. Realize that God's love can and will make a difference if you offer it in generous portions without expectation of receiving anything in return.

"Love is willing self-sacrifice without any expectation of reciprocation, that is offered even when the person who is receiving that love does not deserve it." (Cite: Paul David Tripp in What Did You Expect?).

I want to encourage you to step out in faith and begin to offer God's love to those you live in close contact with. Do this for God's glory and the blessing of those you serve. And I believe God will use your loving kindness to soften the hearts of your neighbors so that they might be able to come to see and know the God who fashioned them in His image and desires a relationship with them.

> **"Love is willing self-sacrifice without any expectation of reciprocation, that is offered even when the person who is receiving that love does not deserve it." -Paul David Tripp**

As you begin to contemplate where to begin, realize first that Jesus was a servant. In the final hours before he would walk that lonely road to Golgotha, he gathered for a last supper with his disciples. Surely those who gathered with him qualified to be his neighbors. They were the people beyond his family that were closest to him. It had to be a heart-wrenching night for Jesus. Being fully divine, he knew what the next day would hold: his arrest, mock trial, beating and eventually the cross. As he made his way to the table, an argument broke out among his disciples. The reason for the argument was their pride and arrogance. Each wanted to sit in the special place of honor when Jesus established his kingdom. Certainly Jesus must have been saddened by their behavior. But read how Jesus reacted:

...(Jesus) rose from supper. He laid aside his outer garments, and taking a towel, tied it around his waist. Then he poured water into a basin and began to wash the disciples' feet and to wipe them with the towel that was wrapped around him. He came to Simon Peter, who said to him, "Lord, do you wash my feet?" Jesus answered him, "What I am doing you do not understand now, but afterward you will understand." (John 13:4-7 ESV). Note that the one served may not understand why you are serving them. Do it anyway. The Holy Spirit will help them understand why you did it in His time.

Notes and Quotes:

The story continues:

> *When he had washed their feet and put on his outer garments and resumed his place, he said to them, "Do you understand what I have done to you? You call me Teacher and Lord, and you are right, for so I am. If I then, your Lord and Teacher, have washed your feet, you also ought to wash one another's feet. For I have given you an example, that you also should do just as I have done to you. Truly, truly, I say to you, a servant is not greater than his master, nor is a messenger greater than the one who sent him. If you know these things, blessed are you if you do them.*

(John 13:12-17 ESV)

Some versions conclude this passage with the command that we are to "go and do likewise." Because Jesus served, we are to serve. And we must do so humbly for His glory and not our own.

Notes and Quotes:

List below five ways that you can serve your neighbors this week.

Chapter 25- Serving Your Neighbor Can Change the World

In 1994, Angela and I and our two children, were desperately looking for a house to buy and move into in the small town of Fortville, Indiana. We had lived in the area for about six months, and the rental we had been living in was scheduled to be turned into office space for the man who owned the house. Our dilemma was that there was absolutely nothing in the little town to purchase or rent. We had looked for several months when suddenly someone told me about a great older home that had sat empty for years that would be sold at auction. When I heard about it, I dropped everything and went to see the house. It was a fixer-upper, but due to our tight budget I was hoping to find something I could put some sweat equity into and this looked like a great possibility.

The house itself was structurally sound, but cosmetically it was in terrible shape. It had sat empty for nearly five years. When I located the house, there were two people inside preparing it to sell at the auction. First I looked at the old, red-brick exterior. It was charming in many ways. The trees and bushes were over-grown from the lack of care, but we were desperate and I could see potential. When I walked inside, I was greeted by a surprise. The house was filled to the brim with junk. Every place you looked was filled up to about five or six feet high with old papers, boxes, and trash. In order to get from room to room you had to simply follow a little path that had been left uncluttered. Finally I found the workers in the maze of trash and asked about the auction date. One of them said, "As soon as we can get all this trash out of here we will set the date, but that could take weeks." Then they went on to explain to me that the lady who owned the house was in a nursing home with Alzheimer's. Apparently for the years prior to being placed in that nursing home, she had wandered the streets of the little town daily gathering anything and everything she could find and carrying it back to add to her collection of junk.

In spite of all the clutter, the house had great potential, and I was excited that this could be the place God had for my family to spend the next decade of our lives. I left and began the work to

Have you ever served God

and others in a way that

the world might call

outrageous?

try to bid on the house. But I immediately ran into a problem. The rules for the auction stated that the buyer had to put 20% down at the time of the auction and the remaining 80% was due within 30 days. My problem was two-fold. I did not have 20% for a down payment, nor did I have the balance. I had planned to get an FHA loan to purchase whatever we found and our cash was limited. And to get the loan approved and then the money to pay the owner would take more than the 30 days allowed. I went back and told Angela that this was a dead end. We couldn't meet the terms to even bid.

A few weeks later, I went to the auction just to see who might buy the house and how much it would sell for, and I was shocked that no one besides me showed up to even bid on the place. After the people from the auction company backed up their stuff and went home, I called the person who was legally responsible for the home. He told me he too was shocked that no one bid on the home. I told him I was prepared to offer the court ordered minimum for the house but that I would have to secure a loan and could not bid because I could not do it within the time specified. He took my number and said he would talk to the judge in charge of the liquidation and call me back. Ten minutes later, my phone rang and it was the man in charge. He simply said, "We will take your offer, the house is yours." He offered the keys immediately so that I could begin the massive amount of work that needed to be done even before the loan was finalized and the dollars were paid. I felt so blessed.

Angela and I were so excited about God's favor. I could not wait to tell our new church the news of His provision. All the while, I was still perplexed as to why no one else wanted the house. A few days after the news that we were going to get the house, I found out why. I told my story of God's provision with great excitement to someone on Main Street and got an unusual reply. The person said, "You didn't buy the old house on Garden Street, did you? The one next door to Mr. Leonard? OH NO...you're in big trouble!" He went on to educate me on the man who many in Fortville called Scrooge. "He is the town grump!" they said. "Legend has it that he HATES children and eats them for dinner," they said and then laughed.

I didn't laugh. I had two children. And I became fearful for what might be in my family's future. But we were committed at this point and had no other options on the table. I met Mr. Leonard a few days later. He was an elderly man, eighty-six years old at the time. He was quite unusual and certainly he did come across as a busybody who was concerned about every little thing. Legend had it that he was the man who walked the streets of Fortville every day with his old briefcase in hand and stopped often to open it up for pen and paper to write down all the things that were wrong in the town. Then once a month he would go to the town council meetings and give them his unsolicited report. They cringed when they saw him coming. But after a few encounters, I was not as concerned. He really didn't appear to be a man who literally ate children. However, I warned Morgan and Amye about the neighbor to the east and told them to make sure they did nothing to incite him.

While Mr. Leonard was different, so was his wife. One day we came home from church to find her in her flowerbed with her vacuum on. Amye said, "Why is she vacuuming the plants?" We were simply perplexed. When fall came, Mr. Leonard raked leaves three times a day. We had lots of trees, and I didn't rake until every leaf had fallen. Soon I learned to pray for wind and eventually all my leaves would blow into his yard and he would grumble and gripe and complain. But eventually he would rake all my leaves as well.

Life for the first several months was uneventful next door to Glen Leonard, and I began to finally relax and think this just might not be so bad. Then one day it happened. I drove into the driveway and got out of my car headed inside when I heard Mr. Leonard call my name. I walked over to the property line and spoke to Mr. Leonard. He simply asked, "Is your boy inside?" I told him that I was sure that he was. And Mr. Leonard said, "I need to speak to him. Please go get him." My heart sunk. What could Morgan possibly have done? I went inside and called Morgan to come down to see me. I told him that Mr. Leonard wanted to see him and asked him what he had done to deserve such an appointment. "Nothing Dad," he said. "Really, I haven't done anything." With fear and trembling, we both made our way outside to face the man called Scrooge. I said my goodbyes to Morgan before we got there, and prayed that Mr. Leonard would not hurt my son. I also stood close by as Morgan's protector.

Mr. Leonard simply asked Morgan one question. "Do you like to play ball?" Morgan said, "Yes." Mr. Leonard said, "Wait here." He walked away and into his garage, and Morgan looked at me and shrugged his shoulders as if to say, "What's with this?" Moments later Mr. Leonard returned with a ratty old tennis ball that he had found on his walk that day. With feeble hands shaking, he extended his arm and offered it to Morgan. "Here," he said, "I want you to have it. I found it on my walk today and thought you might like a ball to play with." Morgan looked at me and then looked at that old ratty tennis ball and I nodded to him. He

Notes and Quotes:

politely reached out and took it and said, "Thank you." Moments later we were safely back inside and Morgan looked at me and I looked at him and then we both just burst out laughing. But that day started a lasting friendship between Glen Leonard and the Adcock family that would last for the rest of Mr. Leonard's days.

After a year or so I realized that Mr. Leonard would not eat children as everyone said and feared. And I began to actually take a liking to this man. The little house he and his wife lived in was no bigger than 800 square feet. It was in terrible repair. They had been on a fixed income for probably 20 years and I am sure that they simply didn't have the funds to care for it well. But Mr. Leonard was diligent and so meticulous in doing all he could to care for it. One day I got a brilliant idea. I thought it would be a great act of service to the Leonards, and also a great teaching time for Morgan, if Morgan and I would paint the old couple's house. The next time I saw Mr. Leonard out in the yard I approached him and asked if it would be okay if Morgan and I painted his house. Glen was a prideful man and I think my request offended him. He dodged the question and finally said, "I will talk to Feyola about it and let you know what we decide." But he never brought the subject back up. So later that summer I asked again about Morgan and I painting their house. "How much are you going to charge me?" Mr. Leonard asked. "Nothing," I answered. "We just want to do it because you take such pride in your place, and at your age, you don't need to be on a ladder painting." "You aren't going to charge me anything?" he asked. "No, sir." I replied. "Are you going to pay for the paint?" I responded, "Well, if you can't afford the paint I will even buy the paint." "No, I can afford the paint." Over the next few weeks, Morgan and I began to mobilize to paint Mr. Leonard's house. The whole family went to the paint store and got paint chips so he and Mrs. Leonard could choose colors. When they finally did pick the colors they were the most awful ones on the whole paint chart. But at least it would look clean, I thought to myself. Morgan and I worked hard. There was lots of scraping and sanding and caulking that had to be done to the little house. Finally, the day came that we started the finish coat. We had finished three sides of the house and were turning down the homestretch when Mr. Leonard appeared. He wasn't happy with the color. He called me out into the front yard and asked if we would repaint it with a different color. I was a bit taken back. How dare he do this to us! We had been generous and done all this work for free and now he was going to ask us to do even more. Morgan was livid. But this was a great lesson for both of us. We talked about Jesus' call to go the extra mile. And the next Saturday, when we

Notes and Quotes:

thought we would be completely done, we started over with a new color and with a new attitude.

In those weeks that Morgan and I served Mr. and Mrs. Leonard, something seemed to have changed for both families. Mr. Leonard and I had discussions about faith and God. He was not a believer, and I wish I could tell you that he fell on his knees and found Christ. I cannot. But our service to him did soften his heart. This was the man feared by many. He was a hard man to understand and a harder man to love. Yet, our service to him penetrated his heart. In those final days of painting, a letter arrived at our house addressed to Morgan. The return address was next door. Inside was a thank you note from Mr. Leonard along with a $100 bill. Love had changed his heart. In the years that followed, Mr. Leonard gave me all of the tools from his garage. He showed respect and compassion to our family. He watched out for our home when we were away. He reciprocated in whatever way he could think of. I want you to know that loving service changes lives.

Glen was nearing ninety when there was a feeble knock upon our door. I was in the kitchen and looked out to see Mrs. Leonard there. This was unusual because she seldom ever went outside. Angela beat me to the door. Mrs. Leonard simply said, "Can Mark come? Glen has fallen in the kitchen." Angela and I went quickly. I knelt over him and simply said to Angela, "Call 911." I placed my hand upon his chest and silently prayed as my friend drew his final breath.

Again, I would love to tell you that the witness of our family had ushered Glen Leonard into the Kingdom. But I do not know that. I do know that the loving service that we provided did change his heart. And I do know that I had been able to share with him about God's love and he had the chance to receive Christ. He had been taught how to get to heaven. He was always just one prayer away from claiming eternity with God. I have forever wondered if somewhere in those final moments, Mr. Leonard might have voiced that prayer. I will never know until perhaps I get to that Promised Land. But this I do know. God loved Glen Leonard. And love can make a tremendous difference to even the most lost soul.

We must love our neighbors. It can and will impact them and offer light to their darkness. And we never know when one spark or light might illuminate the way to Eternity.

Questions for Discussion:

1. How necessary is it for a Christian to be involved in a local congregation?

Notes and Quotes:

2. Is it a sin for a person to proclaim to be a Christian and yet have no connection to a Body of Believers?

3. Read Acts 2:42-47. How does the local church today resemble the early church talked about here? How is it different today?

4. How well does your congregation do at caring for one another in light of what Acts 2:42-47 says regarding the care provided by the early church.

5. How might the church today learn from this passage?

6. In the world today, we are seldom connected to our neighbors like generations past have been. Is this a problem? Should we be more involved with those who live near us? Why or why not?

7. Have you ever gone out of your way to serve someone in your community? Were your motives right? What did you do? How did they respond?

8. What do you think about Paul David Tripp's definition of love that is highlighted near the margin of page 205?

Concentric Circle #4- Unto the Ends of the Earth...
A Man's Relationship with the World

As we look back over this journey, we see God's master plan begin to come into focus. He saved us for a purpose. Initially, when God penetrated your heart, it appeared all about you. The Rock of Jesus Christ smashed through the surface of your hardened heart and brought salvation, and in that moment, nourishment rushed into your soul. Immediately the ripples of Living Water began their journey outward to effect the world, but the first effects washed over you. You were blessed beyond measure that God loved you enough to save you and give you a new life. The result of that fact is that you began to worship.

But as the water began to reach your Judea, and your family received the gift of God's love, you suddenly realized that this was more than simply personal. This was God's way of breathing hope into the lives of those closest to you. And the Christ in you began to turn your eyes away from self, to see your life to be one of purpose. You became an instrument in the Redeemer's hands. Living Water positively affects everyone and everything it touches.

Eventually the Living Water raced beyond your home to affect the church and your neighborhood. Ring number four looks at a man's responsibility to reach the world for God's glory. Let me restate this, God saved you for a purpose. That purpose began by turning your heart to Him in worship. But in the process, you are more than simply a worshipper. You have been called to be a minister. We must carry the gospel of Jesus Christ to a dark world that is in desperate need of hope. That hope is founded only in Jesus. Let us proclaim that message to the ends of the earth.

Suppose for a moment that there was a raging disease that reared its head and it was taking lives at an alarming rate in countries all around the globe. Death was winning the war as men and women, boys and girls were all being ravaged by a disease that seemed to have no cure. But then you wake up and realize that the answer to saving lives is something rather simple. The only problem, to save those who are dying, you must be inconvenienced. It will require that you go and personally teach them how to address the deficiencies in their lives that lead to death. You realize that you hold the very key to their future in your hands. What would you do? Would you go and share the good news so they do not have to die?

Chapter 26- Go, Make Disciples of All Nations

Go therefore and make disciples of all nations, baptizing them in the name of the Father and of the Son and of the Holy Spirit, teaching them to observe all that I have commanded you. And behold, I am with you always, to the end of the age."

(Matthew 28:19-20 ESV)

We call it the Great Commission. Any man who has been involved in the church for very long has heard about it. We are saved for a purpose. One purpose is to set our gaze and our worship on the Almighty. But there is something more. We, the church, are his delivery system to carry the message of Hope in Christ to a desperate world. We are designed to be proclaimers of the Message. We are His plan 'A' to reach the lost for His glory and for their good. And we must realize that God has no plan 'B.' If the world is to hear of Jesus and his saving, amazing grace, then we must go and carry Living Water to a world that is parched and thirsty, a world dying without any hope or spiritual nourishment.

Men, if we really believed that those who do not receive Jesus Christ as Lord and Savior of their lives will spend eternity in hell, then we would make ourselves available and go herald the Good News. But many of us have fallen for the false doctrine that believes that people simply get to go to heaven at the end of life because God is a loving God and He would not send anyone to hell. Or we have fallen into the faulty belief that every religious road leads to God. Neither of these teachings are true. Jesus is the only way. And how will they know if no one tells them about Jesus?

How then will they call on him in whom they have not believed? And how are they to believe in him of whom they have never heard? And how are they to hear without someone preaching? And how are they to preach unless they are sent? As it is written, "How beautiful are the feet of those who preach the good news!" But they have not all obeyed the gospel. For Isaiah says, "Lord, who has believed what he has heard from us?" So faith comes from hearing,

Notes and Quotes:

and hearing through the word of Christ.

(Romans 10:14-17 ESV)

"If people will go to heaven simply based on their native religious preferences, then there is no urgency for any of us to go to them. But if they will not go to heaven because they have never heard of Christ, then there is indescribable urgency for all of us to go to them. If people are dying and going to hell without ever even knowing there is a gospel, then we clearly have no time to waste our lives on an American dream." (Cite: David Platt in Radical. Page 143).

What does it mean when Scripture says that we must go into all the world? To go to all nations includes the one in which we live. The heart of this message and calling can be summed up in one word... evangelism. To evangelize the lost means to proclaim Christ to them so they might come to know him personally as their Lord and Savior. This is a huge calling that is intended by God to fall upon the heart of every Christian regardless of gender. But as leaders in our homes, families and churches, I believe we as men bear a tremendous responsibility to carry the gospel message into the world.

What Must We Do?

We Must Overcome Being Simply Religious- If we are to accomplish what Jesus commanded us to do in the Great Commission, then we have to destroy the complacency that has lulled the church into slumber. As I mentioned in the section regarding the church, the church has fallen asleep. We have come to the place where we are religious but have little relationship with the God who calls for our undivided attention.

>*You hypocrites! Well did Isaiah prophesy of you, when he said:*

>*"'This people honors me with their lips,*

>>*but their heart is far from me;*

>*in vain do they worship me,*

>>*teaching as doctrines the commandments of men.'"*

(Matthew 15:7-9 ESV)

Man of God, have you fallen into Satan's trap of simply acting in a religious way? All the while having a heart that is far from the God who desires an intimate, heart-to-heart relationship with you? A person whose actions do not flow out of his/her heart is an actor. In order to be authentic, we must have an engaged heart. Don't fall for just doing Christianity. James says, "... be doers of the word, and not hearers only, deceiving yourselves." (James 1:22 ESV) We must be so that we might do. Remember this is about identity in Christ.

We Must Care About What God Cares About

What the church needs in order for the Great Commission to be accomplished is for men and women to begin to care about the things that God cares about. Unfortunately, most of us, even after we come to know Christ, still struggle with an ungodly attitude that is consumed with what we care about and unaware of what God cares about.

In the Old Testament God brought about the collapse of Israel by sending in the Assyrian army to plunder them and to take them captive. Why would God do such a thing? The answer to this question is twofold. First, the people all throughout history had turned their gaze and hearts away from God and participated in worshipping false gods. But secondly, the people of Israel experienced the wrath of God because they failed to care about the things that God cared about. In that day the prophet Amos spoke about why God would bring such wrath to Israel. The paraphrase is "...because of your hard-hearted injustice of the poor, because you have not been compassionate to those who have less than you, because you have profaned the holy, I will pour out wrath upon you."

God did exactly what He said He would do. Why? Because the people refused to care about what God cared about. As you read the Word of God, it is quite obvious that He cares about every single person He ever fashioned in His image. But there is one category that seems to have moved the Almighty to a place of great compassion, that category being "the least of these."

As Jesus walked this earth, he taught us about the things that God cares about. As he fed the hungry on the side of the sea, and healed the lepers who were outcasts, and as he gave a scandalous woman Living water at a well in a country scorned by the religious, Jesus was constantly teaching us about what and who God loved.

Even in his first public statement in the temple he proclaimed why he came. He read from the scroll of Isaiah these words:

> *"The Spirit of the Lord is upon me,*
>
> *because he has anointed me*
>
> *to proclaim good news to the poor.*

Notes and Quotes:

In the space below, write a brief but personal mission statement that reflects your own agenda.

Notes and Quotes:

He has sent me to proclaim liberty to the captives

and recovering of sight to the blind,

to set at liberty those who are oppressed,

to proclaim the year of the Lord's favor."

(Luke 4:18-19 ESV)

After he read those words he simply said, "Today this Scripture is fulfilled in your hearing." He was announcing that his coming to earth was to offer good news to the poor and freedom to the oppressed. It was all a part of God's plan that Jesus would come to give the blind new eyes to see. These are the things that God cared about then, and these are the things that God cares about today. Evangelism is all about going and doing God's business in the world.

Realize that this calling is not a suggestion, it is a commandment. Every Christian must go in order to please God. In fact, it is startling to see the criteria that Jesus said he would use when he judges the world. He did not say that he would determine who was given heaven by how much money they gave to the church. Nor would he base his decision on how many prayers were said or how many services were attended. No he said that the Day of Judgment would look at how a person cared for the "least of these."

"When the Son of Man comes in his glory, and all the angels with him, then he will sit on his glorious throne. Before him will be gathered all the nations, and he will separate people one from another as a shepherd separates the sheep from the goats. And he will place the sheep on his right, but the goats on the left. Then the King will say to those on his right, 'Come, you who are blessed by my Father, inherit the kingdom prepared for you from the foundation of the world. For I was hungry and you gave me food, I was thirsty and you gave me drink, I was a stranger and you welcomed me, I was naked and you clothed me, I was sick and you visited me, I was in prison and you came to me.' Then the righteous will answer him, saying, 'Lord, when did we see you hungry and feed you, or thirsty and give you drink? And when did we see you a stranger and welcome you, or naked and clothe you? And when did we see you sick or in prison and visit you?' And the King will answer them, 'Truly, I say to you, as you did it to one of the least of these my brothers, you did it to me.'

"Then he will say to those on his left, 'Depart from me, you cursed, into the eternal fire prepared for the devil and his angels. For

I was hungry and you gave me no food, I was thirsty and you gave me no drink, I was a stranger and you did not welcome me, naked and you did not clothe me, sick and in prison and you did not visit me.' Then they also will answer, saying, 'Lord, when did we see you hungry or thirsty or a stranger or naked or sick or in prison, and did not minister to you?' Then he will answer them, saying, 'Truly, I say to you, as you did not do it to one of the least of these, you did not do it to me.' And these will go away into eternal punishment, but the righteous into eternal life."

(Matthew 25:31-46 ESV)

A Different View of the Great Commission

One of the things that having four different Gospels affords us is perspective. Some might be concerned that not every word and detail recorded by the Gospel writers is identical. But I find great vitality in the different voicing of what each writer remembered and absorbed as they experienced life with Jesus. If four different people witnessed a car accident and they were all looking from different places, they would all have a different perspective to share. The same is true with the Gospels. I want to look at the Great Commission now from Mark's account.

Afterward he appeared to the eleven themselves as they were reclining at table, and he rebuked them for their unbelief and hardness of heart, because they had not believed those who saw him after he had risen. And he said to them, "Go into all the world and proclaim the gospel to the whole creation. Whoever believes and is baptized will be saved, but whoever does not believe will be condemned.

(Mark 16:14-16 ESV)

We Must Go

A proper understanding of this term, "Go into all the world," would be best read, "as you go." The Greek language is a complex language. I have no desire to spend lots of time trying to explain what would require years of Greek training and study. But realize that the word 'Go' in the Great Commission is not a verb. It is actually a passive participle. The verb we are called to do is to proclaim. The best understanding of the word 'Go' should be voiced, "As you go." As you do life, realize that you carry in your heart the very thing that will cure the disease of sin that leads to death. Unless the people of the world receive the cure, they will surely die. We need to realize that this is not a call to

Notes and Quotes:

Who are the people in your world that God is calling you to share about Him?

Notes and Quotes:

grandstand and to take a mission trip to Africa. No, this is to happen daily as you go and do life. When you leave the company of the church and go into the world, you have opportunity to fulfill the Great Commission.

Where We Must Go

In order to understand this, we need to understand a good definition of "the world." In the third ring we looked at the definition of "the church." The church included every person who had been born again into the family of God regardless of what denomination they might affiliate with. The church includes every person who has received Christ.

The world, then, is every person who has NOT received Christ. This means that you go into the world every day when you walk out of your house and go to work. Why? Because you rub shoulders with those who are unsaved every day. They are the people in your neighborhood who live in spiritual darkness.

What We Must Do

God does not call us to save anyone. In fact, we are incapable of a task such as this. But every one of us can proclaim. Our job in fulfilling the Great Commission is to simply speak the Truth for God. We are the ones called to herald the gospel message. If you proclaim, then you have succeeded. Some people get caught up in results. How many have you won for the Kingdom? Our eyes should not be focused upon how many we have won, but upon simply speaking for God and offering a word of Hope and Truth to those who do not yet know Jesus Christ as Lord and Savior of their lives. We live in a day that God's Word is "out of season." We must still proclaim it even if no one will heed the call of Truth. Paul writes to Timothy and says, "...preach the word; be ready in season and out of season; reprove, rebuke, and exhort, with complete patience and teaching." (2 Timothy 4:2). The call to live out the Great Commission is founded not upon results and response from those who hear, but upon obedience to the ones of us who proclaim. Men, we need to carry the message of the gospel to the world regardless of how they respond. We must do it because God said we must. Leave the results to Him.

Why We Must Go

Out of all these 'W' questions, the 'why' is the most important. Why must we go? Why must we proclaim? We must go and proclaim because if the people do not come to know Christ, then they will be condemned. That is simply a nice way of saying that if a person does not come to know Jesus they will go to hell! This fact should be enough to get us out of bed every morning. The problem that I see with the church being silent when it comes to proclaiming the gospel message is a problem with unbelief. Notice that in Mark's account, the context of the Great Commission was an encounter with Jesus where he rebuked them for their unbelief. He had told them that He would rise again on the third day, yet when he did so and word arrived that he had done what he said he would do, some, even some of the disciples, did not believe it. I ask you this very important question. Do you believe that a person who never receives Jesus Christ will be doomed to hell and damnation forever? Really?

If we truly believed this as fact, would we not proclaim and cry out to those we love most, "I love you and don't want you to go to hell!" To be silent is to tell those who do not know the Savior, I don't care enough about you to give you the cure for what is going to kill you. We know the cure. God's plan all along is that we would carry the cure into the world and share it generously and liberally. Yet the church today sits in silence, falling prey to the devil's scheming. We have fallen for a faulty premise that sharing the gospel might offend those who think differently than we do. So we sit by quietly and withhold the very thing that will bring hope and change to our culture.

Men, the Bible teaches that there is only one way to heaven. That is through Jesus Christ. Every person you come in contact with today that does not know him personally is on a straight path to hell. What are you going to do about it?

Notes and Quotes:

Portrait of a REAL Man...Jim Elliot- A Man Willing to Go

Philip James Elliot was born on Oct. 8, 1927, in Portland, Oregon to Fred and Clara Elliot. "Jim" as he became known to his friends, was the son of an itinerant preacher who served in the area surrounding the Puget Sound. At the very early age of eight years old, Jim received Jesus Christ and began to passionately live for the Lord. He was pegged early in life to be a real "go-getter," who was obviously going to make his life count.

Jim excelled at whatever he put his mind to doing. He was an excellent athlete playing multiple sports in high school including football and wrestling. He also was considered to be one of the best actors in his school. In fact, he was recruited by his teachers to enter into professional theater. But Jim's passion was not on the playing fields of life nor in the theater. No, Jim's passion was found in Christ and the tremendous call he felt to carry out the Great Commission.

At Wheaton College in Illinois, Jim learned that "there is one Christian worker for every 50,000 people in foreign lands, while there is one to every 500 in the United States." He preached in youth groups in the Wheaton area, and one summer he visited Mexico where he stayed with a missionary family to learn Spanish for six weeks. There, he felt his missionary call to South America.

In his junior year of college, Jim met the woman he would one day marry. Her name was Elisabeth. She too felt a call to be a missionary. After college they agreed to each go their separate ways and place their individual callings to be missionaries at the head of any selfish pursuit. But God soon made it known that it was His plan that together they would serve Him.

By 1950, Jim had participated in numerous short-term missionary endeavors, most of them to Latin America. But the door had not yet opened to what he felt God had created him to do. So he continued to study and prepare for the day God would offer opportunity. It was around this time that he wrote in his journal, "God, I pray Thee, light these idle sticks of my life and may I burn for Thee. Consume my life, my God, for it is Thine. I seek not a long life, but a full one, like you, Lord Jesus." Perhaps Elliot even at this early part of his life had an understanding of what God had created him to do.

In the summer of 1950 Jim heard about the Auca Indians of Ecuador. Immediately his heart was moved to compassion for them. After a ten day prayer vigil, Jim believed that this was the people he was called to go to. But one didn't just go to the Auca's. Their tribe was remote and missionaries had to establish themselves in the culture of Ecuador. Jim and Elisabeth worked diligently in the ministry. Together they translated the New Testament into the Quechua Indian language. In 1952 they found themselves finally in the country that God had called them to, but it would take time to find the illusive people of the Auca tribe. All the while Jim and Elisabeth ministered to the people of Ecuador who had never heard the name of Jesus spoken.

Along the journey, Jim and Elisabeth met several like-minded couples who also felt called to reach the Auca people. In all there were five couples who prepared a strategy to reach the people of the Auca tribe. The name of their strategy was simply called Operation Auca. Great wisdom led the men to understand that this mission was too dangerous for their wives and children, so they set out to find the Auca people and to deliver the message that God loved them.

Those who served with Jim Elliot were Ed McCully, Peter Fleming, and Nate Saint, the pilot. Roger Youderian would join the group later. All five would be martyred on a beach in Ecuador. The following is an account provided by Rit Nosotro in an article written in 2003 and made available to hyperhistory.net. Other accounts can be found in Elisabeth Elliot's book entitled, Through Gates of Splendor.

The men discovered the first Auca huts with the help of a missionary jungle pilot, Nate Saint. As the plans for contact with the Aucas continued, Roger Youderian, a young missionary was asked to join them. The men's first attempt to contact them was by airplane. Nate Saint would fly the men around the camp shouting friendship words in the Auca language through a loud speaker and dropping down gifts in a basket such as beads, cloths, machetes and a photograph of each man. The Aucas realized they were friendly and allowed them to land on an island they called Palm Beach. The Aucas responded by sending back up a parrot and feathered head dresses.

Encouraged by this progress, after three to four months of gift dropping, they decided to make a base on the Curray River, "Palm Beach". Unexpectedly after a week, four Aucas came to Palm Beach. The five men gave them food and gifts as a sign of peace.

After a few days of transferring their equipment to their new campsite they started to set up shelter. After they had set up shelter they shouted Auca phrases into the jungle. The men were always ready for visits of the Auca and carried firearms, but made an agreement not to use them unless necessary. Four days later two Auca women and a man appeared on the other side of the river at the edge of the jungle. Stunned, the missionaries started frantically shouting out phrases in the Auca language. The man replied speaking in his own language and frequently pointing at one of the girls. Jim immediately jumped into the river and swam across. Frightened and a bit surprised the Aucas backed up into the jungle. Finally after a little persuasion, they were able to convince the men to come into their camp. One of the men gave them knives that greatly pleased them. The younger Auca woman went up to the plane and started making motions with her hands at the plane. The man also moved toward the plane examining it intently. The missionaries promptly named the man "George" and the young girl "Delilah." By the signs that they made they understood that the Indians were interested in a ride, so Nate started up the engine and flew off the narrow strip with "George" in the back of the plane. Nate steered the plane in the direction of the village realizing his opportunity to use his passenger as propaganda. "George," who was wild with delight, was hanging out the plane window screaming Auca phrases to his fellow villagers.

When they got back to their campsite, the missionaries showed the Indians modern things such as rubber bands, balloons and balls. Then they had lunch of hamburgers with mustard. Toward the end of the visit, the Indians showed signs that they wanted to stay the night on the beach with them. The missionaries hospitably set up a hut and said that they could sleep there for the night. All of a sudden, Delilah gave a shrill cry and headed off toward the jungle with George following close behind. Soon after, the older woman left.

Encouraged by this visit, the men felt that it was time to go in and try to minister to them. On the morning of January 8th, after numerous songs of praise and considerable prayer, the men radioed their wives saying that they were going to go into the village and would radio them at about 4:30. "Operation Auca" was under way. He wrote to his father five days before his departure for "Palm Beach", ...they have never had any contact with white man other than killing. They have no word for God in their language, only for devils and spirits. I know you will pray."

The next day, Nate and Ed were flying back to Shell Mera when they saw a group of twenty or thirty Aucas going toward Palm Beach. As soon as they saw that, they got very excited and turned around and landed at Palm Beach. They shouted, "Guys, the Aucas are coming!" As soon as the three others heard that, they flew into action straightening up their camp. Little did these five men know that this would be their last few hours of life. The last radio contact they made with Shell Mera was Jim calling his wife saying, "We'll call you back in three hours." As they lived their last minutes during the attack, they did not injure one Auca.

The women back at the base were praying the entire time for their husband's time with the Aucas and asking God to keep them safe. At 4:30 there was no reply, which immediately put the women in alarm. An hour later helicopters and planes from the Ecuadorian Air Force, the US Army, Air Force and Navy swarmed along the Curray River looking for any sight of the missionaries. Finally, one of the helicopters radioed in saying that they had found their bodies on the beach. Jim Elliot's body was found down stream with three others. Their bodies had been brutally pierced with spears and hacked by machetes. All of the plane's fabric had been ripped off as if they had tried to kill the plane. Nate Saint's watch had stopped at 3:12 p.m. So it was concluded that the Indians had attacked them at that time. Their wives received the news and replied, "The Lord has closed our hearts to grief and hysteria, and filled them with His perfect peace."

These martyrs are known worldwide and continue to be an encouragement for many missionaries. After their deaths, there were many conversions to Christianity among the Indian tribes of Ecuador. After Jim Elliot's death, Elisabeth Elliot and her daughter Valerie continued working with the Quechua Indians and later moved to work with the Auca Indians. Forgiveness allowed them to have amazing success with the once murderous Indians.

Jim Elliot's life was lived honorably and he was known to have looked for God in everything he did. Jim Elliot once said, "He is no fool who gives what he cannot keep to gain what he cannot lose." He gave his all in faith to the Auca people, and he cannot lose in the Kingdom of Heaven.

Concentric Circle #5- A Man's Relationship with Eternity

When the ripples finally land upon the shores of Glory,

When temporal past has a hold no more,

When feeble bodies cease their bidding

And the soul begins its upward stare;

When the pains of sin and agitation

Are but a distant memory,

When lust and greed all pass away;

Then my heart will burst in pleasure,

For my life will be set free,

And my gaze will find its focus

Upon the One who died for me.

When the time of men has ceased its journey,

When breath has stopped its earthly quest,

When all failure is but a shadow

And darkness has been dispelled to rot;

When evil whimpers in its folly,

And a crown adorns the brow,

When my anxious thoughts are banished

And my fear has been relieved;

Then my heart will burst in pleasure,

For my life has been set free,

Then my soul will sing forever

From the shores of Eternity.

~ Mark Adcock

Chapter 27- Understanding the Race of Life

I have fought the good fight, I have finished the race, I have kept the faith.

(2 Timothy 4:7 ESV)

Those words of the Apostle Paul are chiseled in the stone that marks my paternal grandfather's grave. Papa Claude died when I was only ten years old. I never got to know him well. I wish I had been given that opportunity. But God had a different plan. Still his life has affected mine in many ways. Like the evening of September 29, 1989. I knelt at an altar at the Church at the Crossing in Indianapolis, Indiana. People gathered around me to pray for me. It was the night I was ordained into the ministry. Many gathered and prayed. When the final amen was said and I arose from that place, a woman who I did not recognize stood close by with a message to be spoken to me. She said, "I am your Papa Claude's step daughter, Lois, and I am here to represent Him on this most special occasion." Lois was the one I spoke of in the Portrait of a REAL Man earlier. She was the ten year old little girl who had been saved by her father who drowned in the process. Her mother years later married my Papa Claude who had been widowed.

What Lois did not know that evening was that my heart was grieving for my family was not able to attend due to living in Europe. And there was a longing in me that desired they be present and represented. They were there, that night, through the precious gift of legacy.

Though I never really knew my Papa Claude, he has often spoken into my life. You see, I have walked a similar road to my grandfather. He too was a pastor and church planter. Years ago my father gave me a small scrap of paper about five inches square. Upon it these words are typed:

To Whom it May Concern:

"This is to certify that on the Twenty-seventh day of July, Nineteen-hundred and Thirty-eight, at the state camp grounds of the church of God Dixon, Miss; during the 1938 camp-meeting

Notes and Quotes:

In the space below, write

five words that you think

will describe what heaven

will be like.

Rev. C.L. Adcock was duly ordained to the Christian ministry." Six signatures of local pastors who acknowledged his call are listed as witnesses of the ordination.

Seldom do I preach that my grandfather's ordination papers are not in my Bible. I stand upon his shoulders. Though he died a very early death, God has allowed me to walk in his shadow and continue what he began. Generational faith is like that. It is like a relay race where one runner finishes their race and hands the baton to the next. I hold in my hand today a baton that represents many who have run the race before me. And symbolically now, I offer that baton to you.

In Exodus 20 there is a small but powerful phrase that adorns the second commandment. It simply says, "But I lavish unfailing love for a thousand generations on those who love me and obey my commands." (Exodus 20:6 NLT). Men, realize that your impact can continue to a thousand generations even once you finish the race if you will but love the Lord and walk in righteousness and obedience. Finish strong, Oh man of God. The future of your family tree will be forever blessed if you cross the finish line of life with the baton of faith in hand, ready to pass it on to those you love.

Have you ever wondered what heaven will be like? The older I get, the more I think about heaven. I am but in my early fifties now and imagine my life will continue for decades still, but I have begun to realize there is a finish line in sight. And the closer I get to that line, the faster I run and the more excited I get about crossing over into Eternity. As I run the race set before me, I am learning that I was made for this. God set my feet upon this path and He didn't do so haphazardly but with a purposeful plan to lead me Home.

For I know the plans I have for you, declares the LORD, plans for welfare and not for evil, to give you a future and a hope.

(Jeremiah 29:11 ESV)

God's plan is to give you a hope and future. The culmination of that verse is Eternity with Him in the place prepared for all who have been blessed to receive the gift of salvation.

Preparing for the Finish Line- What must we do to finish strong?

We must make sure that our hearts are right with God- Scripture teaches that it is appointed unto man once to die and after this we will experience judgment. (see Hebrews 9:27) Men, we must live every day as if it were our last day on earth. When we die the opportunity to make things right with God comes to its end. For those of us who have been born again, death is not to be feared. Jesus died so that we can live forever. But we must be ready when the race is done.

We must eagerly await THE Day- I find that many Christians have no understanding of death. For the Christian man, we should anxiously anticipate the awesome gift of Eternity. Hebrews 9:28 says that when Christ returns the second time, He will not come to deal with sin, but "to save those who are eagerly waiting for him."

We must look from a different place and have a different perspective- In order to have an appropriate anticipation of Heaven, we must look from a spiritual perspective, not a worldly perspective. One reason that Christians have no longing for Heaven is because they are so attached to the things of this world. We must, as we run towards the finish line, rid ourselves of the worldly so that we might see and understand spiritual things. A man who has no spiritual understanding will be unable to long for heaven. Paul writes, "...But our citizenship is in heaven, and from it we await a Savior, the Lord Jesus Christ..." (Philippians 3:20 ESV). This world is not our home. Heaven is the place we belong. This world is but a training ground for Glory! Pray and ask God for a spiritual perspective.

We must persevere- Men, the race is long in many respects. I am alarmed at how many men are falling out of the race in the final trimester of their lives. This is not a sprint. It requires tenacity and strength in order to finish. Spiritual nourishment is vital. And exercising your faith will give you a strong core that will help you finish the race. There is a direct link, according to Scripture, between perseverance and the rewards of Heaven.

For you have need of endurance, so that when you have done the will of God you may receive what is promised.

(Hebrews 10:36 ESV)

And let us not grow weary of doing good, for in due season we will reap, if we do not give up.

(Galatians 6:9 ESV)

Blessed is the man who remains steadfast under trial, for when he has stood the test he will receive the crown of life, which God has promised to those who love him.

(James 1:12 ESV)

Notes and Quotes:

What in this world seems to hold your attention?

Do you have a Godly longing for heaven?

Notes and Quotes:

We must learn to long for Heaven- As I mentioned earlier, my daughter, Amye, was a distance runner. One of the things that developed over the latter parts of her career was an anticipation and longing for the finish line. With the help of her coaches, she began to pace herself in races so that the last mile was one of the fastest miles of the race. As she would turn toward the finish line and begin the final home stretch, there would begin to rise up within her a longing to be done. That longing would fulfill itself in a kick that would last until her final strides were done.

I write this on a day when I will attend the funeral of a dear woman in our community that will mark her strong finish. She endured the race for 92 years. Her legacy is founded in a 72 year marriage that was built upon faith in Jesus Christ. Over the past six months, she knew that the finish line was drawing nearer and nearer. Doctors told her the cancer would take her life. She was not afraid. In her final lucid moments she showed no fear. She simply ran faster and faster into the arms of her Maker. Why? Because she had a longing to go to the place prepared for her. She went willingly with great anticipation. May it be so for you and me as well.

What Will Heaven Be Like?

As a pastor, I am often asked this question. Scripture gives us glimpses of what Heaven will be like, but because Heaven is God's Home, and because He is indescribable, we probably can't comprehend a place so precious. Look at what we do know from God's Word.

John 14:2 In my Father's house are many rooms. If it were not so, would I have told you that I go to prepare a place for you?

Revelation 5:9-13 And they sang a new song, saying, "Worthy are you to take the scroll and to open its seals, for you were slain, and by your blood you ransomed people for God from every tribe and language and people and nation, and you have made them a kingdom and priests to our God, and they shall reign on the earth." Then I looked, and I heard around the throne and the living creatures and the elders the voice of many angels, numbering myriads of myriads and thousands of thousands, saying with a loud voice, "Worthy is the Lamb who was slain, to receive power and wealth and wisdom and might and honor and glory and blessing!" And I heard every creature in heaven and on earth and under the earth and in the sea, and all that is in them, saying, "To him who sits on the throne and to the Lamb be blessing and honor and glory and might forever and ever!"

Revelation 21:4 He will wipe away every tear from their eyes, and death shall be no more, neither shall there be mourning, nor crying, nor pain anymore, for the former things have passed away."

Revelation 22:1-5 Then the angel showed me the river of the water of life, bright as crystal, flowing from the throne of God and of the Lamb through the middle of the street of the city; also, on either side of the river, the tree of life with its twelve kinds of fruit, yielding its fruit each month. The leaves of the tree were for the healing of the nations. No longer will there be anything accursed, but the throne of God and of the Lamb will be in it, and his servants will worship him. They will see his face, and his name will be on their foreheads. And night will be no more. They will need no light of lamp or sun, for the Lord God will be their light, and they will reign forever and ever.

We learn from these passages that Heaven is a place. It is not some spiritual la la land. It is a physical place with homes prepared for us... actually mansions. I have never lived in a mansion. But one day I will.

Heaven is a place of activity. Some have said they don't want to go to heaven because it seems to them like it will be boring. Nothing could be further from the truth. Heaven will be an awesome place of worship and celebration. We will join with the angels and the saints. Our fellowship will be phenomenal. Our worship will be better still.

Heaven is a place where tears will flow no more. A place where sadness has no home and sickness has been banished. It is the only perfect place available to us. The Garden of Eden was destroyed centuries ago by sin. But there is a place even better for sin will have no opportunity to enter. A place where temptation is squashed in victory. A place of perpetual, never ending, heart bursting JOY and PEACE.

Heaven is a place where every person gets a mansion overlooking a flowing, beautiful stream of living water. I have been asked if I could pick any place to build a retirement home, where would I build it. I always choose, in my dreams, a mountain setting overlooking a beautiful, rushing stream. They don't have those here in Indiana. But I will get to enjoy that in Heaven.

Heaven is a place where fruit is always in season. My favorite fruit is the grape. I love when they are in season. A grape in season is plump and juicy. But out of season they leave much to be desired. While I love grapes, I hate raisins. I want my fruit fresh and ripe. I will have my daily fill of the best fruits when I get to Heaven.

Notes and Quotes:

Notes and Quotes:

Heaven will hold nothing evil or profane. I am so tired of the assault of evil in this world. I enjoy sports but have grown weary of attending events where scores of fans shout profanities and douse me with drinks that emit the pungent smells of decay and ruin. In Glory I will bathe in streams of Living Water and breathe the crisp glorious odors of Heaven. I will no longer need to cover my eyes or my ears in an attempt to find a small corner that offers purity. No, I will bask in that which is pure.

In his book, In Light of Eternity, Randy Alcorn speaks about what won't be in heaven.

"This joy and fulfillment in heaven…will erupt not only from positive experiences, but also from what is not there. No arthritis, no handicaps, no cancer, no mosquitos, no taxes, no bills, no computer crashes, no weeds, no bombs, no drunkenness, no traffic jams and accidents, no septic tank backups, no door locks, no phone calls selling storm windows at dinnertime. No mental illness. No pretense, no wearing masks. Close friendships but no cliques, laughter but no putdowns. Intimacy, but no temptation to immorality." (Cite: In Light of Eternity. Page 54).

> **The more I learn about God, the more excited I get about heaven.**
>
> **~ Randy Alcorn**

Heaven will be a wonderful place. But don't forget the most important fact about Heaven. "Heaven is God's home, the dwelling place of the One who is infinite in creativity, goodness, beauty, and power. How could the home of anyone like that be less than thrilling?" (Cite: Ibid. Page 55-56).

As you can see, Heaven will be wonderful when we get there. For now, let us realize that as long as God gives us breath, then, for us, the race continues. Don't quit until you have crossed the finish line! Don't stop running until the Living Water reaches the shore of Glory. And when you arrive there, listen for the wonderful voice of God to say, "Well done thou good and faithful servant."

NOT HOME YET

An old missionary couple had been working in Africa for years and were returning to New York to retire. They had no pension; their health was broken; they were defeated, discouraged, and afraid. They discovered they were booked on the same ship as President Teddy Roosevelt, who was returning from one of his big-game hunting expeditions.

No one paid any attention to them. They watched the fanfare that accompanied the President's entourage, with passengers trying to catch a glimpse of the great man. As the ship moved across the ocean, the old missionary said to his wife, "Something is wrong. Why should we have given our lives in faithful service for God in Africa all these many years and have no one care a thing about us? Here this man comes back from a hunting trip and everybody makes much over him, but nobody gives two hoots about us."

"Dear, you shouldn't feel that way", his wife said. He replied "I can't help it; it doesn't seem right."

When the ship docked in New York, a band was waiting to greet the President. The mayor and other dignitaries were there. The papers were full of the President's arrival. No one noticed this missionary couple. They slipped off the ship and found a cheap flat on the East Side, hoping the next day to see what they could do to make a living in the city.

That night the man's spirit broke. He said to his wife, "I can't take this; God is not treating us fairly". His wife replied, "Why don't you go in the bedroom and tell that to the Lord?"

A short time later he came out from the bedroom, but now his face was completely different. His wife asked, "Dear, what happened?" "The Lord settled it with me", he said. "I told Him how bitter I was that the President should receive this tremendous homecoming, when no one met us as we returned home. And when I finished, it seemed as though the Lord put His hand on my shoulder and simply said; "But you're not home yet." Author Unknown (http://www.godswork.org/emailmessage43.htm)

"As long as we're still here in the parched wastelands of the present earth, God calls us to offer refreshment to a world full of people dying of thirst. What should we offer them? Exactly what they thirst for — a person and a place. Jesus is that person. Heaven is that place." (Cite: Randy Alcorn In the Light of Eternity. Page 164).

Oh Lord,

Help me finish strong. Help me to become that REAL Man of God. In these days while I have breath and life, give me the strength to set the pace. May these legs be strong and able to sustain this run of faith so that those who come behind me might see the One who saves.

And when this earthly vessel begins to weaken due to age and world decay, give me strength to walk a brisk pace so those who notice my

Notes and Quotes:
In the words of A.W.
Tozer, pray that you
might become athirst
or God.

Notes and Quotes:

weakened state will see my gaze is fixed on Jesus, the One who made me for this race.

And when I can no longer manage to walk along the road of life, when mobility has left me and I am laid upon a bed, help me shout to those who will listen of the One who died for me. Give me strength to sing with vigor the great songs of victory.

And when my voice begins to falter and my strength is almost gone, help me whisper of Your mercy that has blessed me all my days. May the final words I ever speak be words of gentle bidding, to the ones I love the most, to run fast and never stop until they reach the place of calling along the shores of Eternity.

And when I can no longer whisper, may my heart still beat for You. May Your Presence be enough then to give me purpose in that day, to somehow offer a simple pulse of praise to Thee.

And when my breath begins to leave me in shallow gasps unheard, may the feeble hiss of dying somehow worship Thee.

Help me, Lord. May my life reflect Your glory and the greatness of Your plan, from this day until Glory, give me strength to be Your man. Amen.

May God help us all to Be Strong and to Show Ourselves to be Men of God.

Appendix One: What Does it Take to Become a Christian?

In the third chapter of the Gospel of John, Jesus speaks to Nicodemus about being born again. I love this visual picture of becoming a Christian. Every conversion is an act of God. While we often speak about accepting Christ, Scripture teaches that no one can come to Christ "unless the Father has enabled him." (John 6:65). I have come to view my calling like that of a doctor in the delivery room. I am blessed to be one who is in the delivery room when new life is suddenly born. In fact, I often get to be the "catch man;" the person who gets to first receive the new born and embrace them as they come into the family of God. There is no greater privilege than to be used by God in this way.

When someone comes to me to ask for me to help in beginning this journey of faith, there are numerous things to teach them about the process of new birth.

I usually begin with the same passage of Scripture that the evangelist had shared with me the night I came to Christ. 1 John 1:9 says "If we confess our sins, he is faithful and just and will forgive us our sins and purify us from all unrighteousness." However, I want to caution against a modern day phenomenon that often leads to a misunderstanding of Christianity. For many, a one time prayer of confession is thought to bring about a new title, that of being a Christian. But confession alone does not always bring new life. I have struggled in my ministry when people have pronounced themselves to be Christians because they prayed a prayer of confession years and years prior but never experienced anything that would look like the transformation mentioned in Romans 12:2. We must ask ourselves the question, "Is confession all that is required for a person to be a Christian?"

Many claim to be Christians because they believe in God. Often I hear people say, "Well, I must be a Christian because I have always believed in God." Romans 10:9-13 says "9That if you confess with your mouth, "Jesus is Lord," and believe in your heart that God raised him from the dead, you will be saved. 10For it is with your heart that you believe and are justified, and it is with your mouth that you confess and are saved. 11As the Scripture says, "Anyone who trusts in him will never be put to shame." 12For there is no difference between Jew and Gentile—the same Lord is Lord of all and richly blesses all who call on him, 13for, "Everyone who calls on the name of the Lord will be saved.""

In this passage of Scripture, belief is required if we are to experience salvation. This belief is not just a private, silent belief, but one that is confessed or professed with our mouths.

Certainly in order for someone to become a Christian, they must confess their sins to the Lord and ask for his forgiveness. Scripture also teaches that belief is a requirement for someone to "be saved." So, in my understanding of Scripture, both confession and belief are required in order for a person to become a Christian. But is there more required?

A study of Acts 2:38 indicates that repentance is also required if someone is to become a new creation. 38Peter replied, "Repent and be baptized, every one of you, in the name of Jesus Christ for the forgiveness of your sins. And you will receive the gift of the Holy Spirit." This concept is restated in Acts 3:19, "19Repent, then, and turn to God, so that your sins may be wiped out, that times of refreshing may come from the Lord..."

While we often try to simplify what it means to become a Christian so that everyone can easily understand, the truth is that we become a Christian when numerous things converge in a short period of time.

First, the Holy Spirit must draw us. Let us not forget that being born again as described to Nicodemus in John 3 is not an act of our will, but rather it is an act of God's will. Just as none of us could be born the first time of our own will, neither can we be born again by an act of our own will. God has to draw us into a relationship with him.

Secondly, we must believe. John 3:16 says that *"whosoever believes in him shall not perish but have eternal life."*

Thirdly, we must confess. 1 John 1:9. Because God is holy and we are sinful, something must be done to deal with our sin problem before we can have a relationship with God.

Finally, according to Peter's teaching in Acts chapter 2, we must repent. Repentance is turning and going in a new direction. Over the years, I have been given the opportunity to teach others this great lesson. Knowing the One to whom you sing is more than having a new title...the title of Christian. It means that you have a new life!

2 Corinthians 5:17 says "Therefore, if anyone is in Christ, he is a new creation; the old has gone, the new has come!"

Made in the USA
Columbia, SC
25 August 2018